Technology Application in Aviation, Tourism and Hospitality

Azizul Hassan · Nor Aida Abdul Rahman
Editors

Technology Application in Aviation, Tourism and Hospitality

Recent Developments and Emerging Issues

 Springer

Editors
Azizul Hassan
Tourism Consultants Network
The Tourism Society
London, UK

Nor Aida Abdul Rahman
Malaysian Institute of Aviation Technology
(UniKL MIAT)
Universiti Kuala Lumpur
Subang, Selangor, Malaysia

ISBN 978-981-19-6618-7   ISBN 978-981-19-6619-4 (eBook)
https://doi.org/10.1007/978-981-19-6619-4

© The Editor(s) (if applicable) and The Author(s), under exclusive license to Springer Nature Singapore Pte Ltd. 2023
This work is subject to copyright. All rights are solely and exclusively licensed by the Publisher, whether the whole or part of the material is concerned, specifically the rights of translation, reprinting, reuse of illustrations, recitation, broadcasting, reproduction on microfilms or in any other physical way, and transmission or information storage and retrieval, electronic adaptation, computer software, or by similar or dissimilar methodology now known or hereafter developed.
The use of general descriptive names, registered names, trademarks, service marks, etc. in this publication does not imply, even in the absence of a specific statement, that such names are exempt from the relevant protective laws and regulations and therefore free for general use.
The publisher, the authors, and the editors are safe to assume that the advice and information in this book are believed to be true and accurate at the date of publication. Neither the publisher nor the authors or the editors give a warranty, expressed or implied, with respect to the material contained herein or for any errors or omissions that may have been made. The publisher remains neutral with regard to jurisdictional claims in published maps and institutional affiliations.

This Springer imprint is published by the registered company Springer Nature Singapore Pte Ltd.
The registered company address is: 152 Beach Road, #21-01/04 Gateway East, Singapore 189721, Singapore

Introduction

In the current digital era, technology has a tremendous impact on decision-making, operations, and value proposition of commercial services. Thus, countries are seeing a significant increase in academic and professional interest in the fields of aviation, tourism, and hospitality. It is common knowledge that the use of technology may facilitate and speed up corporate operations and decision-making.

Transportation companies that arrange road, sea, and air travel are part of the tourism industry. The industries of aviation, tourism, and hospitality are interrelated and rely on one another. This book offers the most recent analysis and research on how technology is used in aviation, tourism, and hospitality.

This book includes a variety of thorough and in-depth top-quality research papers from reputable writers and editors. This will especially emphasize the major approaches, current trends, and future problems related to the implementation of technology in the aviation, tourism, and hospitality industries. The 13 chapters in this book focus on three key areas: technology and strategy, technology apps and framework, pandemic COVID-19, and future research in the fields of aviation, tourism, and hospitality.

Chapter 1 by Ali, Rahman, and Hassan explains the purpose of this chapter is to examine the value of technological application for passenger safety. At the end of the chapter, a list of potential future study topics is also presented.

Chapter 2 by Sharin and Sentosa highlights that in order to develop, enhance, and market this product globally, this paper focuses on identifying the strengths, weaknesses, opportunities, and threats associated with existing ecotourism destinations in Malaysia. It also examines the mechanisms that are currently available, identifies initiatives that can be implemented to attract both domestic and international tourist segments, and makes strategic recommendations. This article also built an empirical methodology to guarantee ecotourism's sustainability, which would be able to confirm Malaysia's allure as a regional ecotourism destination. This integrated model will synchronize the linkages between the supply and demand of ecotourism experiences in Malaysia, as well as the appeal of ecotourism product qualities as a multicultural tourism destination.

Chapter 3 by Nordin discusses the repercussions of the pandemic are evaluated, along with the use of technology by aviation actors in the post-COVID-19 era and their response plans to these problems. Only a tiny number of the procedures, proposals, and ideas generated during earlier pandemics have been implemented in civil aviation procedures and operations for air travel. This article discusses and highlights many activities and different strategies used by the aviation stakeholders throughout this pandemic.

Chapter 4 by Mukherjee, Rajendran and Wahab examines the many digital technologies used in Halal tourism as well as the challenges the industry confronts. Cyber-physical systems, the Internet of things, cloud computing, big data, artificial intelligence, and advanced robotics are some of the digital technologies used to promote Halal tourism through the thorough analysis of current research and contextual synthesis. Halal tourism stakeholders confront challenges embracing digital technology, including Muslim visitors' safety and security being at risk, digital technology suppliers struggling to maintain facilities up to date, the need for standardizing Halal phrases, and regional marketing initiatives.

Chapter 5 by Sarol, Mohammad, and Rahman discusses that customers of airlines will benefit from using Artificial Intelligence (AI) to get more precise information about things like reserving flights, timetables, and updates. This chapter provides a multi-focus discussion on initiatives for implementing Chatbot systems in the aviation industry, a discussion on AI technology used to improve communication, enhance natural language interactions, and the usability response from a few airlines' passengers on the improved systems.

Chapter 6 by Mustafa discusses how technology is being used in the hotel industry as it becomes the new standard for how hotels operate all around the world. In order to maintain a competitive edge, several studies have been done to report the most recent hotel technology trends and innovations. As a result, this chapter sheds light on how the hotel industry has recently changed, developed, and used numerous technological advancements to substitute human labor. This chapter also shows how these technologies are being used in various hotel industry areas. The tactics hotels are employing to alter their communication channels, financial transactions, food and beverage operations, marketing and promotional tools, as well as the usage of AI in hotel service delivery to replace human labor, are presented in this chapter. At the conclusion of this chapter, the effect of technology application in the hotel industry is also covered.

Chapter 7 by Yusriza serves three purposes. First, it discusses the importance of technological innovation in the airline catering industry and explains how it improves process effectiveness and efficiency. The second part of this chapter addresses the ongoing and impending digital transformation of the airline catering industry. The third part of this chapter provides case studies of several airline caterers and their use of digitalization advances.

Chapter 8 by Mayor-Vitoria praises the situation and significance of rural tourism for Spain as well as discusses how recent technology advancements are completely suited to this kind of tourism and may aid the nation in the short term in expanding and diversifying its tourist offering. Additionally, effective technology use can create jobs at all levels of the supply chain and should be viewed as a source of sustainable opportunities that will enable Spain to maintain its position as a global leader in terms of visitor numbers as well as in terms of environmental conservation and protection.

Chapter 9 by Mohd, Aziz, and Ismail deliberates that the capacity of Mobile Augmented Reality (AR) technology to enhance visitors' destination interactions through dynamic digital engagement has led to an increase in the use of the technology by companies in the tourism industry. By enhancing important travel-related information media, mobile augmented reality (MAR) travel apps like "Iskandar.my" are able to pique users' interest during travel while yet allowing for some room for tourists to appreciate the real landscape. This study examines the technology foundation of the "Iskandar.my" MAR travel applications and elaborates on the app's service and design facets.

Chapter 10 by Sharin, Shamsudin, and Sentosa aims to discover the elements influencing the online shopping habits of Malaysian SME rural tourists during the COVID-19 pandemic. This is being done to gauge how the COVID-19 pandemic has affected consumer behavior in terms of rural tourism based on factors such as product, price, and time savings. Due to increased customer loyalty and retention through online mechanisms in higher numbers given the constrained circumstances, this pandemic has begun to change the tourism industry. Product, price, and time-saving factors as digital sustainability domain have been highlighted as a strategic direction which translated on the predictors of rural tourism business in Malaysia, despite the fact that some SME rural tourism destination and attraction found it hard and difficult to adapt to the e-marketplace ecosystem. Detail route on the manufacturing process of the digitainability of the rural tourism model has been created by an advanced quantitative analysis employing first order confirmatory factor analysis (CFA) of structural equation modeling (SEM).

Chapter 11 by Wan-Chik, Zamri, and Hasbullah highlights that the COVID-19 pandemic has had a significant influence on airport industry because of the travel ban, restricted borders, and "new norm" of some regular operating practices. The COVID-19 pandemic's effects on airports have prompted the deployment of technologies that can improve operations in an effort to get airports back operating within the established norm. This study's goal is to investigate whether using technology may help the airport sector get back on track after the COVID-19 catastrophe. It looks into how airports are using technology and how it can help with operations recovery and airport reopening. Thirty-three pieces of literature on airports' use of technology between 2020 and 2021 were evaluated for this study.

Chapter 12 by Jamaluddin and Rahmat overviews the current use of AI technology in the travel, tourism, and hospitality industries focused on operations, facilities management, supply chain, and marketing is presented in this article. From a business perspective, they safeguarded data collection, provided comprehensive services, supported consumer involvement, and increased worker productivity and efficiency. Additionally, the use of innovative engaging and interactive service delivery methods that connect and engage with clients might improve the perceived quality of the provided services. The future applications of AI in the tourism industry are also highlighted in this study, including self-driving cars, crop and forest monitoring, pest management using AI, decision support systems, forest safeguards, virtual reality, and AI dimensions of travel and tourism.

The final Chap. 13 by Rahman, Hassan, Ahmad, and Singh deliberates that global travel, tourism, and the hospitality industries are currently feeling the effects of the COVID-19 pandemic. The problem of traveler safety and health has taken on essential importance in the recovery strategy for the hotel industry. Both tourists and hotel service providers are adopting technology more quickly as a result of the unexpected COVID-19 pandemic. This chapter explores the many contactless technologies utilized in the hospitality industry and suggests a research cluster for further studies. Virtual reality, Chatbots, robotics, contactless payments, voice searches, mobile check-in, recognition technologies, and many more topics are covered in this chapter.

Azizul Hassan
Nor Aida Abdul Rahman

Contents

Part I Strategies

1 Technology Strategy and the Safety of Travelers 3
   Azlina Mohd Ali, Nor Aida Abdul Rahman, and Azizul Hassan

2 The Digitainability Strategic-Technology Connection:
   A Mechanism for Ecotourism Sustainment in the Midst
   of the Pandemic 13
   Farah Hida Sharin and Ilham Sentosa

3 Strategy and Technology Framework in the Pandemic Era
   Among Aviation Players 29
   Mohd Norazali Nordin

4 Technology Strategy in Boosting Halal Tourism Activities 41
   Aroop Mukherjee, Salini Devi Rajendran, and Siti Norida Wahab

Part II Recent Developments

5 Mobile Technology Application in Aviation: Chatbot
   for Airline Customer Experience 59
   Sufi Dzikri Sarol, Mohammad FakhrulNizam Mohammad,
   and Nor Aida Abdul Rahman

6 Technology in Hotel Sector 73
   Eshaby Mustafa

7 Digital Advancements in Airline Catering Sector 89
   Fathien Azuien Yusriza

8 Technology Framework for Rural Tourism Development
   in Spain 101
   Fernando Mayor-Vitoria

9 **Iskandar.my: Framework of Mobile Augmented Reality Travel App** 113
   Nur Shuhadah Mohd, Maimunah Abdul Aziz, and Hairul Nizam Ismail

Part III Emerging Issues

10 **Defender or Attacker? An Approach to Dynamic Sustainability in the Dynamic Business Climate of Rural Tourism** 131
   Farah Hida Sharin, Mohd Farid Shamsudin, and Ilham Sentosa

11 **Technology Application in Airports Reopening and Operations Recovery Due to COVID-19 Pandemic** 143
   Rita Zaharah Wan-Chik, Nur Syaza Syazwina Binti Zamri, and Siti Salwa Binti Hasbullah

Part IV Directions for Future Research

12 **Artificial Intelligence Technology in Travel, Tourism and Hospitality: Current and Future Developments** 169
   Zaharuzaman Jamaluddin and Abdul Khabir Rahmat

13 **Contactless Hospitality Technology in Post-COVID-19 Era: Future Research Clusters** 179
   Nor Aida Abdul Rahman, Azizul Hassan, Md Fauzi Ahmad, and Reshminder Kaur Satvindar Singh

Editors and Contributors

About the Editors

Dr. Azizul Hassan is a member of the Tourism Consultants Network of the UK Tourism Society. Dr. Hassan has been working for the tourism industry as a consultant, academic, and researcher for over two decades. His research interest areas are technology-supported marketing for tourism and hospitality, immersive technology applications in the tourism and hospitality industry, and technology-influenced marketing suggestions for sustainable tourism and hospitality industry in developing countries. Dr. Hassan has authored over 150 articles and book chapters in leading tourism outlets. He is also part of the editorial team of 25 book projects from Routledge, Springer, CAB International, and Emerald Group Publishing Limited. He is a regular reviewer of a number of international journals.

Dr. Nor Aida Abdul Rahman is an Associate Professor, Universiti Kuala Lumpur (UniKL), Kuala Lumpur, Malaysia, and Head of Aviation Management, Universiti Kuala Lumpur—Malaysian Institute of Aviation Technology (UniKL MIAT), Selangor, Malaysia. She has worked as internal and external trainer in management, supply chain, Halal logistics, and postgraduate research. Her research work has appeared in several reputable academic journals such as Industrial Marketing Management, Journal of Humanitarian logistics and supply chain, International journal of quality and reliability management, International journal of supply chain management, and others. She has also published a number of book chapters and refereed conference proceedings, and part of the editorial team of book project with Routledge. She is a panel of WG in MS2400 Halal Supply Chain standard and TC10 for Halal supply chain standard (SMIIC). She earned Ph.D. degree in Management (supply chain management) from Brunel University, London, UK. She is also serving as Academic Advisor in college, a chartered member for Chartered Institute of Logistics and Transport Malaysia (CILTM), HRDF Certified Trainer, Chairman (Academic Committee) for Malaysian Association of Transportation, Logistics and Supply Chain Schools (MyATLAS), Vice President (Research Journal) for Institute for Research in Management and Engineering UK (INRME), JAKIM Halal Certified Trainer, UniKL Halal Professional Board and a member of Academy of Marketing, UK.

Contributors

Abdul Aziz Maimunah UniKL Business School, University Kuala Lumpur, Kuala Lumpur, Malaysia

Ahmad Md Fauzi Faculty of Technology Management, Universiti Tun Hussein Onn Malaysia, Johor, Malaysia

Ali Azlina Mohd Universiti Kuala Lumpur (UniKL), Kuala Lumpur, Malaysia

Hasbullah Siti Salwa Binti Foundation Centre, Universiti Kuala Lumpur—Malaysian Institute of Information Technology (UniKL MIIT), Kuala Lumpur, Malaysia

Hassan Azizul Tourism Consultant Network, The Tourism Society, London, UK

Ismail Hairul Nizam Faculty of Built Environment and Surveying, Universiti Teknologi Malaysia, Johor Bahru, Malaysia

Jamaluddin Zaharuzaman Faculty of Business and Accountancy, Universiti Selangor, Selangor, Malaysia

Mayor-Vitoria Fernando Universidad Internacional de Valencia - VIU, Valencia, Spain

Mohammad Mohammad FakhrulNizam Universiti Kuala Lumpur, Kuala Lumpur, Malaysia

Mohd Nur Shuhadah Kulliyyah of Languages and Management, International Islamic University Malaysia, Muar, Malaysia

Mukherjee Aroop College of Business Administration, Prince Sultan University, Riyadh, Saudi Arabia

Mustafa Eshaby School of Tourism, Hospitality and Event Management, Universiti Utara Malaysia, Changlun, Malaysia

Nordin Mohd Norazali Malaysian Institute of Industrial Logistics, Universiti Kuala Lumpur, Kuala Lumpur, Malaysia

Rahman Nor Aida Abdul Technical Foundation/Aviation Management Section, Universiti Kuala Lumpur—Malaysian Institute of Aviation Technology (UniKL MIAT), Selangor, Malaysia

Rahmat Abdul Khabir Malaysia Institute of Transport, Universiti Teknologi MARA, Selangor, Malaysia

Rajendran Salini Devi School of Food Studies and Gastronomy, Taylors University, Subang Jaya, Malaysia

Sarol Sufi Dzikri Malaysian Institute of Aviation Technology, Universiti Kuala Lumpur, Kuala Lumpur, Malaysia

Sentosa Ilham Department of Management and Entrepreneurship, Universiti Kuala Lumpur (UniKL) Business School, Kuala Lumpur, Malaysia

Shamsudin Mohd Farid Department of Marketing and International Business, Universiti Kuala Lumpur (UniKL) Business School, Kuala Lumpur, Malaysia

Sharin Farah Hida Universiti Kuala Lumpur (UniKL) Business School, Kuala Lumpur, Malaysia

Singh Reshminder Kaur Satvindar Universiti Kuala Lumpur—Malaysian Institute of Aviation Technology (UniKL MIAT), Selangor, Malaysia

Wahab Siti Norida Faculty of Business and Management, Universiti Teknologi MARA, Puncak Alam, Selangor, Malaysia

Wan-Chik Rita Zaharah Technical Foundation/Aviation Management Section, Universiti Kuala Lumpur—Malaysian Institute of Aviation Technology (UniKL MIAT), Selangor, Malaysia

Yusriza Fathien Azuien Malaysian Institute of Aviation Technology (UniKL MIAT), Universiti Kuala Lumpur, Selangor, Malaysia; Politecnico Di Torino (POLITO), Torino, Italy

Zamri Nur Syaza Syazwina Binti Aviation Management Programme, Universiti Kuala Lumpur—Malaysian Institute of Aviation Technology (UniKL MIAT), Selangor, Malaysia

Part I
Strategies

Chapter 1
Technology Strategy and the Safety of Travelers

Azlina Mohd Ali, Nor Aida Abdul Rahman, and Azizul Hassan

Abstract Recently, travelers have been looking for comprehensive technology that always allow them to access their regular activities while on their vacation. The pandemic outbreak of COVID-19 affected the whole world especially in tourism industry. The result of lockdowns and closures of international and national borders can be seen in the global crisis and disruption within and beyond the tourism industry. Tourism continues to be one of the sectors hardest hit by the coronavirus pandemic and the outlook remains highly uncertain. However, many country has starts to recover especially those in tourism industry. A number of technological approaches and requirements by travelers have had an impact on the worldwide tourist sector. Consequently, many technologies have been introduced in the aviation, travel, tourism and hospitality sector. This chapter aims to explore the importance of technology application for a safety of the travelers. Specifically, a set of future research agenda is also provided at the end of the chapter.

Keywords Safety · Travel · Pandemic · Air travel · Tourism · Travelers · Technology

Introduction

Technology plays significant role in travel, tourism and hospitality sector. Technology not only helps to improve daily business operation, monitoring performance and decision making process, but also play a significant role to ensure positive customer experience among the travelers. Technology allows the travelers to feel

---

A. M. Ali (✉)
Universiti Kuala Lumpur (UniKL), Kuala Lumpur, Malaysia
e-mail: azlinamdali@unikl.edu.my

N. A. A. Rahman
Technical Foundation/Aviation Management Section, Universiti Kuala Lumpur—Malaysian Institute of Aviation Technology (UniKL MIAT), Selangor, Malaysia

A. Hassan
Tourism Consultants Network, The Tourism Society, London, UK

© The Author(s), under exclusive license to Springer Nature Singapore Pte Ltd. 2023
A. Hassan and N. A. A. Rahman (eds.), *Technology Application in Aviation, Tourism and Hospitality*, https://doi.org/10.1007/978-981-19-6619-4_1

safe throughout their journey (Dorcic et al., 2019; Lee, 2022). Following recent COVID-19 outbreak that hits many business sector globally, technology application has become the main strategy for touchless activities in every business sector. The popularity of mobile technology in travel and tourism is also increased due to the fact that travelers looks for online mode transaction, online ordering, touchless payment and virtual communication. According to Dorcic et al. (2019), Lukanova and Ilieva (2019) and Cavusoglu (2019), the application of mobile technology, Artificial Intelligence (AI), service automation, communication technology and many other technologies are significant to be adopted by the travel, tourism and hospitality players in order to achieve smart tourism initiative. The recent COVID-19 outbreak has led to air travel players to be more careful in providing service, especially during facilitating the travelers at the airport to ensure the safety of the travellers (Rahman et al., 2020, 2021a, b). For instance, biometric technology application and Chatbot were used by airport and airline players to protect travelers from the spread of the virus. In fact, mobile application in measuring travelers' health was also developed which allow the travelers to make health declaration especially with regards to vaccination status. This kind of technology is vital to ensure the safe of the travelers during their travel journey.

At present, travelers always looking for unique, meaningful, safe and memorable travel experience. The latest technology application allows the traveler to ease their journey. For instance, comprehensive technology that allow travelers to access their regular activities while on their vacation. From air travel perspective for example, technological innovation adopted by the airlines and airport provide better facilitation and experience to the passengers or travelers. In fact, the International of Air Transport Association (IATA) (2019) also plays a significant role to the global airlines that provides rich information on the latest trend of technologies to the aviation players. It is acknowledged that IATA continuously work with governments and industry to make the best use of modern technology for the safety of the travelers and achieve greater efficiency.

In general, technology and safety are crucial components. Safety is the highest priority in air transport especially the safety of the travelers. Technology and safety should be considered in order to motivate people to work towards attaining an Accident-Free Environment (ACE) (Satish et al., 2020). Everyone in the organization has a responsibility to prevent accidents from occurring in the first place. Employers in the construction sector are stressing behavioral techniques to increase their employees' awareness of potential dangers as well as the application of the maximum number of safety precautions in the workplace (Nnaji & Karakhan, 2020). With recent pandemic, issue on safety, traveler's health and the spread of the viruses are widely discussed. Standard procedure in facilitating the travelers at the airport is strictly monitored, the use of technology such as biometric application, touchless procedure has been expediting and improved. Travelers become less confident to travel due to Covid-19 outbreak. However, with current advancement of the technology adoption by the airline and airport, the confident of the passengers or travelers has been increased and the tourism activities starts to recover again with the help of technology. Technology has become the key strategy for post recovery strategy for many aviation players across the globe including airlines, airport, ground handling organization, airline catering, MROs (maintenance, repair and overhaul) and manufacturing firms.

On the other hand, technology used to improve the travelers' knowledge and skills in order to explore the unknown territory and lead to a safer environment in travel industry. Technology has made travelers easier to plan the trip because it saves time and helps in efficient planning. Travelers may find all the information they need to arrange the perfect trip on the website. Travelers can acquire all the necessary information about their selected destination by spending just a few hours surfing the internet. Another factor that travelers must consider is their packing habit. People can now improve their packing process due to technological advancements. Packing is a challenging chore because forgetting something essential might ruin your journey and trip. The technology allows travelers to pack a lot of stuff without having to worry about exceeding the weight limit. When it comes to staying connected with loved ones, such as family, technology is available everywhere, allowing them to keep connected with the rest of the globe while travelling. This can make travelers and family members feel safer, even if they are in different places. In both situations, communication is also done in real time.

Safety and Travel

Safety is a basic need of travelers. People are extremely sensitive to matters of safety and security when it comes to making decisions about tourism, and even relatively modest crises in one region of the world can cause significant shifts in the demand for tourism in other regions. Back to the history 11th September 2001 which terrorist attacks on the USA, many travelers have raised concerns about the safety and well-being of travelers' welfare and so on. Recently, the pandemic of COVID-19 is hitting close in everyone home since March 2019. This situation has an impact on the global tourism industry, and a study shows that COVID-19 pandemic has greatly affected travel risk and management perceptions (). Report by the United Nations World Tourism Organization (2020) estimated that global international tourist arrivals might decrease by 58% to 78% in 2020; Fig. 1.1 shows the international tourist arrivals, 2019 and Q1 2020 (% change); and the COVID-19 pandemic has caused a 22% fall in international tourist arrivals during the first quarter of 2020.

The COVID-19 pandemic has challenged the existing economic and tourism systems, has led the world to a recession, and has limited the potential of travelers to their homes It is critical to consider tourists' perceptions of travel safety and threat when deciding on the best place to travel to. The implications of this epidemic could have far-reaching implications for many sectors of human life and industry, including travel management, because roughly half of the world's population has imposed unprecedented limits on movement on a worldwide scale (Rahman et al., 2021a, b). Having this limitation, travelers now more alert and ready with safety requirement as well as the technology advancement skills in their travel planning.

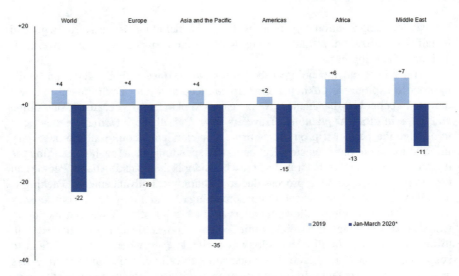

Fig. 1.1 International tourist arrival. *Source* UNWTO (2020)

Safety in travel refers to protection of travelers from potential injury or death during visit to the unknown and known places (Rittichainuwat & Chakraborty, 2012). Travelers' safety and technological advancements are intimately connected. For example, having technology such as the Wi-Fi connections, digital technology, drone's technology, as well as other types of applications could be convenient to travelers in order to access the unknown area. Safety and technology encompasses all current technology in travelers' world that currently being applied. Despite the fact that travelers can utilise a travel agency, technological access is a unique approach because travelers can acquire detailed information on anything they are looking for. Example with Wi-Fi connection, travelers can access their real time driving direction and traffic updates. Wi-Fi is particularly vital for air travelers who engage in activities throughout their flight. With the airline's on-board connectivity experience, passengers may browse the internet, stream videos, check social media, and more throughout flights.

Technology and Safety

Safety has long been an important consideration for travelers due to the nature of intangible and experiential of travel environment. Travelers' safety perception is important in the destination choosing process since they are more vulnerable to unanticipated incidents when they move away from home (Wang, 2014). Concerns about safety in the context of travelers are connected to several categories of travel hazards, such as health/epidemic risk, risk in the country, politic and social aspects among management and people in the visiting location, and so on.

Safety is defined as protection against unintentional incidents, while security is protection against deliberate incidents (Anichiti et al., 2021). According to the Oxford Dictionary (n.d.), safety means protection against any danger, injury, or risk, while security refers to the prevention of and protection against foreseeable dangers; unlawful activities; and protection of a country, a building, or a person against attack or danger. Since the worldwide pandemic, the safety of travelers has become a major concern. Despite this, technological advancements may provide solutions to all of these issues, as travelers currently use high-end devices and cutting-edge equipment with or without access restrictions.

In the context of aviation or air travel, safety is connected to the safety of the travelers on board. It is vital to ensure the aircraft is airworthy Historically, safety concept in the aviation sector refer has been implemented since 1903 in the Wright brothers' first flight. Safety is related to any measures taken against the threat of an accident. Historically, the Wright Brother's first successful heavier-than-air manned flight on 7 December 1903 was simply a 12-s short journey with a flying distance of 120 feet at a windy town known as Kitty Hawk, North Carolina, USA. The Wright Brothers' remarkable milestone has initiated the journey of human flight and related research. After a century of progress, flying faster and staying longer in the air has transcended beyond a dream. However, along with the development of aircraft technology, safety programmes are equally important, which help control and reduce potential hazards related to human operations. For instance, the understanding of human factors associated with unsafe behaviours in the 1990s resulted in the improvement of human-machine interface design.

The development of aviation safety manual for the safe of air travelers is continuously progressing throughout the years. Essentially, the evolution of safety in the air travel sector could be divided into three main eras, namely (1) technical, (2) human factors, and (3) organizational era, which have been ongoing from the 1950s until today (Fig. 1.2).

Technology as a Key Strategy to Survive in Travel Industry

Many people overstate the significance of technological innovation and expansion in the travel industry as ways of facilitating tourist transit in the twenty-first century (Stipanuk, 1993). Technology and the travel sector are both extremely important nowadays. In recent years, according to tourism research, the Internet and digital technologies have become firmly embedded in our lives. The most significant benefit provided by technology is access to reliable information, which allows for the creation and sharing of knowledge among huge numbers of individuals while simultaneously reducing costs and enhancing efficiency (Zeqiri et al., 2020). The information obtained has made it easier for travelers to recognise the territory. The concept of travel has been associated with the sensation of entering strange or unknown terrain

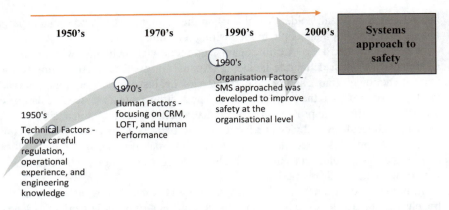

Fig. 1.2 The evolution of safety in the air travel sector—technical era, human factors era, and organizations factor. *Source* The authors

(van Nuenen & Scarles, 2021). Traveling through unfamiliar territory in seeking of travel experience necessitated the use of technology by a traveler who was competent in the use of technology. Traveling with technology provides for a more interesting and thrilling experience for the travelers. Technology world explains how computer hardware, software, networks, and systems operate and interact with one another. In the field of travelers, the destination has emerged as the essential methodological approach (Afsahhosseini, 2020).

Technology 4.0 has embracing increased the technological development within the travelers' framework. Tourism 4.0 refers to a new tourism value eco-system that is based on a highly technology-based service production paradigm and supported by the common principles of Industry 4.0, which include interoperability, virtualization, decentralisation, real-time data gathering and analysis capability, service orientation, and modularity, among other characteristics (Stankov & Gretzel, 2020). It is possible to improve user engagement with systems and enrich the tourist experience itself because to the significant capabilities of Tourism 4.0 technologies, which can provide new ways to support in behaviour change and even long-term transformation of users.

Figure 1.3 shows the Human-centered design (HCD) and the effects on tourist experience. A combination of subject-oriented and object-oriented aspects has been demonstrated to increase user satisfaction. This interactive system focuses on the avoidance of goal-limiting effects while also enabling goal-surpassing experiential results to be realized.

Many organisations in the aviation industry have recently created technology strategies to ensure the safety of passengers. There is one technology that introduce by the airport is contactless tech. Contactless services have acquired entirely new value during the COVID-19 outbreak. Powered by a number of technologies (sensors, RFID and NFC tags, facial recognition and modern biometrics), touchless services have been adopted in airports and travel hubs to ensure better safety and control over passenger traffic (DIGITEUM TEAM, 2021). In other industry, contactless tech also

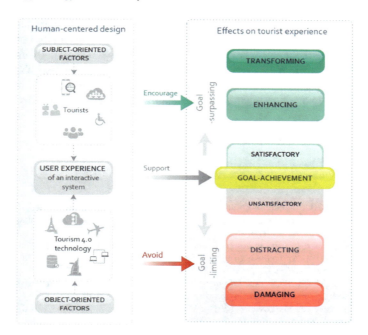

Fig. 1.3 HCD effects tourist experience. *Source* The authors (2022)

plays a special role in the hospitality sector. Before the pandemic, hotels invested in voice-controlled elevators, digital keys and smart hotel rooms to provide better and more comfortable service, increase efficiency and reach sustainability goals. Today, touchless technology is also the source of confidence and security for guests, staff and management.

Furthermore, technology is intelligence, and data sharing between travelers and any other linked organisations is necessary throughout travel. For instance, information about the territory that travelers wish to visit. Travelers' identification can also be quickly obtained when they enter an unfamiliar region. International organisations have developed coordinated and routine exchange of traveler data, including biometrics for identity verification and travel eligibility, enhancing security and facilitating international travel and trade between partner countries.

Conclusion

The pandemic outbreak of COVID-19 emerged in December 2019 in China till present affected the whole world. The result of lockdowns and closures of international and national borders can be seen in the global crisis and disruption within and beyond the tourism industry. As a conclusion, travelers are safe with current technology strategy that have introduce recently. There will be no major concerns for travelers because technology is readily available everywhere. The advancement of technology has contributed in greater communication, ease, and a sense of security for travelers. More research are call to examine how technology improve certain process in the aviation multi sector such as airline catering, air cargo, airline organization, airport terminal operator, MRO and manufacturing firm.

References

Afsahhosseini, F. (2020). Technology in tourism. In *Culture, People and Technology: The Driving Forces for Tourism Cities Proceedings of 8 th ITSA Biennial Conference 2020.* Jakarta.

Anichiti, A., Dragolea, L. L., Hârșan, G. D. T., Haller, A. P., & Butnaru, G. I. (2021). Aspects regarding safety and security in hotels: Romanian experience. *Information, 12*(1), 1–22.

Cavusoglu, M. (2019). An analysis of technology applications in the restaurant industry. *Journal of Hospitality and Tourism Technology, 10*(1), 45–72.

DIGITEUM TEAM. (2021). *5 Technologies for Travel and Tourism Industry in Post-COVID Era.* https://www.digiteum.com/technologies-travel-tourism/. Accessed 20 Mar 2022.

Dorcic, J., Komsic, J., & Markovic, S. (2019). Mobile technologies and applications towards smart tourism–state of the art. *Tourism Review, 4*(1), 82–103.

International Air Transport Association (IATA). (2019). *Technology to drive advances in passenger experience and infrastructure.* https://www.iata.org/en/pressroom/pr/2019-10-15-01/. Accessed 20 Mar 2022.

Lee, M. (2022). Evolution of hospitality and tourism technology research from Journal of Hospitality and Tourism Technology: A computer-assisted qualitative data analysis. *Journal of Hospitality and Tourism Technology, 13*(1), 62–84.

Lukanova, G., & Ilieva, G. (2019). Robots, artificial intelligence, and service automation in hotels. In S. Ivanov & C. Webster (Eds.), *Robots, artificial intelligence, and service automation in travel, tourism and hospitality* (pp. 157–183). Bingley.

Nnaji, C., & Karakhan, A. A. (2020). Technologies for safety and health management in construction: Current use, implementation benefits and limitations, and adoption barriers. *Journal of Building Engineering, 29*, 101212.

Oxford Learner's Dictionaries. (n.d.). *Safety.* https://www.oxfordlearnersdictionaries.com/definition/english/safety?q=Safety. Accessed 20 Mar 2022.

Rahman, N. A. A., Hassan, A., & Rahman, M.S-U-. (2021a). Tourism and air transport sustainability in Bangladesh: The role of technology. In A. Hassan (Ed.), *Tourism marketing in Bangladesh: An introduction* (pp. 42–50). Routledge.

Rahman, M. K., Gazi, A. I., Bhuiyan, M. A. & Rahaman, A. (2021b). Effect of Covid-19 pandemic on tourist travel risk and management perceptions. *PLoS ONE, 16*(9 September), 1–18.

Rahman, N. A. A., Rahim, S. A., Ahmad, M. F., & Hafizuddin-Syah, B. A. M. (2020). Exploring Covid-19 pandemic: Its impact to global aviation industry and the key strategy. *International Journal of Advanced Science and Technology, 29*(6s), 1829–1836.

Rittichainuwat, B. N., & Chakraborty, G. (2012). Perceptions of importance and what safety is enough. *Journal of Business Research, 65*(1), 42–50.

Satish, R., Murugabhoopathy, K., Rajendhiran, N., & Vijayan, V. (2020). Technology strategy for improved safety management in steel industry. *Materials Today: Proceedings, 33*(7), 2660–2664.

Stankov, U., & Gretzel, U. (2020). Tourism 4.0 technologies and tourist experiences: A human-centered design perspective. *Information Technology and Tourism, 22*(3), 477–488.

Stipanuk, D. M. (1993). Tourism and technology. Interactions and implications. *Tourism Management, 14*(4), 267–278.

van Nuenen, T., & Scarles, C. (2021). Advancements in technology and digital media in tourism. *Tourist Studies, 21*(1), 119–132.

Wang, P. (2014). The influence of tourists' safety perception during vacation destination-decision process: An integration of elaboration likelihood model and theory of planned behavior. *Communications in Computer and Information Science, 450 CCIS,* 219–229.

World Tourism Organization (UNWTO). (2020). *International tourist numbers.* https://www.Unwto.Org/News/Covid-19-International-Tourist-Numbers-Could-Fall-60-80-in-2020. http://stats.areppim.com/stats/stats_ita.htm#ita_actual. Accessed 20 Mar 2022.

Zeqiri, A., Dahmani, M., & Ben Youssef, A. (2020). Digitalization of the tourism industry: What are the impacts of the new wave of technologies. *Balkan Economic Review, 2,* 63–82.

Azlina Mohd Ali is a Lecturer of Universiti Kuala Lumpur (UniKL), Kuala Lumpur, Malaysia with specialization in aviation management and safety management research. She has more than 10 years of working experience in the academic sector and currently pursuing her Ph.D. degree in management (safety management in aviation). Her research interest includes safety management, aviation management and tourism management). She actively participated in presenting papers at the conferences.

Dr. Nor Aida Abdul Rahman is an Associate Professor, Universiti Kuala Lumpur (UniKL), Kuala Lumpur, Malaysia, and Head of Aviation Management, Universiti Kuala Lumpur—Malaysian Institute of Aviation Technology (UniKL MIAT), Selangor, Malaysia. She has worked as internal and external trainer in management, supply chain, Halal logistics and postgraduate research. Her research work has appeared in several reputable academic journals such as Industrial Marketing Management, Journal of Humanitarian logistics and supply chain, International journal of quality and reliability management, International journal of supply chain management and others. She has also published a number of book chapter and refereed conference proceedings, and part of the editorial team of book project with Routledge. She is a panel of WG in MS2400 Halal Supply Chain standard & TC10 for Halal supply chain standard (SMIIC). She earned Ph.D. degree in Management (supply chain management) from Brunel University, London, UK. She is also serving as Academic Advisor in college, a chartered member for Chartered Institute of Logistics and Transport Malaysia (CILTM), HRDF Certified Trainer, Chairman (Academic Committee) for Malaysian Association of Transportation, Logistics and Supply Chain Schools (MyATLAS), Vice President (Research Journal) for Institute for Research in Management and Engineering UK (INRME), JAKIM Halal Certified Trainer, UniKL Halal Professional Board and a member of Academy of Marketing, UK.

Dr. Azizul Hassan is a member of the Tourism Consultants Network of the UK Tourism Society. Dr. Hassan has been working for the tourism industry as a consultant, academic, and researcher for over two decades. His research interest areas are technology-supported marketing for tourism and hospitality, immersive technology applications in the tourism and hospitality industry, and technology-influenced marketing suggestions for sustainable tourism and hospitality industry in developing countries. Dr. Hassan has authored over 150 articles and book chapters in leading tourism outlets. He is also part of the editorial team of 25 book projects from Routledge, Springer, CAB International, and Emerald Group Publishing Limited. He is a regular reviewer of a number of international journals.

Chapter 2
The Digitainability Strategic-Technology Connection: A Mechanism for Ecotourism Sustainment in the Midst of the Pandemic

Farah Hida Sharin and Ilham Sentosa

Abstract The COVID-19 crisis has contributed significantly to a global decline in tourism activity. A dynamic environment during the outbreak of COVID-19 significantly impacted on the resilience of the ecotourism industry. As a result, the focus of this paper is on identifying the strengths, weaknesses, opportunities, and threats associated with existing ecotourism destinations in Malaysia, on examining available mechanisms for developing, enhancing, and marketing this product globally, on identifying the initiatives that can be implemented to attract both domestic and also international tourist segments, and on making strategic recommendations. Additionally, this article established an empirical model to ensure the sustainability of ecotourism, which will be capable of verifying Malaysia's attractiveness as an ecotourism destination in the region. This integrated model will synchronise the relationships between the attractiveness of ecotourism product attributes as a multi-cultural tourism destination (supply) and the behavioural intentions of tourists seeking ecotourism experience (demand) in Malaysia. These attributes have been investigated because it's not only as supply-side qualifying factors, but also as indicators of prospective tourists' perceived value. According to current trends in demand for ecotourism, Malaysia is undoubtedly facing stiff global competition and is well positioned to become the region's preferred destination for ecotourism. Additional information is required to comprehend segments of the ecotourism market, as there is tremendous potential for growth both locally and globally.

Keywords Tourism industry · Ecotourism · Sustainability · Creative entrepreneurs

---

F. H. Sharin (✉)
Universiti Kuala Lumpur (UniKL) Business School, Kuala Lumpur, Malaysia
e-mail: farah.sharin@s.unikl.edu.my

I. Sentosa
Department of Management and Entrepreneurship, Universiti Kuala Lumpur (UniKL) Business School, Kuala Lumpur, Malaysia

© The Author(s), under exclusive license to Springer Nature Singapore Pte Ltd. 2023
A. Hassan and N. A. A. Rahman (eds.), *Technology Application in Aviation, Tourism and Hospitality*, https://doi.org/10.1007/978-981-19-6619-4_2

Introduction

The tourism sector is one of the largest contributors to exports, the economy and employment, not only in the Malaysia but also in many cities and local communities over the world. Tourism supports millions of people's livelihoods and teaches billions more about their own and other cultures, as well as the natural world. It can account for more than 20% of a country's GDP in some cases and is the world's third largest export sector overall. Simultaneously, tourism propels cities and benefits local, coastal, rural, and remote communities by generates jobs for specialists and professionals, particularly for women, migrants, students, and older workers (Economic Commission for Latin America and the Caribbean, 2020).

Regrettably, the tourism industry has been significantly harmed by the coronavirus (COVID-19) pandemic and subsequent containment measures. According to revised projections, the potential shock could result in a 60–80% decline in international tourism in 2020, depending on the severity of the crisis (United Nations World Tourism Organization, 2020a). Tourism is one of the sectors hardest hit by the COVID-19 pandemic, which has wreaked havoc on economies, livelihoods, public services, and opportunities across the globe (United Nations, 2020). By 20 April 2020, 100% of the world's tourism destinations will have implemented travel restrictions in response to the COVID-19 pandemic. This could result in the loss of 100–120 million jobs and up to US$1.2 trillion in exports (United Nations World Tourism Organization, 2020b). The level of disruption caused by the COVID-19 pandemic has been significantly greater than that caused by previous crises such as the 2008–2009 financial crisis and also the SARS infection, fundamentally altering the global travel industry. For instance, a number of Commonwealth small states, including small island developing states (SIDS), rely on international tourism for up to 90% of their exports and a sizable portion of their GDP.

The fundamental nature of tourism has shifted, and recovery is expected to be as gradual as the reopening of various economies. Even if the virus is contained, this sector is unlikely to fully recover in the near future. Recovery prospects are contingent upon the duration of the crisis and the time required to recover (Kampel, 2020). Additionally, the impact of the virus outbreak on tourism is likely to be asymmetrical and highly localised within countries, with some destinations being disproportionately vulnerable due to their reliance on the sector (Organisation for Economic and Cooperation and Development, 2020). Malaysian tourism is also not immune to COVID-19's effects. Table 2.1 summarises international tourist arrivals and revenue receipts in Malaysia from 2010 to 2020. According to the figures below, international tourist arrivals and receipts for Malaysia are increasing year after year, but due to the global pandemic and travel restrictions imposed by all countries, the number is expected to decline significantly by 2020.

Not only that, the Malaysian government's analysis indicates that the country's tourism industry has grown complacent. Existing tourism products are becoming stale and unattractive as a result of a lack of creativity and innovation caused by an excessive reliance on government and a silo mentality. Due to its inability to cultivate

Table 2.1 International tourist arrival and receipts for Malaysia

Year	Arrivals (million)	Receipts (MYR billion)
2010	24.6	56.5
2011	24.7	58.3
2012	25.3	60.6
2013	25.72	65.4
2014	27.44	72.0
2015	25.72	69.1
2016	26.76	82.1
2017	25.95	82.1
2018	25.83	84.1
2019	26.10	86.1
2020	4.33	12.7

Source Ministry of tourism, arts and culture, Malaysia (2021)

a service culture, it has experienced a real or perceived decline in service quality relative to ASEAN neighbours. Additionally, insufficient destination management strategies have resulted in unsustainably developed physical infrastructure and negative visitor experiences. Finally, Malaysia has lagged behind in adopting Smart Tourism as a result of an over-reliance on traditional marketing and promotion. As a result, the industry must continually reinvent and transform itself to remain competitive (Ministry of Tourism, Arts & Culture, Malaysia (2020).

Other than that, apart from immediate assistance to the tourism sector, countries are concentrating their efforts on recovery efforts. These include considerations for removing travel restrictions, restoring traveller confidence, and reimagining tourism's future. Given the high degree of uncertainty surrounding the pandemic's duration and associated contingency and easing measures, forecasting the short, medium, and long-term impact on tourism is difficult (Economic Commission for Latin America and the Caribbean, 2020). While preserving livelihoods in the sector is critical, rebuilding tourism presents an opportunity for transformation, with an emphasis on leveraging its impact on visited destinations and strengthening communities and businesses through innovation, digitalization, sustainability, and partnerships (United Nations, 2000). With the vaccines being widely distributed, the economy is opening up in distinct phases, and the Government is determined to foster a climate conducive to balanced economic recovery and to provide certainty and clarity for businesses.

Ecotourism in Malaysia

The definition of tourism can be concluded as the sum of the activities, processes, and the outcomes that result from the interaction and relationships between tourism suppliers, tourists, host governments, host communities, and the surrounding environment in order to attract, transport, host, and manage tourists and other visitors (Cooper et al., 2005; Ritchie & Goeldner, 2000). Camilleri (2018) brings the concept of tourism to a close by elucidating the inherent motivations of tourists to travel. Additionally, it defines the various components of tourism. Tourists visit destinations within their reach and, if their visit exceeds twenty-four hours, they require lodging. Both leisure and business travellers can take advantage of attractions and recreational activities (Osman & Sentosa, 2013). While ecotourism is currently trendy, it is a one of travelling activities that involves the attractions of natural, places a premium on nature preservation, and requires tourism activities to have a minimal impact on the degradation of environment while also respecting indigenous cultures and ways of life (Wallace, 2019).

Attractions serve as the fundamental reason for travelling to a destination. According to the Ministry of Tourism, Arts & Culture, Malaysia (2020), this ministry as part of its strategic move, enhances the appearance of tourism product categories by adding value to the existing tourist experiences through product development, strengthening enablers and removing impediments for the growth and development and one of it that can be focused is ecotourism. The beauty and challenges of combining adventure and ecotourism are undeniable. Ecotourism as a niche in tourism has indeed flourished and made a name for itself in academia and the industry over the last two decades. The very principle of ecotourism, which seeks to strike a sustainable balance between protecting and conserving natural resources and promoting community well-being, has unquestionably garnered enormous positive support on a global scale. This has resulted in a plethora of conferences, grants, projects, and discussions within the global ecotourism community, with numerous exemplary success stories despite a variety of obstacles (Manohar et al., 2020).

The definition of ecotourism as stated is "responsible travel to natural areas that conserves the environment, sustains the well-being of the local people, and involves interpretation and education" (The International Ecotourism Society, 2015). The uniqueness of ecotourism is about uniting conservation, communities, and sustainable travel. This means that those responsible for the implementation, participation in, and marketing of ecotourism activities should adhere to the following ecotourism principles: (a) Minimize physical, social, behavioural, and psychological impacts; (b) Increase environmental and cultural awareness and respect; (c) Provide positive experiences for both visitors and hosts; (d) Provide direct financial benefits to conservation; (e) Generate financial benefits for both local residents and private industry; and (f) Provide memorable interpretative experiences to visitors that help raise awareness and respect for the environment and culture (The International Ecotourism Society, 2015).

The ecotourism product has been proposed as a tool for conserving and managing the cultural heritage together with natural of deserts. Ecotourism, as one of the fastest growing segments of the global tourism industry, has the potential to serve as a financially, environmentally, and sociocultural viable option for promoting sustainable development in the desert biome. Numerous factors contribute to the development of ecotourism in deserts, all of which must be carefully considered in light of nature conservation goals and local socioeconomic well-being. Numerous ecotourism destinations have been developed in Malaysia with the dual objective of economic development and resource conservation of the indigenous people. To accomplish these lofty goals, it is really important to understand and incorporate the participation of local communities into all ecotourism activities. The critical justification for such participation is found in the link between economic benefits and environmental conservation via small businesses.

There are several established ecotourism destinations in Malaysia, including the Forest Research Institute Malaysia's FRIM Canopy Walkway, which is one of the main attractions for visitors (FRIM). Since its inception in 1992, the walkway has attracted visitors from around the world, generating significant revenue for FRIM's management. Ramlan et al. (2013) assessed visitors' perceptions of the FRIM Canopy Walkway's attractiveness as a nature-based tourism product and discovered that the attractive attribute and feature of the FRIM Canopy Walkway is the 'view from the walkway'. The crucial elements for the sustainability of FRIM Canopy Walkway are the best marketing strategies and management practices for the ecotourism product itself by the FRIM's management, particularly the Ecotourism and Urban Forestry Programme.

Additionally, one UNESCO World Heritage Site in Sabah, Borneo called as Kinabalu Park that become one of the hotspots of region's biodiversity. Sheena et al. (2015) discovered that it is critical for ecotourism operators to segment the ecotourists to several group. It can be grouped by their interest to the primary ecotourism attributes and also previous and current experience. Three categories of ecotourist can be identified which are soft, structured and hard ecotourists by analysing and segmenting process. The ecotourism operators are able to meet the ecotourist's expectation and measure the trip characteristics of ecotourists for services and preferred travel arrangement. This is supported previously by Weaver and Lawton (2002), who significantly aided in clarifying and enhancing the understanding of the segmentation of the ecotourist.

Besides, there is several proposal and latest on-going project of ecotourism in Malaysia. The Perak River Tourism Corridor (PRTC) is an area along the river that has been proposed as the state's future tourism focal point. It was chosen based on the unique characteristics each possesses in representing Perak's new and authentic tourism characteristics. The proposed PRTC will represent the state's tourism image as heritage-education-adventure; similarly, the area should be able to represent the wonderful archaeological resources and Old Perak realm as new tourism experiences; the PRTC also represents the hinterland-adventure aspects of the state that have yet to be tapped for future tourism offerings (Aziz et al., 2020a).

On the other hand, Aziz et al. (2020b) demonstrate the process of developing a master plan as a critical and systematic effort to develop a long-term guide for Pahang's Mossy Forest Park development. The Parks Master Plan serves as a framework and guide for the related authority in achieving the vision of a better parks system. Mossy Forest Park in Cameron Highlands, Pahang was redeveloped with the ultimate goal of establishing a strong and positive 'brand' for the forest while also highlighting Pahang State's image as Malaysia's ultimate nature tourism destination.

Other studies have discovered that ecotourist segments remain close yet distant due to differences in ecotourism settings and participants at the time. For instance, ecotourists value involvement in high-risk adventures or activities (Weaver & Lawton, 2002). The preference for physically intensive activities distinguishes domestic ecotourists. Given that hard ecotourists were more willing to try extremely trying activities, it would be advantageous for management to offer a package that included highly challenging activities to appeal to this kind of segmentation.

Conceptual Development

To create a conceptual model for this study, the researchers was applied among the major theories underlying the community-based tourism development which are the Murphy's Ecological Model, the theory of Social Exchange and the theory of Community Attachment.

Murphy's Ecological Model

In her book "Community Development through Tourism", Beeton (2006) discussed a few of theories relating to community-based tourism planning and development. Beeton (2006) emphasised ON the significance of this model, which is frequently used to explain the relationship between tourism and local communities. Murphy is the leading authority on the community's tourism position and role. He pioneered this theory in 1983, contrasting the local community with the visiting community or their origin. This Murphy's model emphasises the importance of local community participation in all stages of tourism planning (participatory planning), but in the case of small-scale planning, more community members must be encouraged to participate in the tourism decision-making process. The ultimate goal of this exercise is to establish community-based tourism development that results in increased community empowerment.

Community Attachment Theory

This theory is used to explain how local residents perceive tourism's influence or contribution to their well-being. McCool and Martin (1994) identified that the community attachment is the social integration and the involvement of people in a community lifestyle that results in a sense of attachment and acts in the best interests of the community. Similarly, Buttel et al. (1979) also clarified that the community attachment as the establishment of an awareness of or the community's social network. A community's level of attachment is determined by the amount of time an individual has spent there since birth or as a child (Harrill, 2004; McGehee & Andereck, 2004; Jurowski et al., 1998; Um & Crompton, 1987). While McCool and Martin (1994) discovered that residents with a stronger sense of community have a more favourable view of tourism's contribution to the well-being of local community life than unattached residents. Regardless, both parties acknowledged that tourism had a negative impact on the environment. However, Um and Crompton (1987) discovered that residents with a stronger sense of negative perception will affected to tourism's sustainability, owing to the fact that the many forms of taxation will be imposed on residents by the government due to the development of tourism's facilities and infrastructure. Harrill (2004) suggested that those involved in community-based tourism development should educate or inform community members about the negative environmental impacts of tourism development and the economic burden imposed by taxation. Individuals who are not affiliated with a community must be educated about the positive effects of tourism on community development.

The Social Exchange Theory

Social exchange occurs voluntarily between certain actors within a community for the purpose of achieving collective benefits (Blau, 1994; Emerson, 1976; Homans, 1958). This theory has been implemented to a numerous of fields, including sociology, economics, and social psychology, in order to analyse the changes that occur within society (Wang & Pfister, 2008). This theory is used in tourism research to better understand how communities perceive the tourism products (Andereck et al., 2005; Sirakaya et al., 2001; Jurowski et al., 1998). Wang and Pfister (2008) looked from the angle of non-economic impact which are from the socio-psychological and sociological aspects where the residents value tourism positively because they also gained from tourism development through improved infrastructure, performances, elements of culture and arts, choice of food and shopping, recreational opportunities, historic places and community service. According to Beeton (2006), power relations is important to ensure balance between the community and tourists so that the exchange that takes place benefits both parties. Community power refers to social power and political power. An understanding of how the power relations influence the community is important to achieve a balanced community development.

As a result, community perception has an effect on their participation in organised tourism activities, and their support is critical for the successful implementation of community-based tourism (Andereck et al., 2005).

Integrated Empirical Model

The current study contributes to the development of an integrated ecotourism model for the process of community development in villages engaged in ecotourism development, as illustrated in Fig. 2.1. This framework is based on Deacon and Firebaugh's Input-Throughput-Output Model (1988). This model is based on System

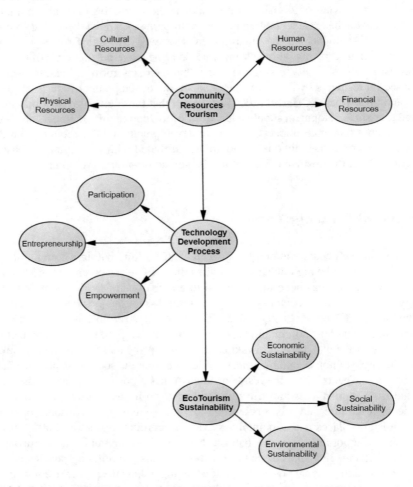

Fig. 2.1 Input-throughput-output model. *Source* Deacon and Firebaugh (1988)

Theory, a holistic approach for comprehending and explaining complex and organised phenomena in which each component has a strong relationship with the others and contributes to the whole (Constantine, 1986).

According to Deacon and Firebaugh (1988), the model's three components, input, throughput, and output, are suitable and applicable to all types of management systems. Each sector is distinct in its approach to resource management and achievement of its distinct objectives. According to Goldsmith (2005), this model has been widely applied to financial and resource management, while Pennings et al. (2006) used it to explain the political system approach.

This research framework was developed to better understand the relationship between community development and ecotourism development in a community system. The model's three components, Input-Throughput-Output, illustrate how community development influences and contributes to ecotourism development. The Input-Throughput-Output Model was adapted for this study based on the requirements for ecotourism development. The first component consists of the physical and social aspects of the ecotourism destination, which are comprised of four primary components: financial resources, human resources, cultural resources, and physical resources, all of which are regarded as community input. The second component encompasses all human aspects of the community that are transformed through the process of technology development (participation, entrepreneurship, and empowerment), also referred to as throughput, during the implementation of the homestay programme, which consists of three components: entrepreneurship, participation, and empowerment. Proper implementation of ecotourism would undoubtedly result in improved coordination, increased tourist visitation, increased participation, increased family unity, and supplementary income, all of which are necessary for ecotourism's success (Fig. 2.1).

According to Kiper (2013), the findings stated that the failure of sustainable of ecotourism products is occurs due to the conflict of interests by the stakeholders especially during the process of decision making. This is due to the complexity of ecotourism and the multifarious nature of stakeholders which they are diversified, have differing levels of interest, and have unique viewpoints (Darley & Moswete, 2012). In addition, Thahir et al. (2021) identified a lack of training in the tourism industry's workforce, which has an effect on service quality. Employee certification in the tourism industry can help increase visitor satisfaction. Standardization of skill training should be strengthened to maintain the workforce's awareness and motivation for sustainable tourism.

Cini et al. (2015) discovered that young tourist among university's student in South Africa, Mexico, the United States of America, Germany, and Italy has limited knowledge of ecotourism even in their own country, and the researchers identified that activities such as educational visit, field research trip and ecotourism's workshops are meaningful to boost people's knowledge especially young generation. This finding is consistent with a previous study by Sangpikul and Batra (2007), which stated that environment education and ecotourism should occur in the same alignment is either via formal or informal platform. The formal platform can be organised by including educational institutions as partnerships such as schools, colleges, or universities that creates and offer the special programme on the ecotourism and environmental awareness. Whereas Kasim and Wickens (2018) substantiate this point by demonstrating that awareness, intentions, and attitudes toward ecotourism are considered critical factors in the growth of ecotourism. The tourist may be created through their own travel experiences or through knowledge which can be gained through non-formal sources such as physical or social media.

According to Hawariyuni et al. (2018), homestay accommodations built specifically in ecotourism areas to attract tourists are unable to provide adequate services and a comfortable environment with sufficient privacy. Most of the homestay accommodations allow guests to stay with the owner's family members, with no physical barriers between them. Additionally, Sarina (2019) identified many issues and problems such as unethical, unregistered homestay operators that may tarnish the good name of registered homestay as well as lack of homestay regulations and policies monitored by local government. Aside from that, the operators lack creativity and entrepreneurial skills to adapt to tourism disruption, specifically digitalisation facilities such as internet access, online booking platforms, and e-marketing.

According to Chai-Arayalert (2020), it promotes ecotourism in destinations and enables the ecotourist to know and experience about ecotourism destination by using modern media in a smart-learning application. Thus, this application will be able to removes the barriers to young people to understand on ecotourism products by tailoring an online learning channel to their specific needs. All of the above-mentioned strategies should be backed up by the capability of the entrepreneur in the numerous creative industries, which is concerned with the strategy execution, organisational design, and crucial element which leadership style within a cultural context (Bujor & Avasilcai, 2016). This concept refers to those gifted and successful entrepreneurs who are capable of transforming their ideas into products or services for society (United Nations Conference on Trade and Development & United Nations Development Programme, 2010). Creative businesses are more active in promoting innovation for their business organisation.

In addition to these factors, trust in the government's capability is a critical component of ecotourism sustainability. Wong and Lai (2021) investigated the factor that influenced the Macao's resident to support tourism's industry during and after the COVID-19 pandemic, and it demonstrated that how the government enforcement's actions can bolster support especially during recovery process. The community satisfaction with government action, the study found, increases community trust and support for tourism recovery. The tourism industry, like all others, has been impacted by the advancements of technology and innovations. The impact of technology is readily apparent in its effect on transportation, the sector's bedrock. The number of tourist would not achieved 300 million in 1970 to 3.6 billion in 2016 without the technological advancements in larger, faster, and more fuel-efficient aircraft carriers. The other aspect of technology that has an effect on tourism is digital advancements, particularly in information and communication technology. The travel industry has changed dramatically as a result of ICT, which has altered booking patterns and contributed to the rise of tech-savvy millennials, who are now tourism's leaders. The digital technology has been impacted on housing and local transportation as a result of the sharing economy's growth. Technological advancements are giving significantly impact on the future of tourism (World Tourism Organization & Global Tourism Economy Research Centre, 2017). According to Kiper (2013), tourism requires sustainable development, and there is a much stronger connection between tourism and the environment than there is in other sectors.

Following the Ministry of Tourism, Arts & Culture, Malaysia (2020), six strategies have been established to achieve tourism transformation in accordance with the National Tourism Policy 2020—2030. The first strategy is to strengthen the governance capacity of Malaysian tourism-related agencies in order to better leverage their tourism core competencies. The second strategy is to establish the Special Tourism Investment Zones (STIZs) to spur the development of high-value, innovative tourism products and services in response to the growing sophistication of the market. The third strategy is to embark on a comprehensive digital transformation journey in order to transform Malaysia's tourism industry into one that is smart. The fourth strategy is to increase the demand of sophistication by deepening the tourist experience in order to facilitate customised and discerning travel. The fifth strategy is to align with the National Tourism Policy with the United Nations Sustainable Development Goals (UNSDGs) by reaffirming tourism's role as a catalyst for sustainable, responsible, and inclusive economic development. The sixth strategy is to foster the development of service culture through the development of capacity and human capital development that cascades seamlessly from the macro to the destination level. Four action strategies for Smart Tourism were introduced by the government, which are firstly, the tourism player should optimise e-marketing usage by stepping up synergy between the government and tourism industry players in driving digitalisation. Secondly, embracing the knowledge sharing economy to innovate the informal tourism sector and rural tourism. Thirdly, leverage on the analytical of big data to assist the decision making and future planning. Lastly, increase the visitor arrivals to rural areas through digitalisation.

Conclusion and Recommendations

The expectation that ecotourism demand will not reach pre-crisis levels until 2023 also provides an opportunity and some space for tourism destinations to reshape the industry in a more sustainable, innovative manner that benefits travellers, local communities, the environment, and local economies equally. The COVID-19 crisis has established itself as a unique global challenge, necessitating international cooperation and collaboration in order to mitigate the pandemic's social and economic consequences.

At the outset, the researchers sought to investigate Malaysia's ecotourism policy, to identify the strengths and weaknesses of existing ecotourism destinations in Malaysia, to investigate mechanisms for enhancing and promoting this product globally, to identify initiatives that can be implemented to attract international tourist segments, and to recommend sustainable policies to the government especially to the Ministry of Culture, Arts and Tourism, Malaysia.

On the other hand, using the aforementioned literature, the study will be able to provide a new perspective on stakeholder's management. As a result of the integrated empirical model proposed, it was demonstrated that the complexity of ecotourism due to the numerous numbers of stakeholders with disparate interests. Perhaps it is instructive to examine such complexities as a means of more effectively managing ecotourism through communication among the various stakeholders, coordination of their actions, and adaptation processes. Malaysia has immense potential to enhance its presence in the global tourism market and any improvement recommended if implemented will make significant strides in developing the tourism industry and educating the locals in these issues.

The practitioners and the researchers in future will be able as well to gain valuable insights on ecotourism products and its sustainability from the findings of this paper. During their presentations, the practitioners and the researchers would be able to convey the findings of this research on the mechanism of survival for innovative businesses. The latter mechanisms are vividly illustrated in the descriptive research, which aims to broaden the debate and instil a sense of the critical nature of stakeholder management in addressing ecotourism challenges.

Entrepreneurs with innovative ideas who wish to investigate a viable revenue stream for ecotourism products and community development strategy may use the model specified in this research as a benchmark for best practises. Besides, the creative entrepreneurs in the ecotourism industry should take advantage of this "rest" period to assess the situation, boost their creativity, and strategize the best mechanism for pandemic recovery in the future. The true obstacle is to pursue the creative entrepreneurship must overcome as the important action to strike a balance between the financial aspect of the business and the creativity artistic. Numerous measures have been implemented in the region's countries to mitigate the pandemic's economic and social effects on tourism and to prepare the sector for recovery.

References

Andereck, K. L., Valentine, K. M., Knopf, R. C., & Vogt, C. A. (2005). Resident perceptions of community tourism impacts. *Annals of Tourism Research, 32*(4), 1056–1076.

Aziz, A., Ajuhari, Z., & Bidin, S. (2020a). Recreation and tourism resource assessments along the Perak River Tourism Corridor. In M. Mariapan, E. L. A. Lin, S. Bidin, A. Zawawi, Z. A. Z. Abidin, & N. J. Jumaat (Eds.), *Ecotourism in Malaysia: Current scenario* (pp. 1–13). Universiti Putra Malaysia.

Aziz, A., Ajuhari, Z., Bidin, S., & Yaakob, S. S. N. (2020b). Re-development of Mossy Forest Park in Cameron Highlands, Pahang: A case study for preparing a Master Plan in Manohar Mariapan. In M. Mariapan, E. L. A. Lin, S. Bidin, A. Zawawi, Z. A. Z. Abidin, & N. J. Jumaat (Eds.), *Ecotourism in Malaysia: Current scenario* (pp. 14–24). Universiti Putra Malaysia.

Beeton, R. J. S. (2006). *Community development through tourism*. Landlinks Press.

Blau, P. (1994). *Structural contexts of opportunities*. University of Chicago Press.

Bujor, A., & Avasilcai, S. (2016). The creative entrepreneur: A framework of analysis. *Procedia—Social and Behavioral Sciences, 221*, 21–28.
Buttel, F. H., Marthinson, O. B., & Wilkening, E. A. (1979). Size and place of community attachment: A reconsideration. *Social Indicators Research, 6*, 474–485.
Camilleri, M. A. (2018). *Travel marketing, tourism economics and the airline product: An introduction to theory and practice*. Cham: Springer Nature.
Chai-Arayalert, S. (2020). Smart application of learning ecotourism for young eco-tourists. *Cogent Social Sciences, 6*(1), 1772558.
Cini, F., Van der Merwe, P., & Saayman, M. (2015). Tourism students' knowledge and tenets towards ecotourism. *Journal of Teaching in Travel and Tourism, 15*(1), 74–91.
Constantine, L. L. (1986). *Family paradigms: The practice of Theory in Family Therapy*. Guilford Press.
Cooper, C., Fletcher, J., Fyall, A., Gilbert, D., & Wanhill, S. (2005). *Tourism principles and practices* (3rd ed.). Pearson Education.
Darley, W. K., & Moswete, N. N. (2012). Tourism survey research in sub-Saharan Africa: Problems and challenges. *Current Issues in Tourism, 15*(4), 369–383.
Deacon, R. E., & Firebaugh, F. M. (1988). *Family resource management: Principles and applications* (2nd ed.). Allyn and Bacon.
Economic Commission for Latin America and the Caribbean (ECLAC). (2020). *Building a new future: Transformative recovery with equality and sustainability (LC/SES.38/3-P/Rev.1)*. Santiago: ECLAC.
Emerson, R. (1976). Social exchange theory. *Annual Review of Sociology, 2*, 262–335.
Goldsmith, A. (2005). Police reform and the problem of trust. *Theoretical Criminology, 9*(4), 443–470.
Harrill, R. (2004). Residents' attitudes toward tourism development: A literature review with implications for tourism planning. *Journal of Planning Literature, 18*, 251–266.
Hawariyuni, W., Rashid, A. Z. b. A., Alaeddin, O., Krishnan, K. S., Sentosa, I. & Nugraha, Y. M. (2018). Establishing Shari'ah compliant homestay in Indonesia: Issues and challenges. *American Scientific Publishers Advanced Science Letters, 24*(1), 289–292.
Homans, G. C. (1958). Social behavior as exchange. *American Journal of Sociology, 63*(6), 597–606.
Jurowski, C. (1998). A theoretical analysis of host community resident reactions to tourism. *Journal of Travel Research, 34*(2), 3–11.
Kampel, K. (2020). COVID-19 and tourism: charting a sustainable, resilient recovery for small states. *A Special Focus on COVID-19 and the Commonwealth, 163*, 1–14.
Kasim, A., & Wickens, E. (2018). Exploring youth awareness, intention and opinion on green travel: The case of Malaysia. *Tourism and Hospitality Research, 18*(4), 1–15.
Kiper, T. (2013). Role of ecotourism in sustainable development. In M. Özyavuz (Ed.), *Advances in landscape architecture* (pp. 773–802). Intechopen and ABEBooks.
McCool, S. F., & Martin, S. R. (1994). Community attachment and attitudes toward tourism development. *Journal of Travel Research, 32*(3), 29–34.
McGehee, N. G., & Andereck, K. L. (2004). Factors predicting rural residents' support of tourism. *Journal of Travel Research, 43*, 131–140.
Ministry of Tourism, Arts & Culture, Malaysia. (2020). *National tourism policy 2020–2030 executive summary*. Putrajaya: Ministry of Tourism, Arts and Culture, Malaysia.
Ministry of Tourism, Arts & Culture, Malaysia. (2021). *Malaysia tourism statistics in brief*. https://www.tourism.gov.my/statistics. Accessed 18 May 2022.
Organisation for Economic and Cooperation and Development (OECD). (2020). *Tackling Coronavirus: Tourism policy responses*. https://www.oecd.org/coronavirus/policy-responses/tourism-policy-responses-to-the-coronavirus-covid-19-6466aa20/. Accessed 15 May 2022.
Osman, Z., & Sentosa, I. (2013). Mediating effect of customer satisfaction on service quality and customer loyalty relationship in Malaysian rural tourism. *International Journal of Economics Business and Management Studies, 2*(1), 25–37.

Pennings, P., Keman, H., & Kleinnijenhuis, J. (2006). *Doing research in political science: An introduction to comparative methods and statistics.* Sage.

Ramlan, M. A., Aziz, A., Mariapan, M., Sheena, B., & Yacob, M. R. (2013). Attractiveness of forest research institute Malaysia (FRIM) canopy walkway as nature-based tourism product. *The Malaysian Forester, 76*(2), 155–163.

Ritchie, J. R. B., & Crouch, G. (2000). The competitive destination: A sustainability perspective. *Tourism Management, 21*(1), 1–7.

Sangpikul, A., & Batra, A. (2007). Ecotourism: A perspective from Thai youths. *The Journal of Hospitality Leisure Sport and Tourism, 6*(1), 81–85.

Sarina, M. N. (2019). *Challenges faced by registered homestay operators from the perspectives of selected stakeholders in Selangor, Malaysia.* Universiti Putra Malaysia.

Sheena, B., Manohar, M., & Azlizam, A. (2015). Characteristics of Malaysian ecotourist segments in Kinabalu Park Sabah. *Tourism Geographies, 17*(1), 1–18.

Sirakaya, E., Jamal, T., & Choi, H. S. (2001). Developing tourism indicators for destination sustainability. In D. B. Weaver (Ed.), *Encyclopedia of ecotourism* (pp. 411–432). CAB International.

Thahir, H., Hadi, S., Zahra, F., Arif, I., Murad, M. A., & Lolo, M. H. (2021). Issues, challenges and strengths of sustainable tourism supply chain after Covid-19 in Togean National Park-Sulawesi, Indonesia: a preliminary findings. In *Proceedings of the International Conference on Strategic Issues of Economics, Business and, Education (ICoSIEBE 2020)* (vol. 163, pp. 274–278).

The International Ecotourism Society (TIES). (2015). *Home.* https://www.ecotourism.org/. Accessed 19 July 2022.

Um, S., & Crompton, J. L. (1987). Measuring resident's attachment levels in a host community. *Journal of Travel Research, 26*(1), 27–29.

United Nations (UN). (2000). *United Nations policy brief: COVID-19 and transforming tourism.* NY, UN.

United Nations Conference on Trade and Development (UNCTAD) & United Nations Development Programme (UNDP). (2010). *All publications: creative economy 2010 report: A feasible development option.* http://www.unctad.org/en/pages/PublicationArchive.aspx?publicationid=946. Accessed 28 July 2022.

United Nations World Tourism Organization (UNWTO). (2020a). *UNWTO launches global guidelines to reopen tourism.* https://www.unwto.org/news/unwto-launches-global-guidelines-to-restart-tourism. Accessed 28 July 2022.

United Nations World Tourism Organization (UNWTO). (2020b). *World tourism barometer may 2020: Special focus on the impact of COVID-19.* UNWTO.

Wallace, R. (2019). Ecotourism in Asia: How strong branding creates opportunity for local economies and the environment. In R. Hashim, M.H.M. Hanafiah & M.R. Jamaluddin (Eds.), *Positioning and branding tourism destinations for global competitiveness* (pp. 192–211). Hershey, PA: IGI Global.

Wang, Y., & Pfister, R. E. (2008). Residents' attitudes toward tourism and perceived personal benefits in a rural community. *Journal of Travel Research, 47*, 84–93.

Weaver, D. B., & Lawton, L. J. (2002). Overnight ecotourist market segmentation in the Gold Coast Hinterland of Australia. *Journal of Travel Research, 40*(3), 270–280.

Wong, J. W. C., & Lai, I. K. W. (2021). Effect of government enforcement actions on resident support for tourism recovery during the COVID-19 crisis in Macao, China. *Asia Pacific Journal of Tourism Research, 26*(9), 973–987.

World Tourism Organization and Global Tourism Economy Research Centre. (2017). *UNWTO/GTERC annual report on tourism trends, 2017 edition—Executive summary.* UNWTO.

Farah Hida Sharin is a Ph.D. Scholar at Universiti Kuala Lumpur (UniKL) Business School, where she specializes in digital marketing intelligence and technopreneurship for rural tourism. She graduated from Universiti Teknologi MARA with a Master of Business Administration

(MBA) and a Bachelor of Business Administration (Hons.) in Marketing. Holding various management positions and being involved in policy development since she was 23 led her to pursue a Doctorate of Philosophy (Management) at UniKL Business School currently. Prior to joining the teaching profession, she worked in both the public and private sectors, including city hall, law firms, real estate and property management, and education. Her interest in the development of graduates directed her to become a basic certified counsellor and a certified HRDF trainer. She also realizes her passion in business through managing the company as co-founder and owner. Due to the knowledge and experience, she always been invited to be adjudicator for local and international academic competition such business plan and marketing plan competition. Her current research interest is dynamic business modeling issues using the techniques of System Dynamics (SD) and Structural Equation Modeling (SEM).

Dr. Ilham Sentosa is an Associate Professor, an eco-system developer, researcher, senior lecturer and business consultant with expertise in smart city management, creative technopreneurship and dynamic business modeling issues using the techniques of System Dynamics (SD) and Structural Equation Modeling (SEM). Dr. Sentosa also recognized as an advanced quantitative analyst with interest in latent variable measurement models (factor analysis, item response), longitudinal data analysis (latent growth curves, growth mixture models), parametric and non-parametric analysis using measurement models approaches. He holds the post of Associate Professor at Universiti Kuala Lumpur (UniKL) Business School, Malaysia, where he teaches a graduate course on advanced structural model analysis techniques.

Chapter 3
Strategy and Technology Framework in the Pandemic Era Among Aviation Players

Mohd Norazali Nordin

Abstract Devastating impact on COVID-19's pandemic on aviation industry affecting millions of aviation players and users around the world. This unprecedented crisis has led to billion dollars' losses and expenses to the stakeholders in the industry. This pandemic has been thoroughly documented in recent scientific literature, with various studies analyzing various aspects of the changes triggered by COVID-19. Several studies have reported that COVID-19 has a positive long-term effects in air travel industry. In recent years, there are numerous technology has been implemented in the industry in order to remain competitive during these pandemic outbreaks. This paper provides an assessment that outlines the effects of the pandemic, technology application among aviation players in post COVID-19 era and recovery strategy among aviation players to encounter these issues. Despite many practices, recommendations, and suggestions arising during previous outbreaks, only a small number have been applied to air travel in civil aviation practices and operations. In this paper, several initiatives and multiple approached introduced by the aviation players during these pandemic are discussed and highlighted.

Keywords Aviation · Post COVID-19 · Technology · Strategy · Recovery · Air travel

Introduction

The COVID-19 pandemic outbreak, which occurred in 2019, is still continuing to pose a threat to global health and the economy. It has given a big distraught to the business processes in all industries including aviation industry. The aviation industry has faced a vital change in its business during this pandemic outbreak hits around the world. The aviation industry which have several industries behind it (such as airport, air travel airlines, airfreight business and MROs) have made significant progress in its recovery from COVID-19 pandemic. According to Li et al. (2021), in the

M. N. Nordin (✉)
Malaysian Institute of Industrial Logistics, Universiti Kuala Lumpur, Kuala Lumpur, Malaysia
e-mail: mnorazali4@gmail.com

next few years that will be crucial in battling this unprecedented crisis. Olaganathan (2021) mentioned that, Aviation has generated 3.6 percent of gross domestic product (GDP) of the world by creating about 65.6 million jobs in air travel and aviation related industries worldwide. The pertinent job is including the employment of flight crew, cabin crew, maintenance and technical team, ground team, equipment supplier, training provider such as aviation training school and several others. Among these direct job servant, out of 36.7 million from 65.6 million jobs has served for tourism industry which particularly relying on air travel demand (International Air Transport Association, 2020a). These negative impacts have made exponentially increased billion dollars of losses day by day (Deveci et al., 2022).

Nowadays, air travel demand is seeming to be well as one of the foundations of the global economy in the post COVID-19 era. Travel restrictions, partial lockdowns, and ongoing quarantine measures remain a hindrance to international travel, but vaccine production is increasing, providing a better prospect for recovery and a future of wider operations (Rust et al., 2021). Airports are continuing to concentrate passenger and employee safety, cost reductions in response to planning and to improve the lower levels of traffic. These initiatives are planned to make an airports as safe as possible in order to salvage the air traveller self-assurance as well as remain responsive in this indeterminate times. Airlines also have taken some proactive roles by introducing several exertions to their passenger to regain passenger confidence to fly again. It took 50 years for the air transport market to reach one billion passengers in1987, and then it had exponential growth in less than two decades, topping two billion in2005, three billion in2013, and 4.5 billion in 2019 (Liu et al., 2021).

The tragedy of the terrorist attacks September 11in 2001, the financial crisis of 2008 are two examples of the previous catastrophic events that caused air travellers to lose their faith in the sky. Right after two decade of the event, COVID-19 has hit the world which makes people afraid to fly again due to subsequent rapid spread of this contagious disease and it's almost unrealized. Besides the travel bans set up by countries globally, the airlines and airports have come out with several innovative strategies to rebuild passenger self-assured to fly again after people felt reluctance to travel during pandemic. These supply chain between airport and airlines continue to create and evaluate best practises for the near future of air travel, with a greater emphasis on passenger health and personal safety throughout the journey (International Air Transport Association, 2020b; Airport Council International, 2020). Several concepts have been introduced by International Air Transport Association (IATA), and Airport Council International (ACI), to improve passenger experience and convenience with advanced processing system technology in supporting the resumption of the industry when health mitigations requirement as it needs to be accommodated.

Although the damaging impacts of these contagious diseases have drawn attention from scholars (e.g. Dube et al., 2021; Gössling, 2020; Miani et al., 2021; Sun et al., 2021; Yu & Chen, 2021) on air travel demand pattern, initiatives and strategies taken up by aviation players especially airport and airlines industry through installations of new technology and implementations in their operation in battling this pandemic is robust and bombshell. It is an imperative core factor that aviation industry's immediate business restart efforts and future activities need to focus on long-term implementations in the post-pandemic world. As part of rebooting aviation industry, introduction of new technology playing an imperative role to bring a significant impact to the industry's recovery and resilience planning—so it can properly control the airport and airlines environments—the potential future transmission risk of the disease in the future can be controlled. New understanding of sustainability in technology at the airport such as early passenger health screen checks before on-board, biometric application, face recognition, electronic bag tags, self-service check in from home and touchless technology have brought brighter potential in supporting industry resumption besides sanitized hands and wearing mask at all times. The future of aircraft is depending on its day to day key decision making on aircraft operation efficiency (Tisdall & Zhang, 2020). Increased efficiency of aircraft operation will give direct impact to the financial standing of the airlines through cost reduction in their line besides reduce carbon emission. In the long run, by installing new technology followed by stringent requirements, drastically new aircraft design and concept are probable to emerge using this clean renewable energy technology through these digital technology application to support business. To fit in COVID-19 crisis support by the air traveller and aviation industry users, these initiatives strategy can push this development forward. Therefore, this study focuses on strengthening technology application by the aviation stakeholders to support their business operation, domestic or internationally besides recovery strategy in every technology used during COVID-19 and continuous application of the technology for post COVID-19 era.

Air Travel Restrictions

COVID -19 has had a large impact on the demand of passenger transport, as a combination of fears of contracting and government lockdowns also the spreading of the virus resulted in a reduction of demand. Travel restrictions, the economic crisis and changes in the behavior of passengers have led to a dramatic fall in demand for air travel services. The tourism industry as one of the industry which has directly impacted with the down fall drop of air travel demand around the globe when all the countries starts ban the cross countries travel. According to IATA (2020b), measured by revenue passenger kilometers, passenger air transport fell year-over-year in April 2020 by 90% and remained down by 75% in August. A slump drop in economic activity and commerce has had an impact on freight, which was about 30% lower year over year in April 2020 and is still around 12% lower in August 2020, making the industry even worse. A large amount of the shock due to this pandemic has put airline companies' liquidity buffers in strain, even though an important portion of airline costs are variable, and recent drops in oil prices have caused them to lower operating costs. This crisis can result in a reduction in transport demand that lasts for a long time, especially in cases where transportation is not considered as essential. In prediction, there are two uncertainties that the airlines companies have to face;

health-related measures cost and poor commercial flight recovery strategy (Abate et al., 2020). The combination of these two uncertainties will have a significant negative impacts on the demand of air travel as a whole. The intervention of policy makers is required at this phase in order to reduce the encumbrance of the airlines industry especially during post COVID-19 era to assure their competitiveness in the market can be sustained.

Policy Interventions for Air Travel Sustainability

Different public policy interventions have been made in the aviation industry in the past brings different rationales. Airlines especially aircraft operations become the main target of discussion in this policy intervention specifically in technology adoptions. There is a tendency for these airlines and firms to learn by doing and realise the significant economies of scale which may result in underinvestment in technology, innovation or production which may justify public interest in air travel. Public policies have also been directed toward managing a wide selection of suppliers and expertise, and also ensuring aircraft safety (Dube et al., 2021; Zhang et al., 2021). Recently, airlines and aircraft manufacturer have been a targeted for the policies of green industrial for low-carbon aircraft initiatives especially during flight. Government interventions have become a highlight for the employment issues at a large company such as air transport and travel agencies. In response to the crisis of COVID-19, most of the industries looking at the air transportation sector as a specific measures of performance. In August 2020, governments had providing airlines with support of about USD 160 billion according to (IATA,). The intervention of government in some countries had generally focuses on liquidity of airlines' financial standing for job-retention scheme, sectoral scheme which for those airlines who are operates for the whole country and firm-specific support measures for the companies who are operates to support airlines operations such as MRO industry.

Key Recovery Phases

The COVID-19 outbreaks around the world has change all industry holistically. The aviation industry was impacted with more than 58% of arrival passenger stagnant figure with no changes and the number of losses become higher with more than 795,000 of cancelled flights—passenger figures dropped estimated to lose billions of revenue at the end of the year 2021 (Deveci et al., 2022; Gössling, 2020; Liu et al., 2021). The aviation industry as a whole was not ready for the impact of COVID-19. Integrated with digital transformation in the business provide business intelligence and restore passenger confidence to fly. The key questions for aviation to recover become a greatest discussion among the stakeholders—how to encourage the passenger to fly again to maximize passenger number of flying, how to regain

3 Strategy and Technology Framework in the Pandemic Era …   33

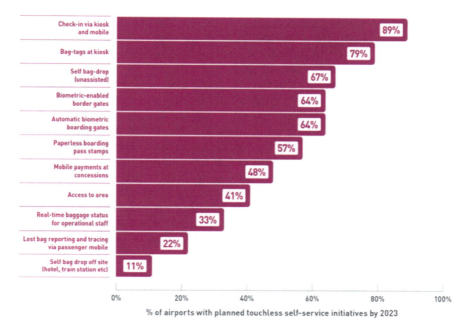

Fig. 3.1 Percentage of airports with planned touchless self-service initiatives by area, by 2023. *Source* Airport Council International (2020)

passenger confidence and passenger demand in the midst of the pandemic and how to improve passenger travels per kilometer. According to IATA (2020a, b), Revenue Passenger Kilometers (RPKs) fell 94% year-on-year in April, the biggest drop in the history of our time series that dates back to 1990. The massive contraction builds year-on-year decline about 55% starting March, 2020. By looking Fig. 3.1, aviation industry has to propose strategies and initiatives to foster air travel demand. There are three key recovery phases need to be matched in the point of interventions to return: restore, reshape and react (Ebbutt, 2022).

Restore—Get the Aircraft Flying

One of the initiative to make the industry progress is to reconfigure the operations of the flight by restoring passenger's confidence in flying. The airlines need to promote the safety of the air traveler in flight by presenting the safety measures and preventive action to the regulators especially the government—to convince them to reopen the border to allow these aircrafts to fly again. According to Deveci et al. (2022), travel bans by the countries have had caused consequent damage impact to the aviation industry. Understanding current data and technology is crucial in ensuring the right decision making at this phase of pandemic. Data underutilization is a common issue among industry players. In airport industry the collected raw data of the passenger need to be utilized by processing the data through tried-and-tested digital system in delivering the value of restoring business as well as reviewing whether new data streams can be generated to support decision making and passenger information, this will become as one of the effort in strengthen infection control efforts and build trust among passengers. As an airline, identifying key physical touchpoints in the passenger journey and understanding how existing technology can be used to replace the previous procedures which these can reduce the risk of cross-contamination (Gössling, 2020). Passengers, airport operators and other stakeholders may also then collaborate to minimize risk from the moment a flight ticket is booked until it lands at the gate and it disembarks at its destination. Fully utilization of mobile apps technology nowadays shows that the technology applications is able to replace a series of activities of passenger processing at the airport and ease airlines processes. These initiatives need to be enhanced to ensure the passenger have faith and confidence to plan their holiday or journey into and through the facilities again.

Reshape—It's Time for a New Normal

Beyond the temporary resumption, the industry has to remain resilient and sustainable to overcome this crisis. Health passport and thermal screen become an essential screening equipment technology at any airports around the globe for health monitoring purposes. Taking preventive measures by choosing the right automation technologies making contactless journey is possible for the safety of passenger and staff besides adds cost efficiencies in the business. Installation of new sensor and surveillance are able to improve operators' in controlling the assets in order to plan and enforce a vigorous hygiene program to manage these contagious diseases from spreading at their operation areas (Abu-Rayash & Dincer, 2020; Jamaludin et al., 2020). Furthermore, the improvement of data utilization can have a broader bearing power drive the efficiency and effectiveness in managing assets. It will allow owners and operators to understand how individual assets works and processes are performing in every angle, and in what condition of the assets they are in. In order to make better operational and investment decisions, operators should consider what data they need to ensure them to perform well. Combination of data from various data collection technology such as machine learning technologies will be core processes to aviation industry in adaptation and application in facing these liquid operations environment.

React—Preparation for Future Pandemics

As it has been treated as the pandemic all around the globe, the players in the industry need to take proactive action in managing these issues. The probability of these pandemic to happen again is obvious. The new challenges will be faced by aviation industry is in COVID-19 issues (Tisdall & Zhang, 2020). As a result of COVID-19, the aviation industry has learned the importance of preparedness, which facilitates rapid response in the event of pandemics in the future. COVID-19 and containment measures have resulted in a critical down drop in air passenger demand for air travel including air freight demand, intimidating the capability of many firms across the air transport area and in the aviation sector as a whole. Similar to how airports prepare for a terror threat by bolstering security, airports need to be 'health aware'—harvesting data about population health and monitoring for health anomalies in the airport environment (Scheelhaase et al., 2022). Efforts must be made to ensure operators can manage health threats effectively and resiliently, which includes adding thermal screening points, allocating space for social distancing, and removing touchpoints (Yu & Chen, 2021). COVID-19 has accelerated the digital revolution in many spheres of life. With the aviation industry striving to get aircraft and passengers back in the air, the digital solutions have a crucial role to play, enabling the industry to use better data and to make better decisions, resulting in better outcomes. Data sharing between airports, airlines, other transport operators, the government and wider stakeholders is essential throughout all three phases of recovery.

Artificial Intelligence in Airlines Operation

In the airline industry, artificial intelligence (AI) systems with machine learning built-in algorithms are widely been used to accumulate and analyze flight data about route distances, altitudes, aircraft types and weights, weather conditions, etc. The carrier also can visualize aircraft operations at the gate or through an on-board video camera so that they can analyze their ground handling procedures and maintain turnaround times by using these AI with built-in with machine learning equipment (Dube et al., 2021). As part of corrective actions, these initiative can improve in cost efficiencies such as preventive aircraft delays, reduces carbon emissions by reducing the time consumption of the equipment whether is in idling mode or in operation. Furthermore, it will promote the energy savings at the aircraft gate, also each fuel consumption use on the ground can be reduced by optimizing aircraft maneuvering processes during taxiing both in terms of unnecessary time waiting to access the aircraft stand or to enter runway and the use of tow tugs rather than use the aircraft's engines. In general, or at least, through aircraft turnaround time and maintenance activities by using AI it will reduce the number of human interactions in ramp and it will not become as one of contribution factor at the main point for the virus to spread (Sun et al., 2021). The successfulness of AI application in aviation industry such as in safety management system in providing structured and unified reporting for Air Navigation Service Providers (ANSPs)—shows a great impact the usage of AI in aviation industry are reliable (Patriarca et al., 2019). The use of AI and data science in airlines can automate their operations, decrease expenses, and increase customer satisfaction. It is also can optimize operations, such as adding, changing, or removing routes, establishing flight times, pricing, and offering products.

Technology Priorities for Airports During Pandemic

According to IATA (2020a, b), Several airports have detained the opportunity to reconsider their normal production and normal business operational processes, including the deployment of innovative technologies and adjustments to space and infrastructure in order to support the global effort in defeating COVID-19. At the same time, airports must find a solution that will benefit them to become more efficient, cut costs, deal with a changing workforce, including the loss of experienced employees, and generate new revenue, all while maintaining high levels of cybersecurity, safety, and aviation security. Information technology, automation and digital transformation are all being evaluated by airports as ways to ensure efficiency, safety and customer experience are all addressed as part of the recovery effort. The 2020 Airport IT Trends Survey revealed a commitment to investing in these areas, as well as new technology, to improve operations and airport business outcomes. There are several plan that need to be put in action by the airport business entities through several implementation stages. These implementation stages are according to few top priorities outlines such as the development of digital technology strategies, cyber security, timely and accurate health information and enabling airport technology application (Airport Council Internation, 2020).

"Touchless" Air Travel Technology

"Touchless" air travel technology is one of the technology that widely been introduce to many airports. The passenger and staff interaction can be minimalized as previous. Body checking, baggage drop service and service at check in counters are now in safe mode and healthy with less "touch" and body contact interaction between passenger and ground staff at the airport. These indirectly meeting the new requirements of social distancing and sanitization. In order to reduce contact between passengers and staff inside the airport, technological solutions must be introduced so that it will permit the passengers to perform functions independently without touching screens or documents. Innovative technologies such as facial recognition and biometrics will become increasingly important to make the travel experience safe, easier and faster for passengers, and also minimize the amount of contact with surfaces and contaminated items. Ultimately it will reduce the possibility of passenger and ground staff to touch the contaminated items during their passenger-flying process. One of the example in Malaysia, a contactless or touchless service provided by Malaysia Airport Berhad is by using biometric face recognition at check in counter. These service can assist the passenger to process their travel journey and make payment during check in process with limited possibility of touching the airport machine and equipment (Olaganathan, 2021). According to ACI (2020), to assure a contactless travel, biometric technologies, AI for bag tracking, crowd monitoring, voice control, and other advancements are successfully being rolled out globally.

Other example is, rather than a close conversation, contactless communication such as walkie talkies and mobile phones is preferred. To reduce physical contact between workers, electronic paperwork has been introduced to replace traditional paperwork such as electronic boarding pass—QR code. Identity verification with biometrics is already a widely accepted solution, and their use will become more widespread as fingerprint scanners and hand scanners are phased out (Element, 2021; Halpern et al., 2021). In the near future, touchless options like contactless fingerprints, iris and facial recognition will be available. Touchless data-entry technologies such as gesture control and touchless document scanning are already being tested. In addition, with mobile apps nowadays, travellers can make airport navigation much easier, collect boarding passes on their phones, avoid lines and human contact, and receive flight alerts.

The Emergence of Mobile Apps

Consumer buying behaviour have change throughout the time. Due to this crisis, people who previously avoided use of mobile application, have suddenly turned to it after they were forced to do so due to lack of access to physical stores during COVID-19 outbreaks. In this case, the air traveller has a very limited access to buy a flight ticket over counter. As people become more accustomed to mobile application, this trend spread through the aviation industry. In recent years, mobile applications have drastically improved the passenger experience. Travelers who are willing to manage their trip journey at their leisure can use mobile applications to check-in, obtain boarding permits, and select desired seats not just limited to buying a ticket flight. Meanwhile, airline, airport authorities and agents use mobile technologies to improve efficiencies and streamline processes. The introduction of apps such as ABOMIS DCS, TAKEFLITE GO, Passenger Document Checker and INK TOUCH shows that how serious the aviation industry strive in their business to ensure the aircraft can fly again through these introduction of mobile application indirectly improving air travel demand. According to Halpern et al. (2021), the benefits of using mobile apps in aviation environment especially in the airport provides a better monitoring and controlling over the passenger by airport authority. The passenger can be segmented easily by the airport operator based on their preferences at the airport and enhance passenger experience during their airport journey. This mobile apps innovation is not just limited for the usage of passenger to do a pre ordering booking for food or flight ticket but the service is now extended to the airport operator to do passenger monitoring at the terminal, security clearance and electronic health screening report can be obtained which this app is interlink with Ministry of Health of their home country. The introduction of these mobile apps ease a lot of problem at the airport. At security checkpoints for instance, smart systems like Thales' Fly to Gate use biometrics and document scanners to recognise and authenticate travellers. BagsID for baggage identification solutions are capable to detect individual bags through unique characteristics which enable contactless baggage handling. All of these technologies are able to ease passenger check in time and improving the experience of the customer.

Conclusion and Recommendations

The COVID-19 catastrophe has already had a considerable impact on people's transportation habits, with significant decreases in airline and public transportation used. Observation from previous crises and overview from previous scholars, the air traveller behaviours will shift in the immediate aftermath of a catastrophe, as people revaluate the costs and benefits of various means of transportation not limited to air transportation (Martin-Domingo & Martín, 2016). The introduction to several digital technology has brought different means to air travel industry. Technology will be critical to the air travel especially in aviation sector for recovery and future development, and the industry as a whole is undergoing a fundamental transformation as it emerges from the pandemic. As part of aviation industry revolution in terms of operation, the quick transition to digitalisation, as well as the adoption and expansion of technology will help to offer a more efficient, cost-effective, and robust aviation system. The technology and solutions discussed have been accelerated in part by the pandemic, and they are also part of the industry's long-term evolution. Whether the passenger perceptions of risk are well founded or not, people's decision making will be influenced by their own perceptions. Health issues becomes the main concern for air travel demand after post COVID-19 era. Upon the lifting of the lockdowns and bans cross countries has been retracted, policy will be a major influence and critical roles in determining whether COVID-19 changes the mobility-related are positive or negative specifically in terms of technology application, energy consumption, health safety, and long term environmental health impact. As recommendation, technology application and adoption in this digital world nowadays showing a lot of improvements and assistance in aviation business besides technology itself is fit for purpose in defeating health issues requirements around the world.

References

Abate, M., Christidis, P., & Purwanto, A. J. (2020). Government support to airlines in the aftermath of the COVID-19 pandemic. *Journal of Air Transport Management, 89*, 101931.
Abu-Rayash, A., & Dincer, I. (2020). Analysis of mobility trends during the COVID-19 coronavirus pandemic: Exploring the impacts on global aviation and travel in selected cities. *Energy Research and Social Science, 68*, 101693.

Airport Council International (ACI). (2020). *Aviation operations during COVID-19 business restart and recovery 2020*. https://www.store.aci.aero/product/aviation-operations-during-covid-19-business-restart-and-recovery/. Accessed 28 Mar 2022.

Deveci, M., Çiftçi, M. E., Akyurt, İZ., & Gonzalez, E. D. R. S. (2022). Impact of COVID-19 pandemic on the Turkish civil aviation industry. *Sustainable Operations and Computers, 3*, 93–102.

Dube, K., Nhamo, G., & Chikodzi, D. (2021). COVID-19 pandemic and prospects for recovery of the global aviation industry. *Journal of Air Transport Management, 92*, 102022.

Ebbutt, L. (2022). Technology's role in rebooting aviation. *MOTT MACDONALD*. https://www.mottmac.com/views/technologys-role-in-rebooting-aviation. Accessed 20 Mar 2022.

Element, S. (2021). How biometrics can help airlines take off again. *Biometric Technology Today, 2021*(1), 8–11.

Gössling, S. (2020). Risks, resilience, and pathways to sustainable aviation: A COVID-19 perspective. *Journal of Air Transport Management, 89*, 101933.

Halpern, N., Mwesiumo, D., Budd, T., Suau-Sanchez, P., & Bråthen, S. (2021). Segmentation of passenger preferences for using digital technologies at airports in Norway. *Journal of Air Transport Management, 91*, 102005.

International Air Transport Association (IATA). (2020a). Air Passenger Market Analysis—April 2020. *IATA Economics Report*, April, 1–4.

International Air Transport Association (IATA). (2020b). *The NEXTT vision in a post-COVID-19 world*. https://www.iata.org/contentassets/bf24e4583c4f4e6398e3ec0b9f6335ed/nextt-vision-post-covid-19-world-1.pdf. Accessed 27 Mar 2022.

Jamaludin, S., Azmir, N. A., Mohamad Ayob, A. F., & Zainal, N. (2020). COVID-19 exit strategy: Transitioning towards a new normal. *Annals of Medicine and Surgery, 59*, 165–170.

Li, X., Lai, P. L., Yang, C. C., & Yuen, K. F. (2021). Determinants of blockchain adoption in the aviation industry: Empirical evidence from Korea. *Journal of Air Transport Management, 97*, 102139.

Liu, A., Kim, Y. R., & O'Connell, J. F. (2021). COVID-19 and the aviation industry: The interrelationship between the spread of the COVID-19 pandemic and the frequency of flights on the EU market. *Annals of Tourism Research, 91*, 103298.

Martin-Domingo, L., & Martín, J. C. (2016). Airport mobile internet an innovation. *Journal of Air Transport Management, 55*, 102–112.

Miani, P., Kille, T., Lee, S. Y., Zhang, Y., & Bates, P. R. (2021). The impact of the COVID-19 pandemic on current tertiary aviation education and future careers: Students' perspective. *Journal of Air Transport Management, 94*, 102081.

Olaganathan, R. (2021). Impact of COVID-19 on airline industry and strategic plan for its recovery with special reference to data analytics technology. *Global Journal of Engineering and Technology Advances, 7*(1), 33–46.

Patriarca, R., Di Gravio, G., Cioponea, R., & Licu, A. (2019). Safety intelligence: Incremental proactive risk management for holistic aviation safety performance. *Safety Science, 118*, 551–567.

Rust, D. L., Stewart, R. D., & Werner, T. J. (2021). The Duluth International Airport aviation business cluster: The impact of COVID-19 and the CARES act. *Research in Transportation Economics, 89*, 101135.

Scheelhaase, J., Ennen, D., Frieske, B., Lütjens, K., Maertens, S., & Wozny, F. (2022). How to support the economic recovery of aviation after COVID-19? *Transportation Research Procedia, 62*, 767–773.

Sun, X., Wandelt, S., Zheng, C., & Zhang, A. (2021). COVID-19 pandemic and air transportation: Successfully navigating the paper hurricane. *Journal of Air Transport Management, 94*, 102062.

Tisdall, L., & Zhang, Y. (2020). Preparing for 'COVID-27': Lessons in management focus—An Australian general aviation perspective. *Journal of Air Transport Management, 89*, 101922.

Yu, M., & Chen, Z. (2021). The effect of aviation responses to the control of imported COVID-19 cases. *Journal of Air Transport Management, 97*, 102140.

Zhang, L., Yang, H., Wang, K., Bian, L., & Zhang, X. (2021). The impact of COVID-19 on airline passenger travel behavior: An exploratory analysis on the Chinese aviation market. *Journal of Air Transport Management, 95*, 102084.

Mohd Norazali Nordin is a Lecturer at Industrial Logistics Section, Universiti Kuala Lumpur Malaysian Institute of Industrial Technology, Malaysia. Nordin has completed his MBA with distinction at Universiti Kuala Lumpur, Business School and obtained his first class degree honors in Aviation Management at Universiti Kuala Lumpur, Malaysian Institute of Aviation Technology. Currently, he is one of active researcher under aerospace cluster majoring in airport management at Universiti Kuala Lumpur. He has more than 9 years of teaching experience at the university level. He is also work as the coordinator of Polytechnic Mauritius Limited—Diploma in Logistics (PML-DIL) of Industrial Logistics Section at Malaysian Institute of Industrial Logistics, Universiti Kuala Lumpur. His areas of interest for teaching and research include Airport Management, Air Freight, Aerospace Management, and Logistics. Currently, he is plan to develop a framework for sustainable airport operation in Malaysia.

Chapter 4
Technology Strategy in Boosting Halal Tourism Activities

Aroop Mukherjee, Salini Devi Rajendran, and Siti Norida Wahab

Abstract The usage of digital technology has been aided by the growing number of Muslim tourists around the globe each year. The birth of the Fourth Industrial Revolution has shifted consumer behaviour and attitudes concerning the use of digital technology in their daily lives. The Halal tourism business is facing various hurdles as a result of the global economy's transition owing to technological disruption. Thus, the purpose of this chapter is to explore the various digital technology utilised in Halal tourism as well as the issues that the business faces. Through the exhaustive study of existing research and contextual synthesis, cyber-physical systems, the internet of things, cloud computing, big data, artificial intelligence, and advanced robotics are among the digital technology utilised to boost Halal tourism. Meanwhile, Muslim tourists are at risk of safety and security, digital technology providers are facing a hard time keeping facilities up to date, Halal terms required standardisation and regional marketing programmes are among the issues Halal tourism stakeholders face in adopting digital technology. Since the research on Halal tourism is currently mounting, this study could contribute to that body of knowledge and provide useful information to both practitioners and scholars.

Keywords Halal tourism · Technology adoption · Tourism 4.0 · Sustainable tourism · Tourism resilience

A. Mukherjee
College of Business Administration, Prince Sultan University, Riyadh, Saudi Arabia

S. D. Rajendran
School of Food Studies and Gastronomy, Taylors University, Subang Jaya, Malaysia

S. N. Wahab (✉)
Faculty of Business and Management, Universiti Teknologi MARA, Puncak Alam, Selangor, Malaysia
e-mail: sitinorida23@uitm.edu.my

© The Author(s), under exclusive license to Springer Nature Singapore Pte Ltd. 2023
A. Hassan and N. A. A. Rahman (eds.), *Technology Application in Aviation, Tourism and Hospitality*, https://doi.org/10.1007/978-981-19-6619-4_4

Introduction

The tourism industry has the potential to be a big economic force for developing countries such as Malaysia and others that are diversifying their revenue streams. Halal tourism is undoubtedly one of the most important specializations in global tourism. It provides both Muslim and Non-Muslim countries with numerous opportunities to develop their economies (Boğan & Sarıışık, 2019). Halal tourism is defined as tourism activities that are permissible under Islamic law in terms of behaviour, clothes, conduct, and diet, among other things (Ahmed & Akbaba, 2018). Halal tourism is the most recent product to hit the market, and it is a rapidly expanding sector within the industry (Rasul, 2019). The growing Muslim population, the expanding middle class, disposable income, increased access to travel information, and the increased availability of Halal travel services and amenities are some of the primary factors driving the rise of the Muslim travel market. According to the Pew Research Center (2011), the global Muslim population will reach 2.2 billion by 2030, with most Muslims living in the Middle East and North Africa. Muslims are predicted to account for 26.4% of the world's total expected population of 8.3 billion people by 2050. According to the study, Malaysia, Singapore, Indonesia, and Turkey have already begun participating in this sector because of the potential economic benefits (Isa et al., 2018).

Tourism is defined by the United Nations World Tourism Organization (UNWTO) (2013) as the migration of individuals to countries or places outside of their own country or region for personal, business, or professional reasons, or a mix of these reasons. Overall, tourism is a critical industry that, if properly planned and managed, has the potential to contribute significantly to the socio-economic growth of many countries, according to the Organization of Islamic Cooperation (Dabur, 2020). In addition to their current and future abundant tourism resources, their populace travels in large numbers worldwide for business, pleasure, and other purposes. Another potential source of revenue for OIC countries in tourism is the growing popularity of Halal tourism in the area. It is not surprising that Malaysia's a long-standing position as a pioneer in the Halal business. The United Arab Emirates (UAE) was one of the first countries to see the potential of Halal tourism and respond promptly by improving and updating the facilities and services available to Muslim visitors in order to conform to their religious beliefs (Isa et al., 2018).

Another potential source of revenue for OIC countries in tourism is the growing popularity of Halal tourism in the area. In recent years, a rising number of people living in OIC countries have shown a preference for using tourism facilities and services built with Islamic values. According to the most recent estimations, the demand for Halal tourism will continue to expand and is expected to reach $200 billion by 2020 (Dabur, 2020). Additionally, the global Halal tourism market increased from $177 billion in 2017 to $189 billion in 2018, and in 2019, the company is likely to expand even further. It is expected to reach $274 billion by 2024, representing a compound annualized growth rate of 6.4% over the next five years (Salaam Gateway, 2019). Another well-known initiative is the Global Muslim Travel Index

4 Technology Strategy in Boosting Halal Tourism Activities 43

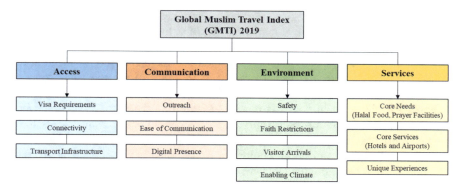

Fig. 4.1 Global Muslim Travel Index (GMTI) 2019. *Source* Mastercard-Crescent Rating (2019)

(GMTI) (2021), created in conjunction with the World Travel Organization by the Mastercard Foundation and Crescent Rating. This score includes several components that determine the overall Halal tourism experience at a given site. As shown in Fig. 4.1, this index analyses a location based on 13 criteria in four areas (access, communications (technology used), environment, and services). In the GMTI 2019, 130 countries were ranked, including 50 from the OIC.

Almost all of the country's most prominent hotels, restaurants, and shopping centres have developed facilities and amenities to satisfy the demands of Muslim travellers in recent years. Almost all hotels feature prayer facilities, including prayer rooms, prayer mats, timetables, and Qibla signs visible in the rooms. Most shopping malls have Halal restaurants and prayer rooms to make it easier for Muslim shoppers to buy (El-Adly & Eid, 2017). Many restaurants are becoming Halal-certified, and Halal cuisine is readily available throughout the country. However, it was not always the case around the world. Muslim travellers are progressively venturing further into European and Asian countries such as France, Italy, South Korea, and Japan, where they may lack Halal cuisine, mosque sites, Qibla signs, and prayer facilities (Saville & Mahbubi, 2021). A technology tool or search engine is required to access and locate all of these, and passengers rely on their cell phones more than ever. It helps in getting values and beliefs, and still, it is also useful for doing things like shopping for Halal products at a local mall, finding a tasty Halal restaurant, or finding the nearest mosque wherever you are travelling while on vacation buy (El-Adly & Eid, 2017).

As the world recovers from the COVID-19 pandemic, more countries are opening up to tourism. Halal tourism platforms are likely to beat more traditional online travel agencies by the end of 2022, generating 35% more money than they did in 2017 (Dabur, 2020). However, compared to more established western online travel businesses, Halal tourism is still in its early stages. Even though it is still a new market, hotels, restaurants, and other companies will be able to demonstrate their sensitivity to Halal standards as the industry matures. Thus, with technology, Halal tourism technology firms appear to have a first-mover advantage. However, it is just a matter of time before giant Western online merchants enter and attempt to control this potentially lucrative market. Thus, this chapter aims to discuss the use of technology in Halal tourism. Understanding the demand factors enables tourism service providers to employ technology in their service delivery (Organisation for Economic Co-operation and Development, 2020). As a result, the Halal tourism sector will require a collaborative effort from all the stakeholders to ensure that the anticipated Halal tourism policy is met by 2030 during the post-COVID recovery phase. Despite the sector's catastrophic status, technological advancements have enabled tourism stakeholders to remain watchful and receive up-to-date information digitally until the industry is fully equipped to welcome passengers again. To that aim, the chapter has highlighted how technology might help stakeholders realize the full potential of Halal tourism and identify the role of technology in connecting the potential of Halal tourism and discuss the extent to which technology influences the future potential of Halal tourism.

Halal Tourism

Muslim Travel Market

The global Muslim population is dispersed across the globe, with significant minorities in Muslim majority countries and minorities in other countries. The Halal tourism market has recently been recognized as one of the world's most promising tourist markets, driven by the rapid growth of Muslims around the world. According to Mastercard-Crescent Rating (2021), GMTI of 2021 statistics shows that the projected number of global Muslim travellers in 2013 was only 108 million. Nevertheless, the total number of Muslim travellers increased by nearly 33% to 160 million in 2019. Although the COVID-19 pandemic has had a direct impact on the travel industry for the past two years, affecting Muslim travellers globally, Muslim tourists are predicted to hit 230 million domestically and abroad by 2026. Alike, statistics gathered from GMTI of 2021 revealed that Malaysia is ranked as one of the top Muslim travel destinations since 2015. Comparable, Zainol et al. (2021) study discovered a broad range of Muslim-friendly facilities and amenities that serve as a feasible choice for the Muslim travel market in Malaysia contributing to the recognition of being a top Muslim travel destination. Following that are Turkey and Saudi Arabia. Uzbekistan, on the other hand, has made the greatest giant leaps. It has launched a few projects in recent years to highlight its lavish Islamic heritage and to promote Ziyarah tourism.

GMTI of 2021 shows that Singapore, on the other hand, is the only non-OIC destination among the top 20 GMTI 2021 destinations, and notably, Singapore has continued to lead the spot since the GMTI's launch in 2015. Non-OIC destinations have been much more interested in developing their potential to attract Muslim travellers than some OIC destinations in a bid to boost more Muslim tourists (Mastercard-Crescent Rating, 2021). Samori et al. (2016) opined that Halal tourism is entirely feasible in both Muslim and non-Muslim countries if appropriately manage the capabilities and capacities according to Shariah compliance in all aspects of tourism activities. Destinations such as Spain, South Korea, and the Philippines, for example, have designed essential information and travelogues that accommodate Muslim preferences by listing the best Halal restaurants and nearby prayer facilities. In the ranking list, the United Kingdom has steadily increased to second place. Meanwhile, Taiwan, Thailand, Hong Kong, South Africa, and Japan remain among the top ten destinations. Even during the COVID-19 pandemic, these destinations attempted to carry out passive marketing to the Muslim market. From a regional standpoint, Western Asia and North Africa are the highest-ranked regions reported in the GMTI of 2021 (Mastercard-Crescent Rating, 2021). This is because these two regions are primarily made up of Muslim-majority destinations. Turkey and the Gulf Cooperation Council (GCC) countries are included in Western Asia. Egypt and Morocco are the most popular destinations in North Africa. Central Asia and South-Eastern Asia come next. Eastern Europe and South America are among the destinations with the lowest GMTI 2021 rankings.

Halal Tourism Faith-Based Needs

Halal tourism is distinct in and of itself. The Halal tourism concept is primarily concerned with Muslim travellers' needs, which may differ from those of other tourists. The Halal tourism market is critical for meeting Muslim tourists' needs, otherwise, Muslim tourists may be hesitant to travel and explore a destination. In general, Muslim tourists prefer to visit a tourist destination that incorporates Islamic aspects, allowing them to enjoy their vacation without jeopardizing their religious obligations, resulting in an amazing travel experience. According to Mastercard-Crescent Rating (2021), GMTI of 2021 statistics, Muslim travellers have identified several faith-based needs that differ in importance. These requirements are categorized as "Need to have", "Good to have", and "Nice to have": as per a previous study by Battour et al. (2021), the absence of any of these needs may lead to Muslim travellers' unwillingness or denial of visiting a specific tourist destination. Table 4.1 presents the detailed requirements of each category of needs.

From Muslim tourists' perspective, Battour and Ismail (2016) opined that special religious requirements and culture will make the Muslim tourists significantly different group meet their needs. As a result, while Muslims' travel intentions may not always be spiritual. Henderson (2016) stated that Muslim travellers always seek to fully comply with the Al-Quran and the Prophet's Sunnah. Hence, in the context of Halal tourism, tourist businesses, marketers and agencies definitely need to give greater attention to the needs of their primary target audience, so that they can improve the products and services offered to satisfy Muslim tourists.

Table 4.1 Muslim travelers faith-based needs

Faith-based needs	Requirements
Need to have	Halal food, prayer facilities, water-friendly washrooms, and safety and security with no islamophobia
Good to have	Social causes, Ramadan experiences, and local Muslim experiences such as heritage sites and interaction with the Muslim community
Nice to have	Recreational spaces with privacy and no non-Halal activities including alcohol, discotheques, or gambling resort in the vicinity

Source Mastercard-Crescent Rating (2021)

Halal Tourism and Sustainability Approach

Definition of Sustainable Tourism

The rapid expansion of the Muslim tourism market introduces new terms to comprehend the concept of tourism tailored to the needs of Muslims. The most frequently used terms to describe the concept are "Islamic tourism", "Halal tourism", and "Muslim-friendly tourism" (MFT). Muslim tourists are one of the fastest-growing businesses in the hospitality industry (Standing Committee for Economic and Commercial Cooperation is one of four standing committees of the Organisation of Islamic Cooperation, 2016; Stephenson, 2014). The growth of the Muslim tourist market has piqued the interest of both industry and academia in recent years. On the other side, sustainability has recently received attention in the literature on tourism marketing (Battour et al., 2021; Bhuiyan & Darda, 2018).

Tourism is one of the key sectors of many economies where sustainability is becoming increasingly important. Tourism incorporates the concept of sustainable development, which is a pressing issue that is integrated into three main interrelated components that may accelerate sustainable tourism, namely economic, environmental, and social sustainability. Azam et al. (2019) mentioned that sustainable tourism may contribute substantially to the global sustainable development goals (SDGs) agenda. There are numerous definitions of sustainable tourism available from various sources. The term sustainable tourism has been defined by several organizations, including the UNWTO and UNESCO, as well as numerous previous studies. Table 4.2 briefly described definitions of sustainable tourism from the selected source.

Halal Tourism Towards Sustainable Development

Halal tourism plays a pivotal role in the 2030 SDGs agenda, and it supports the definition of sustainable tourism. Halal tourism's strict compliance with Shariah principles can contribute to the development of sustainability. However, there is a scarcity of literature on sustainable Halal tourism (Battour et al., 2021). In the

Table 4.2 Selected definition of sustainable tourism

Source	Definition
United Nations World Tourism Organization (UNWTO) (2013)	"To adopt a number of sustainable efforts which include, meeting the needs of tourists, protecting the host region to extend the future opportunities, and providing economic, social, and aesthetic needs of consumers in a balanced manner by utilizing the available resources as well to sustain biodiversity, maintain cultural integrity, and the essential ecological process"
ETE Ecological Tourism in Europe (2022)	"Protects the benefits of economic and social aspects of the industry while minimizing the negative effects on all the aspects (nature, history, culture, and environment) related to the industry development"
International Council on Monuments and Sites (ICOMOS) (2022)	"Activities in tourism that can be managed for the long term and have a positive impact on society, environment, culture, nature, and the economy of the region where it takes place"
Battour et al. (2021)	"That takes full account of its current and future economic, social and environmental impacts, addressing the needs of visitors, the industry, and the environment and host communities"

Source Compiled by the authors (2022)

context of sustainable development, Azam et al. (2019) research identified the SDGs that should be prioritized in order to understand how Halal tourism can be linked to global sustainable goals. The four SDGs found to be significantly correlated to Halal tourism are Good Health and Wellbeing of Society (SDG 3), Gender Equality (SDG 5), Decent Work, and Economic Growth (SDG 8), and Responsible Consumption and Production (SDG 12).

According to Azam et al. (2019), good health and well-being in society (SDG 3) can be achieved through Halal travel packages that guarantee the provision of Halal foods and beverages that are clean, safe, healthy, and nutritious according to the definition of Halal. Furthermore, the travel industry is committed to the safety and overall well-being of travellers while on their travel journey. Similarly, Halal tourism is demonstrating a great emphasis on ensuring gender equality (SDG 5). Numerous Halal travel and vacation agencies have already begun to work toward the SDG 5 goal. For example, women in Dubai were given the opportunity to operate and manage a UAE-based Halal hotel chain, and Air India introduced a separate seating area on a flight for females to avoid sexual harassment, as well as special facilities and equipment such as a separate health fitness area and swimming pool services for Muslim women in Shariah-compliant or Muslim friendly hotels. Furthermore, Islam ensures economic development through decent work and business (SDG 8) which is lawful by Shariah principles. Karia and Asaari (2016) claimed Muslim-owned businesses should consider conducting business according to the Quran and Islamic teaching and preaching by knowing what Halal (lawful) and haram (prohibited) are. For instance, the prohibition on bribery, gambling, stealing and violation of rights of another's property. Aside from the previously mentioned sustainable goals, Halal tourism ensures both responsible production and responsible consumption in order to address SDG 12. According to JAKIM (2015), the Halal travel industry is in charge of upholding certain standards such as cleanliness, sanitation, wholesomeness, environmental hygiene, and animal welfare. Muslim tourists are increasingly concerned with issues such as food safety, health, leisure and entertainment, convenience, information, and ethical considerations such as environmental friendliness in food production and consumption. As a result, Halal food manufacturing and processing will place a greater emphasis on fostering sustainability and a green environment, as well as ensuring the product's safety for consumption (Wahab et al., 2022).

The growing Halal tourism sector contributes to long-term sustainability. Muslim travel companies, agencies, and packages in this sector should incorporate sustainability into their business model. It is important to promote the sustainable concept of the Halal tourism industry throughout all economies in order to improve the efficiency of achieving SDGs.

Technology Needs for Halal Tourism

In recent years, the impact of technology on the tourism industry has been a popular research topic. Perceived benefits and perceived risks influence people's readiness to accept new technology. Perceived benefits include simplicity of use and utility, social impact, and future business growth (Davis et al., 2014). Publicly perceived risks include investment and maintenance costs, safety and security, consumer satisfaction, and dangers linked with outdated or outmoded technology (Haddad, 2020). The application of information technology enables tourism agility and resilience. Tourism is dependent on other connected components such as housing and transportation, attractions and shopping, and merchandise to meet customer pleasure. Innovative technology that uses the internet of things (IoT) provides easy access to comprehensive information sources (Rezai et al., 2015), providing a competitive advantage to business operators and the destination (Ordóñez, et al., 2020). While fostering collaborative efforts and effective risk mitigation strategies to meet customer satisfaction (Mandal, 2019).

A global distribution system provides real-time information and product inventory from tourism merchants. This enables stakeholders to easily access information at all hours of the day and night, and it has the potential to result in considerable business growth at all levels. According to Agrawal (2021), it also broadens the target market and increases profitability. This is because big data improves service quality, expands the number of people it can reach, and promotes corporate profitability by using less energy. The following tourism trends will be metadata management and artificial

4 Technology Strategy in Boosting Halal Tourism Activities   49

intelligence (AI). Given that millennials are the primary market for Islamic tourism (Kamin, 2019) and the future market will be dominated by Generation Z and Alpha (Bitcoin Suisse, 2020), the industry must leverage technology in every aspect of its business encounter, among other things, in order to build, maintain, and sustain relationships with customers and other stakeholders. Crescent Rating's Halal Travel Frontier 2019 (Mastercard-Crescent Rating, 20,211) research found seventeen (17) themes that will influence the future growth of Halal tourism products and will be aided by technological advancements. Table 4.3 divides them into four primary categories, as indicated below:

Table 4.3 Halal tourism future trend

Category	Trend
Industry demand	Competitive business and a demand for improved hospitality services necessitate the hotel industry to enter the Muslim tourism market
	To remain resilient, business owners must modernize their workforce capital
	The destination must be conscious of the issue of diversity
	Increased demand for travel advisory boards
	Business owners should take advantage of the benefits of big data
Sustainable development goals	Destinations take advantage of Muslim travellers' responsibilities for responsible tourism in order to achieve long-term development goals
The shift in consumer preferences	Because of the upcoming consolidation of the Muslim travel sector, there will be more powerful Muslim lifestyle and travel enterprises in the future
	Non-OIC countries are increasing their competency and capacity to attract Muslim tourists
	The influence of educated ladies with greater purchasing power on trip planning and decision-making
	The decrease in Muslim visitors to Islamophobic destinations
	The spread of digital technology in travel behaviour throughout generations
Technology aided travel	Real-time Halal certification and assurance using Augmented Reality (AR) and Artificial Intelligence (AI)
	Augmented Reality (AR) to improve visitor interpretation, particularly in comprehending Islamic heritage
	Continuous AI (Artificial Intelligence) offering in the travel industry via Chatbots and Intelligent Personal Assistants (IPA) to empower Muslim travellers

Source Bitcoin (Suisse, 2020)

Halal tourism demands a collaborative effort from all stakeholders in order to exist, and virtually all parties are leveraging artificial intelligence to that aim. To be competitive, stakeholders must collaborate while still competing with one another in the relationship. Being aware of technology changes is one of the most critical components in obtaining success in today's industry. As a result, Halal tourism stakeholders must be able to fully leverage technology-driven travel to personalize their products and services for various generation gaps and variations in consumer behaviour while still meeting industry standards and embracing the objective of sustainable growth. Technology innovation and adoption in the tourism ecosystem are predicted to raise productivity across all sectors (Boyd, 2002).

Additionally, there are considerable financial repercussions, mainly where litigation is involved and deploying cutting-edge and energy-efficient technology, supporting green practices, making careful supply chain selections, and implementing complete metadata management. More research and development are needed to raise knowledge and compliance among all tourist stakeholders and manage risk more effectively through the use of technology (Malay Mail, 2021). Thus, the need for travel advisory committees is increasing. It is critical that adequate understanding and interpretation of Halal tourism is provided, particularly by businesses and government organizations. Key organizations and companies understand the Halal tourism concept, but there is still much misconception about what it involves. Furthermore, having more and better information about Halal tourism allows people to receive better service, more visitors to visit the nations they visit, and more revenue can be generated.

Development of Industrial Revolution 4.0 in Halal Tourism

With the Fourth Industrial Revolution (IR 4.0) and the introduction of new technologies, huge changes have happened in many disciplines, most notably science and technology, which contributed 75% of these shifts (Lu, 2017). When combining the actual and digital worlds, a product's Halal label meets a dilemma. Collective knowledge is becoming increasingly significant, particularly in research commercialization, which is safe, acceptable, and applicable in all areas of life, including the tourism business. As a result of IR 4.0, market competition in all industrial sectors has become exceedingly strong. Since the beginning of IR 4.0, every company has competed with one another to collect information in order to take appropriate and prompt action. In contrast, the use of digital technology is driving entrepreneurs to examine the possibilities of acquiring a competitive edge. This circumstance is feared to undermine the order of the business model, which occurs on a different scale in each business unit. One of the results will be an improvement in the company's performance, particularly in terms of promoting Halal tourism (Wibawa et al., 2021). As a result, the economic sector will experience rapid growth at macroeconomic and microeconomic levels. It depicts the outcome of the tactics and policies implemented during that time period. A company's performance gives a snapshot of the industry over a specific time period. Halal tourism makes a substantial contribution to the country's economic prosperity.

New potential for the business model economy emerged due to IR 4.0. First and foremost, it is meant to provide a solution to the existing societal challenges. As a result, it will continue to foster innovation in the industry. The information technology and internet-based application systems are used in the IR 4.0 marketing model, and substantial changes in the economic environment will occur. As information technology advances, it will eventually pervade every area of our lives (Pew Research Center, 2021). This will result in the development of new technologies and ways that combine elements from the physical, digital, and basic worlds. With the introduction of IR 4.0, the tourism industry introduced Tourism 4.0, an almost fully digitalized sector. Digital marketing in the tourism sector is a new concept introduced by Turkey to aid in developing the industry's digital marketing. The idea was introduced in 2017 and will continue to grow and attract investment. Thailand is attempting to digitize tourism, improve the E-document system, and transform the way businesses operate and spend money (Pino, 2018).

Designing a digital ecosystem to reach Chinese tourists is central to Tourism 4.0, and in Malaysia, digital technology enhances tourism offers while increasing visitor experience. The Malaysia Smart Tourism 4.0 program aims to take the tourism business to the next level by utilizing the possibilities of digital technology. Partnerships between the public and private sectors will develop a digital environment for targeted marketing (Restanis, 2018). The term Tourism 4.0 refers to the present trend of big data processing obtained from a huge number of tourists in order to provide personalized travel experiences. It is based on several contemporary high-tech computer technologies and is referred to as the Tourism 4.0 model. Many technologies, such as artificial intelligence and the Internet of Things, are utilized in IR 4.0. Big data analysis, cloud computing, virtual and augmented reality, and virtual and augmented reality glasses are among these technologies. Industry 4.0 is being applied to tourism in a new paradigm to improve the public's perception of tourism and the business environment in which it functions (Arctur, 2018).

A few technologies used in Tourism 4.0 include Cyber-Physical Systems (CPS), the Internet of Things, Cloud Computing, Big Data, Artificial Intelligence, and Advanced Robotics. It can be used in Halal Tourism for better service and security. It is critical to note that these six broad technologies are the fundamental technology components of IR4.0, with other technologies layered within and between them. These are essential components of information systems that may assist hospitality and tourism businesses and consumers receive more relevant information for making better decisions and having more pleasant experiences (Osei et al., 2020).

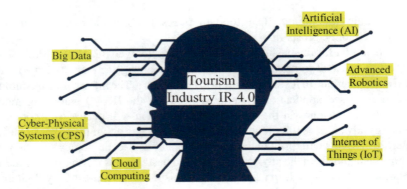

Fig. 4.2 Key technologies of IR 4.0 for the tourism industry. *Source* Osei et al., (2020)

Technology Adoption Challenges in Halal Tourism

Digital technology is viewed as a strategic tool for facilitating Halal tourism. However, there are various potential challenges in implementing technology that can satisfy the needs of Muslim tourists. The use of smartphones enables Muslim tourists to obtain various Halal services such as travel guides, hotels, airport locations, holiday packages, and restaurant guides. Hence, digital technology is crucial in Halal tourism. However, technological adoption comes with its own set of challenges that must be carefully considered before any financial commitment is made by any Halal tourism player. The Halal tourism industry, for example, is exposed to safety and security risks such as data authenticity issues, data privacy violations, and commercial threats such as information leaks because of its use of technology (Berakon et al., 2021). In addition, competitors might easily copy the products and services that are being advertised. Furthermore, it is vital to keep the facilities up to date because new technology may render old equipment obsolete over time. Thus, it requires a lot of time, effort, and money to keep personnel trained and retrained (Beldad et al., 2017). Furthermore, many Halal tourism terms needed to be standardised so that Halal tourism providers could easily guarantee Halal friendliness in airports, hotels, cruises, resorts, restaurants, and parks. It may also make Halal tourism promotion more straightforward, allowing it to meet the needs of both Muslim and non-Muslim tourists. Other challenges include geographic marketing programmes and social networks. The speed with which information about Muslim-friendly venues is disseminated via social media or geographical closeness is still lacking. Geographic marketing programmes, both in non-Muslim and Muslim countries, should be planned and delivered to locations where the majority of Muslims live (Boğan & Sarıışık, 2019). As a result, the adoption of digital technology not only benefits the Halal tourism business and makes it easier for Muslim tourists, but it also helps to create tourism resilience, which is especially important during the COVID-19 endemic phase.

Conclusion and Future Research Directions

This research adds to the current literature on Halal tourism and digital technologies. Despite an increase in the number of studies on Halal tourism, research on technology strategies for boosting Halal tourism activities is still sparse. Accordingly, this chapter identified a number of technologies that can help Halal tourism become more resilient. Given the context of this study, future research should conduct field research with the goal of producing empirical evidence to further validate the findings. Despite this study's conceptual nature, it could serve as a groundwork for future Halal tourism research. More study should be done to progress toward a Muslim-friendly destination model. A mix of qualitative and quantitative research should be conducted to empirically understand Halal tourism. In addition, research on non-Muslims' attitudes toward Halal tourism might be conducted in both Muslim and non-Muslim places.

References

Agrawal, R. (2021). Internet of things in tourism: Challenges and opportunities in "the new normal." *International Journal of Science and Research, 10*(7), 513–516.

Ahmed, M. J., & Akbaba, A. (2018). The potential of halal tourism in Ethiopia: Opportunities, challenges, and prospects. *International Journal of Contemporary Tourism Research, 2*(1), 13–22.

Arctur. (2018). *Tourism 4.0.* https://www.arctur.si/news/2018051409162882/tourism_40/. Accessed 12 Mar 2022.

Azam, M. S. E., Abdullah, M. A., & Abdul Razak, D. (2019). Halal tourism: Definition, justification, and scopes towards sustainable development. *International Journal of Business, Economics and Law, 18*(3), 23–31.

Battour, M., & Ismail, M. N. (2016). Halal tourism: Concepts, practises, challenges and future. *Tourism Management Perspectives, 19*, 150–154.

Battour, M., Salaheldeen, M., & Mady, K. (2021). Halal tourism: Exploring innovative marketing opportunities for entrepreneurs. *Journal of Islamic Marketing, 13*(4), 887–897.

Beldad, A. D., & Hegner, S. M. (2017). Expanding the technology acceptance model with the inclusion of trust, social influence, and health valuation to determine the predictors of German users' willingness to continue using a fitness app: A structural equation modeling approach. *International Journal of Human-Computer Interaction, 34*(9), 882–893.

Berakon, I., Wibowo, M. G., Nurdany, A., & Aji, H. M. (2021). An expansion of the technology acceptance model applied to the halal tourism sector. *Journal of Islamic Marketing.* https://doi.org/10.1108/JIMA-03-2021-0064

Bhuiyan, A. H., & Darda, A. (2018). Prospects and potentials of Halal tourism development in Bangladesh. *Journal of Tourismology, 4*(2), 93–106.

Bitcoin Suisse. (2020). *Halal travel frontier: Trends to watch in 2020.* https://www.bitcoinsuisse.com/outlook/trends-to-watch-in-2020. Accessed 20 Mar 2022.

Boğan, E., & Sarıışık, M. (2019). Halal tourism: Conceptual and practical challenges. *Journal of Islamic Marketing, 10*(1), 87–96.

Boyd, J. (2002). Compensating for Wetland Losses under the Clean Water Act. *Environment: Science and Policy for Sustainable Development, 44*(9), 43–44.

Dabur, N. (2020). *International tourism in the OIC countries: Prospects and challenges—2020.* SESRIC Publication.

Davis, J., Mengersen, K., Bennett, S., & Mazerolle, L. (2014). Viewing systematic reviews and meta-analysis in social research through different lenses. *SpringerPlus, 3*(1). https://doi.org/10.1186/2193-1801-3-511.
El-Adly, M. I., & Eid, R. (2017). Dimensions of the perceived value of malls: Muslim shoppers' perspective. *International Journal of Retail & Distribution Management, 45*(1), 40–56.
ETE Ecological Tourism in Europe. (2022). *Definition of sustainable tourism.* https://www.oete.de/index.php/en/sustainable-tourism/definition-en. Accessed 20 Mar 2022.
Haddad, S. (2020). Robot hotel: Why didn't it works?—Inside the hotel run by robots. *Raconteur.* https://www.raconteur.net/technology/automation/robot-hotel-ai. Accessed 20 Mar 2022.
Henderson, J. C. (2016). Halal food, certification and Halal tourism: Insights from Malaysia and Singapore. *Tourism Management Perspectives, 19,* 160–164.
International Council on Monuments and Sites (ICOMOS). (2022). *Cultural heritage and sustainable development.* https://www.icomos.org/en/focus/un-sustainable-development-goals. Accessed 27 Mar 2022.
Isa, S. M., Chin, P. N., & Mohammad, N. U. (2018). Muslim tourist perceived value: A study on Malaysia Halal tourism. *Journal of Islamic Marketing, 9*(2), 402–420.
JAKIM. (2015). *Manual procedure for Malaysia Halal certification* (Third Revision, pp. 1–67).
Kamin, D. (2019). The rise of Halal tourism. *The New York Times.* https://www.nytimes.com/2019/01/18/travel/the-rise-of-halal-tourism.html. Accessed 20 Mar 2022.
Karia, N., & Asaari, M. H. A. H. (2016). Halal business and sustainability: Strategies, resources and capabilities of Halal third-party logistics (3PLs). *Progress in Industrial Ecology, an International Journal, 10*(2–3), 286–300.
Lu, Y. (2017). Industry 4.0: A survey on technologies, applications, and open research issues. *Journal of Industrial Information Integration, 6,* 1–10.
Malay Mail. (2021). *Minister: Islamic tourism entrepreneurs urged to raise understanding of halal aspects.* https://www.malaymail.com/news/malaysia/2021/10/21/minister-islamic-tourism-entrepreneurs-urged-to-raise-understanding-of-halal/2015009. Accessed 20 Mar 2022.
Mandal, S. (2019). Exploring the influence of IT capabilities on agility and resilience in tourism: Moderating role of technology orientation. *Journal of Hospitality and Tourism Technology, 10*(3), 431–444.
Mastercard-Crescent Rating. (2019). *Global Muslim travel index (GMTI) (2021).* https://www.crescentrating.com/reports/global-muslim-travel-index-2019.html. Accessed 7 Mar 2022.
Mastercard-Crescent Rating. (2021). *Global Muslim travel index (GMTI) (2021).* https://www.crescentrating.com/reports/global-muslim-travel-index-2021.html. Accessed 7 Mar 2022.
Ordóñez, M. D., Gómez, A., Ruiz, M., Ortells, J. M., Niemi-Hugaerts, H., Juiz, C., Jara, A., & Butler, T. A. (2020). IoT technologies and applications in tourism and travel industries. In O. Vermesan & J. Bacquet (Eds.), *Internet of things—The call of the edge: everything intelligent everywhere* (pp. 367–386). Routledge.
Organisation for Economic Co-operation and Development (OECD). (2020). *OECD tourism trends and policies.* https://www.oecd-ilibrary.org/urban-rural-and-regional-development/oecd-tourism-trends-and-policies-2020_6b47b985-en. Accessed 13 Mar 2022.
Osei, B. A., Ragavan, N. A., Kandappan, B., & Mensah, H. K. (2020). "Hospitality Revolution 4.0": A literature review on a unified typology of IR 4.0 technologies for the tourism and hospitality industry in the era of COVID-19. *Asia-Pacific Journal of Innovation in Hospitality and Tourism, 9*(1), 25–45.
Pew Research Center. (2011). *The future of the global Muslim population: projections for 2010–2030.* http://www.pewforum.org/2011/01/27/the-future-of-the-global-Muslimpopulation/. Accessed 29 Mar 2022.
Pew Research Center. (2021). *Experts say the 'new normal' in 2025 will be far more tech-driven, presenting more big challenges.* https://www.pewresearch.org/internet/2021/02/18/experts-say-the-new-normal-in-2025-will-be-far-more-tech-driven-presenting-more-big-challenges/. Accessed 27 Mar 2022.

Pino, M. (2018). Tourism 4.0? Here we explain it to you. *Bitfinancenews.* http://www.bitfinance.news/en/a-cryptocurrency-for-modern-travelers/. Accessed 20 Mar 2022.

Rasul, T. (2019). The trends, opportunities, and challenges of halal tourism: A systematic literature review. *Tourism Recreation Research, 44*(4), 434–450.

Restanis, A. (2018). Smart Tourism 4.0 to be tourism game-changer for Malaysia. *Travel Daily News.* https://www.traveldailynews.asia/smart-tourism-40-to-be-tourism-game-changer-for-malaysia. Accessed 29 Mar 2022.

Rezai, G., Mohamed, Z., & Shamsudin, M. N. (2015). Can Halal be sustainable? Study on Malaysian consumers' perspective. *Journal of Food Products Marketing, 21*(6), 654–666.

Salaam Gateway. (2019). *State of the global Islamic economy report: Driving the Islamic economy revolution 4.0.* https://www.cdn.salaamgateway.com. Accessed 20 Mar 2022.

Samori, Z., Salleh, N. Z. M., & Khalid, M. M. (2016). Current trends on Halal tourism: Cases on selected Asian countries. *Tourism Management Perspectives, 19*, 131–136.

Saville, R., & Mahbubi, A. (2021). Assessing Muslim travellers' preferences regarding food in Japan using conjoint analysis: An exploratory study on the importance of prayer room availability and halalness. *Heliyon, 7*(5), 1–11.

Standing Committee for Economic and Commercial Cooperation is one of four standing committees of the Organisation of Islamic Cooperation (COMCEC). (2016). *Muslim friendly tourism: Understanding the demand and supply sides in the OIC member countries.* Ankara: COMCEC Coordination Office.

Stephenson, M. L. (2014). Deciphering 'Islamic hospitality': Developments, challenges and opportunities. *Tourism Management, 40*, 155–164.

United Nations World Tourism Organization (UNWTO). (2013). *Tourism highlights.* https://doi.org/10.18111/9789284413560. Accessed 30 Mar 2022.

Wahab, S. N., Rajendran, S. D., Ling, E. K., & Mukherjee, A. (2022). A framework for effective food safety controls. *Journal of Emerging Economies and Islamic Research, 10*(1), 44–59.

Wibawa, B. M., Pranindyasari, C., Bhawika, G. W., & Mardhotillah, R. R. (2021). Discovering the importance of halal tourism for Indonesian Muslim travelers: Perceptions and behaviors when traveling to a non-Muslim destination. *Journal of Islamic Marketing.* https://doi.org/10.1108/JIMA-07-2020-0210

Zainol, N. A., Mustafa, E., & Willibrod, A. T. (2021). Muslim tourists' food and beverage needs and preferences during travel. *Journal of Event, Tourism and Hospitality Studies, 1*(1), 121–142.

Aroop Mukherjee is an Assistant Professor at the Aviation and Management Department, College of Business, Prince Sultan University, Riyadh. He has an extensive teaching experience in Management courses. He has more than 17 years of experience in education management. His research interest includes sustainable organization processes and agile, agribusiness management, and supply chain management. He has published her research works in high-rated journals, proceedings, and book chapters and published two research monographs. He serves as a reviewer for journals and academic conferences. He has a black belt certificate in Lean Six Sigma.

Salini Devi Rajendran is a Senior Lecturer I at the School of Food Studies and Gastronomy, Faculty of Social Sciences and Leisure Management. Previously, she held the position of head of the department at one of the top private universities in Malaysia. She has an extensive teaching experience in supply chain management courses. She has completed her Ph.D. in Halal herbal-based food supply chain management at Halal Product Research Institute, Universiti Putra Malaysia. She managed research grants and has published numerous research works in academic journals, and conference proceedings. She is also actively involved in design and innovation research competitions and has won platinum, gold, silver, and bronze medal. She is a professional technologist of the Malaysia Board of Technologists (Ts) and a chartered member of the Chartered Institute of Logistics and Transport (CMILT). Her field of research includes food supply chain management, food risks, and integrity, quality and food safety management, Halal management, and agribusiness.

Siti Norida Wahab is a Senior Lecturer in the operations management program at the Faculty of Business and Management, UiTM Puncak Alam. She has more than 15 years of experience in both the industrial and educational fields. Her previous leadership positions include roles at the managerial level in multinational logistics companies and renowned private universities. Her research interest includes sustainable adoption in logistics and supply chain management. She managed national and international grants and has published her research works in high-rated journals, proceedings, and book chapters. Besides, she supervised a number of M.Sc. and Ph.D. candidates. For excellence, she has won a platinum, diamond, gold, and bronze medalist for the innovation competitions. She also actively serves as a reviewer for journals and academic conferences. Currently, she is a professional technologist of the Malaysia Board of Technologists and a chartered member of the Chartered Institute of Logistics and Transport.

Part II
Recent Developments

Chapter 5
Mobile Technology Application in Aviation: Chatbot for Airline Customer Experience

Sufi Dzikri Sarol, Mohammad FakhrulNizam Mohammad, and Nor Aida Abdul Rahman

Abstract Effective communication between customers and businesses is crucial. Enhancing the communication between customer and company are non-ending efforts that require continuous improvement and approach. In the emergence of new technologies, the transmission of information through technology as a platform adds to more challenging initiatives performed. More enterprises adopt artificial intelligence (AI) to increase operational efficiency, eliminate costly errors, and increase customer satisfaction. Time spent by passengers interacting with airlines is minimized through the use of a practical application that supports their needs, integrated with the natural language processing, conversational agents, or Chatbot's serving as virtual assistants. Artificial intelligence shall assist airline customers in acquiring more accurate related information such as flight booking, schedules, and updates. This chapter offers a multi-focus discussion on initiatives for applying Chatbot systems in the aviation sector, a debate on artificial intelligence technology used in improving communication, enhancing natural language interactions, and the usability response from selected airlines passengers' feedback on the improved systems.

Keywords Airlines · User satisfaction · Automation · Business performance · System interface · Chatbot · Usability

---

S. D. Sarol
Malaysian Institute of Aviation Technology, Universiti Kuala Lumpur, Kuala Lumpur, Malaysia

M. F. Mohammad (✉)
Universiti Kuala Lumpur, Kuala Lumpur, Malaysia
e-mail: mfakhrulnizamm@unikl.edu.my

N. A. A. Rahman
Technical Foundation/Aviation Management Section, Universiti Kuala Lumpur—Malaysian Institute of Aviation Technology (UniKL MIAT), Selangor, Malaysia

© The Author(s), under exclusive license to Springer Nature Singapore Pte Ltd. 2023
A. Hassan and N. A. A. Rahman (eds.), *Technology Application in Aviation, Tourism and Hospitality*, https://doi.org/10.1007/978-981-19-6619-4_5

Introduction

Business entities are gradually enhancing their services and product delivery by continuously investigating the roles of technologies in meeting the growing passengers' needs by improving operational efficiency, product delivery, effective processes, and supporting the interaction between companies and their customers. Similarly, industry players in the aviation sector constantly formulate strategies, approaches, and initiatives to provide effective and better customer services through information technologies (IT). Airlines can adopt various IT technologies for their passengers by enhancing security and safety, improving communication between passengers, ensuring fast information delivery and accuracy, improving flight operations and planning, and many others. The use of technologies allows airlines or airports to operate and manage their businesses through effective communication with their customers and personalising their experience; the advent of digitalised communication helps companies quickly spread information to their large audience.

In order to assist the operations and business of the airlines as well as the aviation sector as a whole, artificial intelligence (AI) has attracted the attention of the industry's key participants. One of the widely popular applications of AI is the Chatbot application developed to support and allow interactive communication between passengers and airlines. In addition to keeping communication between customers and the airlines, the system developed typically acts as a knowledge repository that collects all customers' information and queries useful for future references among existing and potential customers.

The overall goal of this project is to look at how the GPT-3 language model is applied to improve the passenger experience with airlines. In reaching the outcome of the GPT-3 model application, this study emphasises the discussion of three areas; the benefit of AI in the industry, the introduction of GPT-3 models, the development of the prototype, and the usability test among users (who have prior experiences of using existing customer knowledge-based system).

Chatbot Application for Supporting Customer Interactions

AI is a branch of computer science aiming to produce robots behaving like human brains in solving issues or problems that may not be solved using typical conventional approaches (Abduljabbar et al., 2019) or devices that mimic human performance. It can be categorized into strong and weak AI (Dehouche, 2021; Pérez-Campuzano et al., 2021). AI technologies like Chatbots, Recommenders, and Virtual Assistance (VA) can boost companies' branding, build better customer interactions & satisfaction, and tailor the products to the passenger's needs (Rana et al., 2021). The outcome of AI implementation advances the industry, automating processes, analysing data, and engaging engaged employees with customers (Davenport & Ronanki, 2018).

The use of Chatbots in supporting a knowledge-based system assists airlines in rendering effective delivery to customers and improves companies' actual performance in providing fast and quick customer service. Commonly, customers may visit the company's website to search for information or submit questions related to the service or products they obtained from the company. In some instances, airlines may already have developed a knowledge-based system that captures and acquire past customers' inquiries and stores them in the database for the reference of other customers. Availability of this feature or systems' capabilities to search for similar types of past questions for the new customers can improve the company's delivery time to their customers. This capability indirectly enhances customer satisfaction by enabling them to get the answer they are looking for quickly and instantly. However, there could be situations where the customer will be redirected to the customer service officer when they are not getting the answer they are looking for (after communicating and texting with the Chatbot agent through the system). Nonetheless, it helps both sides utilise more productive time in managing time and resources to acquire the solution for the questions faced by the customers.

Implementation of AI in aviation may impact several areas in the industry, such as aircraft design and operations, aircraft production and maintenance, air traffic management, drones, urban air mobility and U-space, safety risk management, cybersecurity, environment, and regulations (European Union Aviation Safety Agency, 2000). In addition, the use of AI may positively affect companies such as minimising higher costs of cancellation (Abduljabbar et al., 2019), enhancing the efficiency and efficacy of businesses and operations (by minimising potential risks errors) (Mat Rahim et al., 2018), and improving customer/passenger satisfaction (Adam et al., 2021; Følstad & Skjuve, 2019; Nordheim et al., 2019).

Minimising Costs

Managing costs effectively is vital to ensuring the efficient utilisation of investments made by the organisation. Adopting AI has long-term labour costs reduction, production time, and optimum utilisation of resources. However, AI implementation might require higher initial physical investment (acquisition of tools, equipment, and devices) and non-physical investment (human resources, training, intellectual development). As an indicative measure, implementing AI tools helps reduce healthcare costs in the health industry and optimise the available system for effective productivity of businesses. The relationship between AI investment and its implications for operational costs of the company portrays the strength of its influence in assisting the companies in managing their expenses. Adopting AI could minimise the organisation's costs without affecting their quality, or both costs and quality are increasing simultaneously (Golding & Nicola, 2019).

Enhancement of Business Operations

The performance of businesses relies heavily upon the interaction among employees, managers, and decision-makers supported by IT systems. AI and IoT-enabled technologies could contribute as an essential technology in supporting airline operations and procedures. For example, AI technology could overcome the recovery issues of airline operations (involving agents, crew and passengers) with less time and cost (Castro & Oliveira, 2007). Hence, airlines should investigate new ways to boost passenger experience (using cutting-edge creative technology) (Chakraborty et al., 2021). Moreover, AI has its advantages that can support the human decision-making process (Robinson et al., 2005), integrate data with business tools (Gupta et al., 2022), and support complex airline operations by eliminating human error-causing factors (Mat Rahim et al., 2018). The human-computer interaction improves inspection efficiency and reliability in aviation, decreases risk and uncertainty, and self-adapts to various aircraft, services, investigation contexts, and operational situations (Donadio et al., 2018). Since enabling communication between customers and companies through Chatbots may be inconvenient; thus, more investigation into using AI to provide accurate and closely imitating human-like conversations is crucial and needed.

In another experiment, agent-based modelling simulation (ABMS) successfully supported the involved company to compare and coordinate the organisation's policies to enhance the coordinating mechanisms of a highly complicated socio-technical air transportation system (Bouarfa et al., 2016). The use of AI is significant as facilitating tools commonly embedded within existing applications and as a tool used to manage and coordinate the right policies used by the organisation. Despite the advantage of AI to business operations, the lack of academic research to integrate AI with business operations increases the chance of project failure and undesirable outcomes (Reim et al., 2020). Therefore, it is paramount that more diverse research investigates the efficiencies of AI implementation in the organisation (specifically in the aviation sector). Moreover, the GPT-3 model is just newly introduced in the industry; therefore, the outcome of more research and experiment in would derive and elaborate on its benefit and advantage to the industry.

Improvement of Customer Satisfaction

Today, technologies have gone beyond enabling businesses and driving businesses to be more competitive within the robust and dynamic markets. Companies directly interact with customers' needs to ensure that the communication between customers and the company is effective and efficiently performed. Moreover, the use of technologies in supporting business operations and processes somehow has minimised the direct interaction among humans through the use of technologies platform. The use of technologies to facilitate business processes, special communication between company and customers, is gradually attracting attention.

Interaction of customers with companies through the use of technological platform facilitates the customer in getting information and with utmost attention (Adam et al., 2021; Følstad & Skjuve, 2019), whereby the use of Chatbots have a significant role in optimising customer service operations (Nordheim et al., 2019). Customers are using Chatbots to seek information and assistance; hence, Adam et al. (2021) suggested that customers should be aware that they are communicating and liaising with the automated agent but not directly with the customer service officer. The situation whereby customers are aware that they are liaising with agents but not with humans allows them to interact more naturally with the system. Although customer trusts the system as a replacement to communicate with the company, Følstad and Skjuve (2019) stated that they would use it to use straightforward and straightforward transactions. In elevating the customer trusts in using the system, factors such as Chatbot-related (expertise, responsiveness), environment-related (risk, brand), and user-related (propensity to trust technology) are needed to enhance the trust in using Chatbots for customer service applications (Nordheim et al., 2019). Given the benefits and advantages of using Chatbots for customer satisfaction, there should be more opportunities for future studies to investigate the outcome and benefits of using the system.

Generative Pre-Trained Transformer 3 (GPT-3) Algorithm

What is GPT-3?

Most business entities work continuously and effortlessly to develop a system that can interact with customers who understand language naturally. The ability to establish a system that can understand the common language and standard language used by customers helps to minimise additional traffic volume of the transaction; reduce human-computer interaction with a customer service officer, and improve the response time performance by the airlines. As such, limited technology capabilities able to support these goals may humidify companies' intention to provide excellent service while satisfying the needs and expectations of their customers. As a result of recent developments in Natural Language Processing (NLP), such as OpenAI's GPT-3 language model, expectations for both parties (companies and customers) are now attainable.

GPT-3 is a predictive language model that produces human-like text (such as responding to questions, composing essays, interpreting language, capturing notes, summarising lengthy texts, and even creating computer coding) than the earlier version (Ibrokhim & Ugli, 2020). Again, Ibrokhim and Ugli (2020) highlights that GPT-3 involves 175 billion parameters as opposed to 1.5 billion machine language parameters (artificial neural networks (ANNs) in the earlier version. It works well by transforming texts into other forms such as numerical or representations while processing millions of readers. Subsequently, GPT-3 decomposes the texts into more easily and readable words and sentences by humans. The language model works by picking up and learning the other languages through continuous exposure to various scales. Although several developments indicate its ability to understand and learn the different languages better intelligently, studies also suggested that some improvements should be needed to accommodate its achievement. For example, it might sometimes fail at the most basic linguistic tasks without specific rules, yet it can thrive at more challenging ones like copying an author or waxing philosophical (Elkins & Chun, 2020). The critical challenge for any artificially intelligent conversation model is to account for a speaker's communicational objectives and motivations via shared attention (Montemayor, 2021). Arising from the critical criteria of the model and studies highlighting the requirement for additional consideration for improvement, the outcome of this study can shed light on some of the capabilities and limitations of the system developed based on the GPT-3 model for enhancing the airline customer experience.

Prototype Development

The prototyping approach uses an AI Chatbot powered by GPT-3 language model to construct the system. Prototyping is a technique for developing strategies that are well-suited to resolve issues between users and system developers that may cause the user's inability to appropriately communicate their expectations or system developers' failure to understand the users' requirements. Therefore, the researcher has built a GPT-3 powered Chatbot in a smaller-scale model (that does not need to suit all users). The model is available to a specific group of consumers, so they may try it out and understand the requirements; before developing the whole system. After creating the system's prototype, the next development cycle to improve and rectify any additional requirements for the existing system is done based on the users' input during the prototype development stage. In developing the Chatbot programs applying GPT-3 as one of the components, the researchers have formulated the component structures (see Fig. 5.1).

The prototype model developed requires a developer interface (Python 3.9), an OpenAI API key, a database (a GitHub account), messaging service (a Twilio account), and cloud application hosting (a Render account), and a user interface (WhatsApp account). The researcher uses Python and Flask frameworks to build the system, and the Visual Studio Code editor is used to write the system's code. An API key from OpenAI uses to access GPT-3. Meanwhile, Twilio handled the message service by Twilio, and the implementation of the Chatbot was using Render as a cloud hosting for the application. GPT-3 and users communicate using the WhatsApp application.

5 Mobile Technology Application in Aviation …   65

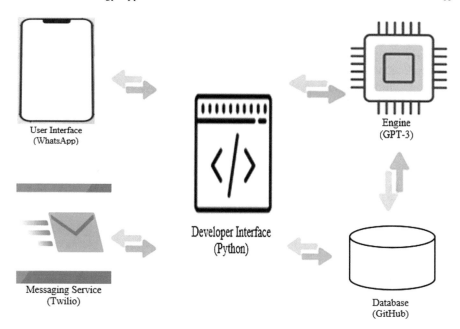

Fig. 5.1 Structure of prototype systems development. *Source* Modified and developed by the authors (2022)

Developing the Interface (Using Python)

Python developed a system installed in a virtual environment. A virtual environment is an interpreter for Python used to install packets without affecting the primary system. The code is more constrained and reproducible since a single location locates all dependencies and site-packages. There are several ways to configure virtual environments, but the commands below used in this development stage:

```
$mkdir AiharaBot_GPT-3
$cd AiharaBot_GPT-3
$Python -m venv venv
$.\venv\Scripts\activate
(venv) $ pip install openai twilio flask pythn-dotenv gunicorn
```

After creating the virtual environments and executing the coding, installation of all packages and dependencies (such as openai, Twilio, flask, pythn-dotenv, and gunicorn) are in the virtual environment are done.

Creating the Repository and Database (GitHub)

The database stores created and acquired data linked to the system, opening a new database in the GitHub App. The procedure for creating a GitHub database is as follows:

1. Login to the website or open GitHub applications to create the database
2. Choose 'New Repository' on the top right corner of the menu
3. Name the repository at the opened dialogue box before its opening in Visual Studio Code.
4. Add Python gitignore file before creating repository—to refrain from uploading the.env file (with API access tokens) and the virtual environment.

Creating the Repository and Database (GitHub)

An API key from OpenAI is required to gain access to GPT-3. The Chatbot program will need this API key; thus, included in a new.env file. The rationale for keeping it behind the.env file is that it is a secret key, and anyone with the API key will have access to GPT-3. The.env file is placed and imported as a variable, and the constructed default gitignore file includes the.env file.

Prompting the Chatbot

The system assigned developed Chatbot with identity before adding Question and Answer (Q&A) criteria. Several created lists of Q & A demonstrate how GPT-3 creates relevant text when prompted. In providing a better overview, users can learn more about GPT-3 by logging in to the OpenAI playground, and within a few instances, GPT-3 will fill in the blanks and duplicate users taught lessons about it.

Meanwhile, a brief text explanation of the system prompted a chatbox. Arising from the description of the system's identification, several Q & A are prepared to guide GPT-3 engine to follow the Q & A structure. The newly added system shall follow the exact format to design the Chatbot system while responding to inquiries (and comments) about airlines' products and services. The GPT-3 algorithm only requires a few samples to bring the system back to life. Finally, converting and exporting the Playground codes to Python are done.

```
import os
import openai
openai.api_key = os.getenv("OPEN_API_KEY")
start_sequence = "\nA:"
restart_sequence = "\n\nQ:"
response = openai.Completion.create(
        engine = "dbase"
        prompt = "I am Aihara.I am your AI personal flight attendant powered by GPT-3"
        temperature=0,
        max_tokens=100,
        top_p=1
        frequency_penalty=0,
        presence_penalty=0,
        stop=["\n"]
        )
```

Code is copied and pasted in an IPBOT.py file once Python imports the conversion and Playground codes. At this stage, the Chatbot is ready to use OpenAI API to produce responses in Python by allowing the API key to inform OpenAI that the system has made the request. At first, initialise the created IPBOT.py file. In the next stage, copying the start and restart sequences directly from the Playground code was performed. Subsequently, add the session prompt variability to set the text written earlier in the playground. It becomes the referred global variables outside of any functions. Its purpose is to teach the system how to speak and respond to questions.

The following part concentrate on Chatbot interaction. The next step was executing the code once the completion of Chatbot prompt. At first, creating a new ask function takes two arguments. The first question is the actual question that is compulsory and becomes the text input from the other end of the chat. The second argument of the chat log is optional. The chat log lists everything conversed; therefore, the Chatbot can understand what is happening. The register is set as equal to None to begin.

```
Def ask (question, chat_log=None):
Prompt_text = f'{chat_log}{restart_sequence}: {question}{start_sequence}:'
Response= openai.Completion.create(
            engine=" devinci",
            prompt=prompt_text,
            temperature=0
            max_tokens=100,
            top_p=1,
            frequency_penalty=0,
            presence_penalty=0,
            stop=["\n"],
            )
Stort = response['choices'][0]['text']
Retrun str(story)
```

Afterward, the response variable is added, which sends a completion request to the GPT-3 engine. OpenAI has provided the create function. This process contains several arguments that will notify GPT-3 on how creative it should be and how many tokens it should use. The API will return a conveniently set response equal to the parse and used response variable. Another transformation is adding a new prompt text variable to the ask function. The *f'* creates a string variable that contains all of the Chatbot's histories and the restart, question, and start sequences required to prompt GPT-3. Finally, argument code is added, which tries to set the prompt = prompt text.

The system has everything it needs for the user to communicate with the GPT-3 bot after all of the required and necessary prompts have been written.

User Interface (Connecting to WhatsApp)

The system has everything it needs for the user to communicate with the GPT-3 bot; after all of the required and necessary prompts have been written. When specific actions on a repository or organisation occur, Webhooks allow sending notifications to an external web server (Github Docs, n.d.); the Webhook link is copied in Render once installed and pasted in the incoming messages section. Once completed, a WhatsApp message sends to the identified number with the join code to initiate communication with GPT-3.

Engine (GPT-3 Algorithm)

- *System's operability and functionality*

The developed system must be measured and analysed for its operability and functionality with the intended users. The objective of the test is to measure the acceptance level of airlines passenger with the systems interface and its usability among passengers who have experience in using the existing system and interacting with airline passengers. Two aspects analysed the operability and functionality of the system: (1) general feedback of the system; and (2) its usability and satisfaction of users with the Interface. The usability and user interface satisfaction analysis uses five elements of QUiS (Questionnaire for User Interface Satisfaction) (Chin et al., 1988).

Users are identified based on their previous experience using the existing information system of any airline. There are two stages categorised users' feedback: the prototype development and the complete development of the system. Users' feedback from the prototype development stage becomes the input for the researcher to provide improvement to the initially created system. Finally, once the system is fully developed, other users are invited to use the system by entering the set of questions to test its usability and functionality.

The outcome of the questions helps determine whether the systems met the passenger's satisfaction. This study adopts descriptive analysis (mean score) to analyse the respondent's acceptance level of the designs.

Two sections separate the layout of the questions: general user input and system interface usability. (see Fig. 5.2). The decision to split the types of questions into three different natures is to ensure that robust and rigorous types of questions are asked to users to measure the capability of the systems developed. For fixed pre-set questions, the researcher provides similar questions to all users to key into the system. Meanwhile, the researcher gave the random pre-set questions keyed in by the users.

Justification of these types of testing is due to the cooperation between the developer (technical expertise that understands the system capabilities) and the user (who perform the system testing based on their expectation and prior experiences). The final question's category provides flexibility to users in posting questions. Random

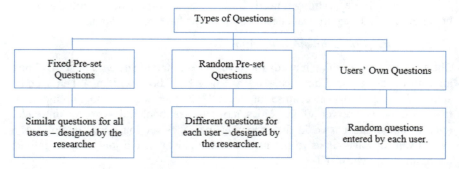

Fig. 5.2 Types of questions designed—user testing. *Source* Modified and developed by the authors (2022)

pre-set queries and users' questions are written in English and Malay to further test and measure the system's capabilities.

- *Result analysis*

Arising from the test performed by the users, the system usability test and its applicability are conducted. The test required users to key in their feedback through a distributed survey questionnaire. Analysis of the operability and functionality of the system separated into two aspects of categories:

(1) general input about the system
(2) the usability and user satisfaction system interface.
(3) The usability and user interface satisfaction analysis adopts five elements of QUiS (Questionnaire for User Interface Satisfaction) (Chin et al., 1988).

Both parts of the assessment are analysed descriptively to explore their usefulness and suitability among users for future exploration and studies. The users' general feedback highlights the effectiveness, efficiency, engagement, error of tolerance, and ease of learning experienced by the users in using the system. Overall, the majority of the elements show that:

1. users agree the system is adequate for retrieving information (90% agreed)
2. efficient to be used (90% satisfied)
3. willing to use the system again in the future (80% agreed)
4. error discovered while using (80% said rarely found)
5. easy to ask questions in the system (80% found it was easy)

The usability and system interface tests adopt the QUiS template developed by Chin, Diehl and Norman (1988) with five elements (overall user reaction to the system, system screen, the terminology used, learning process, system capabilities, etc.).

The test result indicates that the average satisfaction is 7.0 out of 10 scales used in the questions template (Fig. 5.3).

Recommendations and Conclusion

In the past, IT systems enable businesses; however, in the emerging demands of business and customer requirements, IT systems have become the critical drivers to leading the industry. Without the use of technology, in the current situation, it may be complex and challenging for the business to catch up and remain valid in the competitive market. This chapter formulates the explanation based on three areas:

1. What is artificial intelligence?
2. Benefits and the advantage of artificial intelligence in the aviation
3. Development of Chatbot prototype utilising GPT-3—the latest natural language processing (NLP) algorithm
4. User usability and system interface test.

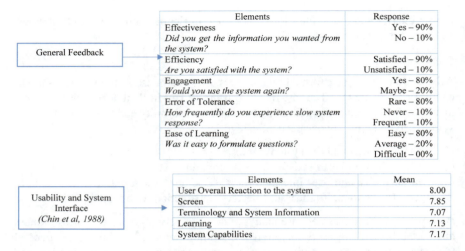

Fig. 5.3 Usability and interface elements. *Source* Modified and developed by the authors (2022)

This chapter offers a brief overview of AI's know-what and know-why advantage of its adoption in fronting the communication between airlines with their customers and the use of AI within the aviation industry. Implementing AI for businesses shall benefit the organisation by minimising costs, enhancing business operations, and improving customer satisfaction. Minimisation of charges does not only come from the context of monetary value but in terms of productivity benefit and return of investment (as a result of putting investment with the technologies). Meanwhile, business operations typically can be seen and realised quickly as most of the implementation of IT systems or artificial intelligence focuses on automating business processes and minimising time consumed in accomplishing tasks, processes, and day-to-day operations.

In the context of improvising customer satisfaction, AI is not new to the business through various initiatives to support their operations in fronting communication with customers. The use of AI Chatbots to replicate or mimic the' honest' communication between passengers and airline companies helps, to some extent, minimise the waiting time, improve quick customer response and reduce the bottleneck of responding to customers by customer service officers. Although existing Chatbot initiatives support customer knowledge-based systems, the ongoing customer demand and the advancement of AI technology motivate future system research and development. As discussed in one of the academic discussions, a lack of research to support managers in the industry with the implementation and integration of AI in the business may increase the chances of undesirable outcomes and failure of the project. Therefore, discussion on developing a customer interface application prototype for airline passengers; and conducting a usability test shall offer an additional view and exposure to how slight improvements can provide more tremendous changes to the existing airlines' operations and customer experience.

References

Abduljabbar, R., Dia, H., Liyanage, S., & Bagloee, S. A. (2019). Applications of artificial intelligence in transport: An overview. *Sustainability, 11*(1), 189.

Adam, M., Wessel, M., & Benlian, A. (2021). AI-based chatbots in customer service and their effects on user compliance. *Electronic Markets, 31*(2), 427–445.

Bouarfa, S., Blom, H. A. P., & Curran, R. (2016). Agent-based modeling and simulation of coordination by airline operations control. *IEEE Transactions on Emerging Topics in Computing, 4*(1), 9–20.

Castro, A., & Oliveira, E. (2007). A distributed multi-agent system to solve airline operations problems. In *ICEIS 2007—9th International Conference on Enterprise Information Systems, Proceedings, AIDSS*. Funchal: The 12th–16th June, pp. 22–30.

Chakraborty, S., Chakravorty, T., & Bhatt, V. (2021). IoT and AI driven sustainable practices in airlines as enabler of passenger confidence, satisfaction and positive WOM: AI and IoT driven sustainable practice in airline. In *Proceedings—International Conference on Artificial Intelligence and Smart Systems (ICAIS) 2021*. Coimbatore: The 25th–27th March, pp. 1421–1425.

Chin, J. P., Diehl, V. A., & Norman, K. L. (1988). Development of an instrument measuring user satisfaction of the human-computer interface. In *CHI '88: Proceedings of the SIGCHI Conference on Human Factors in Computing Systems*. Washington D.C.: The 15th–19th May, pp. 213–218.

Davenport, T. H., & Ronanki, R. (2018). Artificial intelligence for the real world. *Harvard Business Review*, January–February, pp. 108–116.

Dehouche, N. (2021). Plagiarism in the age of massive generative pre-trained transformers (GPT-3). *Ethics in Science and Environmental Politics, 21*, 17–23.

Donadio, F., Frejaville, J., Larnier, S., & Vetault, S. (2018). Artificial intelligence and collaborative robot to improve airport operations. *Lecture Notes in Networks and Systems, 22*, 973–986.

European Union Aviation Safety Agency (EASA). (2000). *Artificial intelligence roadmap—A human-centric approach to ai in aviation*. Retrieved from: https://www.easa.europa.eu/document-library/general-publications/easa-artificial-intelligence-roadmap-10. Accessed 20 Mar 2022.

Elkins, K., & Chun, J. (2020). Can GPT-3 pass a writer's turing test? *Journal of Cultural Analytics, 5*(2), 1–16.

Følstad, A., & Skjuve, M. (2019). Chatbots for customer service. In *CUI '19: Proceedings of the 1st International Conference on Conversational User Interfaces*, pp. 1, 1–9.

Github Docs (n.d.). *About Webhooks*. https://www.docs.github.com/en/get-started/customizing-your-github-workflow/exploring-integrations/about-webhooks. Accessed 20 Mar 2022.

Golding, L. P., & Nicola, G. N. (2019). A business case for artificial intelligence tools: the currency of improved quality and reduced cost. *Journal of the American College of Radiology, 16*(9), 1357–1361.

Gupta, S., Modgil, S., Bhattacharyya, S., & Bose, I. (2022). Artificial intelligence for decision support systems in the field of operations research: Review and future scope of research. *Annals of Operations Research, 308*(1–2), 215–274.

Ibrokhim, M., & Ugli, B. (2020). Will human beings be superseded by generative pre-trained transformer 3 (GPT-3) in programming? *International Journal on Orange Technologies, 2*(10), 141–143.

Mat Rahim, S. R., Mohamad, Z. Z., Abu Bakar, J., Mohsin, F. H., & Md Isa, N. (2018). Artificial intelligence, smart contract and islamic finance. *Asian Social Science, 14*(2), 145.

Montemayor, C. (2021). Language and Intelligence. *Minds and Machines, 31*(4), 471–486.

Nordheim, C. B., Følstad, A., & Bjørkli, C. A. (2019). An initial model of trust in chatbots for customer service—Findings from a questionnaire study. *Interacting with Computers, 31*(3), 317–335.

Pérez-Campuzano, D., Morcillo, P., Rubio, L., & López-Lázaro, A. (2021). Artificial intelligence potential within airlines: A review on how AI can enhance strategic decision-making in times of COVID-19. *Journal of Airline and Airport Management, 11*(2), 53–72.

Rana, J., Gaur, L., Singh, G., Awan, U., & Rasheed, M. I. (2021). Reinforcing customer journey through artificial intelligence: A review and research agenda. *International Journal of Emerging Markets, 17*(7), 1738–1758.

Reim, W., Åström, J., & Eriksson, O. (2020). Implementation of artificial intelligence (AI): A roadmap for business model innovation. *Ai, 1*(2), 180–191.

Robinson, S., Alifantis, T., Edwards, J. S., Ladbrook, J., & Waller, A. (2005). Knowledge-based improvement: Simulation and artificial intelligence for identifying and improving human decision-making in an operations system. *Journal of the Operational Research Society, 56*(8), 912–921.

Sufi Dzikri Sarol has always been passionate about aviation and aims to contribute to the industry in the future. Aside from his studies at the Universiti Kuala Lumpur, he enjoys coding and aspires to be a programmer or apps developer in the future. He has joined and won several competitions at various levels; international robot development (Mindstorm programming), international project management competition (creative project video montage), and national level robot development competition (Arduino software programming).

Mohammad Fakhrul Nizam is a Lecturer at Universiti Kuala Lumpur, Malaysia. Background-wise, he has years of experience in information systems, technology, network administration, and project management. He has an overwhelming interest in establishing and investigating knowledge management and development within aviation, quality, and project. Currently, he is pursuing his studies at the doctorate level in information systems with an interest in knowledge management and quality.

Dr. Nor Aida Abdul Rahman is an Associate Professor, Universiti Kuala Lumpur (UniKL), Kuala Lumpur, Malaysia, and Head of Aviation Management, Universiti Kuala Lumpur—Malaysian Institute of Aviation Technology (UniKL MIAT), Selangor, Malaysia. She has worked as internal and external trainer in management, supply chain, Halal logistics and postgraduate research. Her research work has appeared in several reputable academic journals such as Industrial Marketing Management, Journal of Humanitarian logistics and supply chain, International journal of quality and reliability management, International journal of supply chain management and others. She has also published a number of book chapter and refereed conference proceedings, and part of the editorial team of book project with Routledge. She is a panel of WG in MS2400 Halal Supply Chain standard & TC10 for Halal supply chain standard (SMIIC). She earned Ph.D. degree in Management (supply chain management) from Brunel University, London, UK. She is also serving as Academic Advisor in college, a chartered member for Chartered Institute of Logistics and Transport Malaysia (CILTM), HRDF Certified Trainer, Chairman (Academic Committee) for Malaysian Association of Transportation, Logistics and Supply Chain Schools (MyATLAS), Vice President (Research Journal) for Institute for Research in Management and Engineering UK (INRME), JAKIM Halal Certified Trainer, UniKL Halal Professional Board and a member of Academy of Marketing, UK.

Chapter 6
Technology in Hotel Sector

Eshaby Mustafa

Abstract This chapter presents the discussion on the technology applied in the hotel sector in the new norm for hotels' operation around the world. Various studies have been conducted to report the latest hotel's technology trends and innovation to sustain competitive advantage. Therefore, this chapter offers light on the recent transformation, development, as well as the application of various technological advancement, to replace human labor in the hotel sector. Further, this chapter presents the application of these technologies in several departments in the hotel sector. This chapter offers a significant view on the strategies that hotels are implementing in using technology to transform their communication medium, financial transaction, food and beverage operations, marketing, and promotional tools, as well as the use of Artificial Intelligence (AI) in hotel's service delivery to replace human labor. The impact of the technology application in the hotel sector is also discussed at the end of this chapter.

Keywords Hotel sector · Technology application · Impact of technology · Hospitality industry · Competitive advantage

Introduction

The hotel sector is indeed extremely competitive, and it is very important for hotels to keep up with the latest trends in technology application. Technology can assist hotel in efficiently managing processes of the daily operations, reducing expenses, minimizing employee workloads, increasing productivity and performance of the hotel, and most importantly, improving the level of customer service provided. Furthermore, technology application in hotels may improve tasks that is complicated for human labour. In addition, technology applications helped manage work better and made it easier to fulfill customers' demands. As mentioned in Ezzaouia and Bulchand-Gidumal (2020), Information Technology (IT) refers to a broad variety of digital

E. Mustafa (✉)
School of Tourism, Hospitality and Event Management, Universiti Utara Malaysia, Changlun, Malaysia
e-mail: eshaby@uum.edu.my

© The Author(s), under exclusive license to Springer Nature Singapore Pte Ltd. 2023
A. Hassan and N. A. A. Rahman (eds.), *Technology Application in Aviation, Tourism and Hospitality*, https://doi.org/10.1007/978-981-19-6619-4_6

technologies that allow for the network access, transmission, storage, and modification of data. Technology is developing at an unbelievable rate, transforming not just the expectations of the consumer but also how the hotel sector operates.

Malaysia for example, is one of the hospitality and tourism-led industries with the hotel sector as the main contributor for the overall Gross Domestic Product or GDP of the Malaysia's economy. However, the COVID-19 pandemic crisis has impacted the hotel industries in Malaysia, along with many other developed nations that suffers significant downturn due to travel restriction and bans, events cancellation, and tourists' reluctance to travel. In addressing the significance of the hospitality and tourism sector, Malaysia welcomed almost 13.35 m international tourists and with the tourists' receipt increased 6.8% in the first half of 2019 with a total contribution of RM41.69 billion to the revenues. However, it was recorded that Malaysia loss as much as RM3.37 billion in early 2020 due to the pandemic (Dzulkifly, 2020). In addition, the current contribution of tourism to GDP in most of Asian countries are at a much higher level, for example, Vietnam—7.5%, and Singapore—5% (Ayoobkhan & Kaldeen, 2020). It is estimated by the Malaysian government that the GDP of the county deteriorated by 0.8–1.2% (RM 10.8 billion to RM 17.3 billion). Moreover, the declining number of inbound international tourists to the most popular destinations in all over the world has worsened the condition for the industry.

Admittedly, the comprehensive application of information systems and technologies in the hotel sector, and innovative technology infrastructures play an important role in hotel performance throughout the world in the competitive environment of the industry. The hotel sector is expanding with various new possibilities of technological adoption. Furthermore, the integration of new technological innovations and manual service delivery processes is warranted to keep up within the competition (Napierala et al., 2020). Shin and Perdue (2022) commented that an understanding of the technological innovations is a key strategic management and critical source for hotel industry's sustainability in this competitive world. Some examples of the technology that have been taking over service delivery in the hotel sector are Internet, email, hotel's own website, Wi-Fi, booking engines, mobile notification and promotions, computer hardware and software, computer-based reservation systems (CRSs), global distribution systems (GDSs), customer relation management systems (CRMs), property management systems (PMSs), mobile applications, and social media platforms (Ezzaouia & Bulchand-Gidumal, 2020).

Additionally, the recent COVID-19 pandemic has also acted as a catalyst and fundamental transformation to technology adoption and digital infrastructure in terms of delivery of the core services in the hotel sector as it can reduce the interaction between hotel guests and staffs, as well as enhancing cleanliness (George et al., 2020). For example, contactless hotel check-ins and check-outs, keyless entry to guests' rooms, cashless payment, and self-operated facilities have all became extensively applied in hotels around the world. Next, the review of the recent transformation, development, and application of technology in hotel sector is discussed.

The Transformation of Technology in Hotel Sector

The trends in hotel sector are keen for improvements and cost-savings for hotel businesses, transforming the development plan for hotel buildings, infrastructure, management structure and staffing requirements. Inclusively, the way hotel works using technological application in service delivery and daily operations of hotels are providing opportunities, and important solutions needed to create exclusive and personalized experiences that can lead to customers' satisfaction, service quality and growth in the hotel industry.

The application of technology is most instrumental during the pandemic, endemic and other health crisis to help hotel recover and revitalise their operations. This was mainly due to the requirement of daily operations and communication to facilitate every transaction and all the decisions that must be made by the hotel. In addition, almost every single department in a hotel would also require application of new software, system, or program, as part of their daily operation in the new norm for hotel industry. In a positive note, Ahmad and Scott (2019) mentioned that this was in light with the Malaysian Government second policy target, to implement innovative technology to improve productivity in hotels. Moreover, the need for technology application in the hotel sector are within the context of organisational absorptive capacity theory mentioned by Choo and Tan (2019). Their study assumed that, '(1) absorbing external new knowledge can help a hotel to become more innovative and flexible to achieve a higher level of performance; (2) a hotel with a higher ability for absorbing new knowledge will have a competitive advantage over hotels with lower abilities to absorb; and (3) a hotel requires an internal knowledge-based technology to enable it to efficiently absorb and apply external new knowledge' (Choo & Tan, 2019: 13–14). Recent years have seen enormous efforts from the industry and academics alike in the search of the most fitting technology applications that could reduce direct contact between staffs and hotel guests (Tuzovic & Kabadayi, 2018). Next, the technology as applied in the hotel sector is discussed, presenting all the latest trends for delivering efficient services to hotel guests.

The Recognition Technology

The recognition technology is currently a widespread trend in hotels. It allows for biometric recognition through capturing, analyzing, and storing a person's face or other biometric details, which allows for contactless experience. Although it might be awkward for an industry that demands personal interactions through customer service, it cannot deny that the technological devices used by customers are the most appropriate solution for a high standard of hygiene and personal safety. In addition, the recognition technology will directly improve customer experience and satisfaction by adding the value of a hotel's service delivery. The transformation of service delivery in the hotel sector through technology has been applied at the front office department using self-check-in and check-out operated devices which is more convenient and faster. The payment system has also been improved and become much more reliable using facial recognition technology. Further, it enhanced security in the transaction and provide a more satisfying experience along the customer's journey when staying at the hotel. Imagine staying in a hotel that is using facial recognition for check-in, avoiding traditional metal keys when entering the guest's room and where everything is cashless.

The Artificial Intelligence (AI) Self-Service Technology (SST)

The application of artificial intelligence technology or AI self-service technology (SST) is also taking over several daily operations at the hotel, providing highly efficient, convenient, and novel services to customers (Liu & Yang, 2021; Liu & Zhang, 2021). AI's SST's purpose is to perform tasks that would normally require a human to function. Automation using AI such as using Chatbots to interact with customers, has created a service that is unique, consistent, and efficient. Another example is voice control system that allow guests to interact and request for services at the hotel without the need to go through the reception or concierge. The voice control system can also be set to help hotels reduce operating costs and maintain energy efficiency. Other SSTs application such as service robots, electronic and digital key system, self-service devices, smart hotel room entertainment, and others, have proven its efficiency in delivering service throughout the COVID-19 pandemic (Liu & Yang, 2021). These technologies allow the hotel guests to experience personalized services without the requirement of service professionals (Meuter et al., 2000).

The Internet of Things (IoT)

The applications of the Internet of Things in the hotel sector as presented in Infante-Moro et al., (2021:1) are as follows; "(1) Wearable technology (for example, smart glasses) that allows you to identify and recognize a repeat customer facially (as soon as they enter the hotel) and gives information on their preferences and tastes, so that you can give personalized offers; (2) Smart refrigerators that order online so as not to run out of product stock; (3) Connected minibars that notify you when a product is picked up and needs to be recharged. This information will be used for future visits of the client, as you can prepare their preferences in the minibar; (4) Facilities management, which manages the use and maintenance of facilities such as air conditioning, electricity, and water depending on the client's preferences and their presence (or not) in the room where it should be activated, allowing hotels to make economic savings by avoiding uncontrolled use and providing better customer satisfaction by adapting to their preferences; and (5) Mobile keys that allow customers to enter the rooms without the need for keys through an app installed on their mobile that also gives a notification when the room is available". Many hoteliers are supporting these applications since it offers personalized customer experience, despite its huge cost factor and complexity in its installation, training, and maintenance, among others (Infante-Moro et al., 2021).

The Integrated Hotel Mobile Application Technology

Staying connected to the guest at every point of service delivery is fundamental to ensure guest experience quality service at the hotel. However, this effort remains complicated and necessitates a single point of control, and hotel mobile app is an obvious choice for hosting all these tasks. The hotel mobile app is important in developing customers' experiences, allowing hotel guests to manage online booking through their mobile devices, request service and information relating to hotel's promotion, services, and products (Lee, 2018). Aimed at providing a service that allow hotels to stay connected to their guests, increased productivity, enhanced hotel's performance, as well as increasing guest's experience and drive additional revenue, the hotel mobile app has become a required technology application in the hotel sector. When the hotel mobile app was first launched, it simply provided basic hotel information and services, such as images of the hotel, its location, amenities provided, and information on the facilities at the hotel. Recently, hotel mobile app includes various other functions, such as electronic room key, access to hotel, restaurant and outlet booking services, concierge service, housekeeping and laundry services, maintenance services, as well as updates on ongoing event in and around the hotel.

The Underlying Factors for Technology Application in Hotel Sector

Generally, technology application helped to optimize the communication between service providers in the hospitality industry. It has become an integral part of the hospitality industry that is widely adopted in different tourist sites, hotel departments, transportation services and by other service providers to enhance customer's experience. Currently, the practice of e-service technology, digitalized hotel services and hospitality activities is in the rise especially in managing online reservation, hotel own app, mobile services, e-payments, and others. The need for information for example, is the catalyst for the use of social media, mobile technology, and information technology to ease information search, information sharing, and data exchange. The emerging technology application using Web 2.0 has continuously changing the platform for information search, reservation process and destination choice by providing wide access to a larger database of hotel services. Consequently, technology application as the fundamental answer for information need and demand in the hotel sector is evident. The application of technology and its purpose in the hotel sector is discussed next.

The Application of Technology to Improve Communication

Traditionally, hotel guests are required to call the hotel directly to make room reservations and make other hotel arrangements. However, with the latest application of information technology to support reservation for most hotels in Malaysia, customers now rely heavily of computer-based reservation system or CRS to complete their bookings and make transactions. This has enhanced the efficiency of Malaysia's hotel operations among international and domestic tourists, by helping to manage language barrier (Teck & Karuppiah, 2020). This issue is significant whereby it can affect the perception of guests towards the hotel's service and reputation. Adding to this, hotel guests are now more sophisticated, using online reservations mobile application, and other platforms that helped them to compare prices and providing comments and feedbacks on their experiences. However, one of the main challenges of the current hotel industry is the demand to implement technology to improve communication and the hotel management team must seriously address the issue of applying technology to meet customers' needs and demands more effectively.

For example, the application of own mobile communication app that can be installed in smartphones has helped hotels to improve the efficiency of interaction with their guests. The mobile app is also developed for other hospitality and tourism operations such as menu ordering and food delivery, virtual museum, virtual tours, and transportation reservations, to name a few. The Ritz Carlton, Malaysia, was the first five-star hotel that introduced the mobile communication app in the early 2000s. Each of their in-house guests will get a personal phone with pre-installed phone numbers for room services. Due partly to this technology application, The Ritz Carlton was selected to run as one the best hotel in Malaysia in 2002. In addition, the technology application to aid communication between the hotel and their guest has helped saving the cost of retraining the hotels employees to improve communication and indirectly improve customers' perception towards the hotel's services. In another view, Hotel Sama-Sama offers a touch screen device for menu selection for the convenience of their restaurant's guests. As a result, the hotel received compliments from their customers and the occupancy rate of the hotel increased by 15% since the app was introduced. This shows the importance of using the communication app to create a competitive advantage and reduce face-to-face interaction between the customers and staffs, which helped to improve communication between them.

The Application of Technology for Mobile Payment in Hotel Sector

In the last decade, the preference of payment system in the hotel sector has increasingly shifted towards mobile payment gateways (Sun et al., 2020). Psychological factors such as technology acceptance and adoption have influenced customers' continuous usage on mobile payment especially in the hotel sector (Khanra et al., 2021). During the COVID-19 pandemic, technology has developed at a rapid pace, especially in consumer behaviour and business operations in the hotel sector. From the financial aspect in hotel business, mobile wallet or m-wallet was introduced as a mobile payment option (Lew et al., 2020). According to Matemba and Li (2018), m-wallet enables users to store their debit or credit card information, pay for goods and services, and transfer money to third party. The application of m-wallet has helped making the transactions much more efficient and effective. Moreover, according to research by Australia's Biosecurity Laboratory, COVID-19 may remain infectious on common surfaces including banknotes, thus highlighting the risks from paper currency, among other surfaces (Gale, 2020). The application of m-wallet and other online transaction platform helped reduce the usage of paper money and avoid the risk of cross contamination caused by it.

Mobile payment can be divided into two categories. According to Smart Card Alliance (2007), remote mobile payment and proximity mobile payment are the two most common mobile payment categories, preferred by many consumers. Remote mobile payment (MP) is more practical for online shopping using a mobile phone while proximity mobile payment is frequently applied at locations that has compatible point-of-sale (POS) system and vending machines (Smart Card Alliance, 2007). Moreover, it was mentioned that the most common form of proximity mobile payment is the Near Field Communication (NFC)-based MP systems (Smart Card Alliance, 2007). The application of NFC based mobile payment is very popular in the restaurant business (Cobanoglu et al., 2015) as it offers a more secure option of payment and eliminates the need for cash. NFC technology application allows customers to the NFC-enabled payment cards and mobile phones for over-the-counter payments without internet connections (Karjaluoto et al., 2019). It allows customers to pay easily using mobile device for the transaction process that occur in front of the, without having to give their cards to the merchant (Cobanoglu et al., 2015). Moreover, NFC-based mobile payment also offers customer analysis, improve decision-making, increase their revenue per available seat hour (RevPASH) and directly improve customer satisfaction due to service efficiency (Kimes & Collier, 2014). In addition, NFC-based mobile payment also provides a reward system for customer's purchases through point-based programs (Makki et al., 2016). However, although contactless payments are easier, faster and more convenient to use, the use of NFC in Malaysia is still in its early stages (Lew et al., 2020).

The Application of Technology in Food and Beverage Operations

The number of usages of e-commerce mobile apps has experienced a significant rise among active users and new users since the COVID-19 pandemic hits Malaysia. In a study by Hasanat et al. (2020), it was found that most of mobile business apps users used the food delivery services offered on the platform. Similarly, the increase of online traffic on the food delivery websites in the nations of Southeast Asia, for example, Malaysia, Indonesia, Thailand, and Singapore during the pandemic (Karimi-Zarchi et al., 2020).

The challenges from the COVID-19 pandemic forced reinventions of hotels' business model especially in restaurant business, by limiting their menu and offering virtual experiences instead. Recently, hotel restaurants shifted their focus to food delivery by selling packaged meals and promoting them using various social media platforms including live streaming. AirAsia for example, through its e-commerce arm AirAsia Fresh, sells grocery packages of everyday items such as fruits and vegetables. In another case, hotels in Penang, Malaysia, has been promoting the hotel's food and beverage item by selling them by the roadside, opposite the hotel's property (Chin, 2020). The hotel was forced to find alternative sources of income to increase their revenue during the movement control order period in Malaysia since the restrictions of dining in was introduced.

Operating in the new normal requires dramatic changes for hotel's daily operations. The COVID-19 pandemic stressed the need for people to follow social distancing measures and these trends affect the food service industry (Kim et al., 2021). As a result of the coronavirus's highly infectious disease, demand for food delivery services has skyrocketed, and consumers are increasingly accepting contactless delivery options. To avoid human interaction between delivery staff and customers, contactless food delivery systems were highly in demand, prompting hotel industries to adopt "contactless" options in their daily operations. As an example, the trends of hotels using robots to deliver services while hotel staffs are working from home, are taking place recently (Lau, 2020). Robots are now replacing human labour in the preparation of food and beverage in room dining services, replacing human waiters delivering customer's orders, delivering housekeeping items, and the use of vending machines to dispense facemasks and hand sanitizers. The application of robots to handle most of the hotel's service delivery helped reduce the risk of human contact to prevent the spread of COVID-19.

The Application of Technology for Marketing and Promotional

Social media platforms provide hotels an opportunity to establish relationships with their clients, strengthen the hotel's online reputation, and create trendy content. Social media also enables hotel to support their decision making and encourage booking process, through the search in booking engine, online reviews and real experience shared by social media influencers. Therefore, the application of social media as a hotel marketing and promotional tool is inevitable. The increasing number of online users during the pandemic also highlighted the demand for creative visual content, allowing users to have a taste of what they can experience, by engaging with the product or service.

In addition, the emergence of Web 2.0 in providing online social platforms encouraged the application much more significantly (Lau, 2020). Using social media as a marketing and promotional tool proved to be low-cost and effective online information sharing, encouraged social networking, provide consumers a detailed information about products, brands, services, and its description. Hotels can reach a wider market base using social media and it has speed up the communication process. Increasing number of hotels advertisement in social media platforms such as Facebook, Instagram, Twitter and TikTok for example, has boost sales for accommodations, food and beverage promotions, and tour packages, among others. Many hotels chose to advertise more flexible hotel packages and arrangement, due to uncertainties of travel regulations in Malaysia. In addition, Lau (2020) mentioned that hotels also took advantage of using live streaming platforms to promote to hotel customers, such as showcasing cooking demonstration, 3D virtual room and site tour, and virtual events with the objectives to generate more interest and entice interest among customers.

The Application of Artificial Intelligence (AI) and Robots in Service Delivery

Artificial Intelligence or AI has increasingly applied to help smoothen hotel operations during the COVID-19 pandemic. Self-check-in and check-out machines for example, has started to make way in the hotel's front office department and the application has skyrocketed since the pandemic hits. These AI experiences provide access to guest's rooms by using biometric identification such as thumb print and other virtual recognition method. The application of AI delivers a solution for contactless check and check out procedures, body temperature checks and biometric recognition to help control the spread of COVID-19. This technology implementation leads to more efficient and effective service and will be more convenient to guests who values time and speed of service.

As an example, more hotels are currently using self-service kiosks as a substitute to front desk operation, to minimize customer's waiting time during registration and improve performance quality. The Henn-Na Hotel in Japan is a prominent example that used the application of service robots at the front lines when greeting and registering their guests. The Henn-na Hotel in Japan, open its doors in 2015 and is the world's first automaton hotel. Another example is Connie, a service robot receptionist that uses IBM's AI platform to engage with guests and react to their inquiries at the Hilton Hotel (Revfine.com, 2021).

Robots are designed as intelligent physical device that are assigned with specific level of autonomy, intelligence, interactivity, movement, and sensory abilities to allow it to operate (Wirtz et al., 2018). In the hospitality and tourism industry, there are three types of robots designed to fit the purpose in this sector: industrial robots; professional service robots; and personal service robots (Lukanova & Ilieva, 2019). Industrial robots and professional service robots can perform back-office operations, and personal service robots are technology embodied with adaptable interfaces (Ho et al., 2020). Service robots are more suitable in front office operations because it has AI technologies, which allow it to do sophisticated tasks, and communicate with hotel guests (Lukanova & Ilieva, 2019). One example is the Travelmate, a service robot used for baggage and luggage systems that can follow guests to their rooms (Chatterjee, 2020). Travelmate's application removes the need to carry, drag, or push guest's luggage to and from their room. Currently, recent innovations were largely focused on developing machines that can serve customers in hotel sector and complete various other hotel service and operation tasks (Ivanov, 2017, 2019; Ivanov & Webster, 2019).

Several tasks and hotel operation that are currently implementing AI and robot technology are:

- Greet and welcome customers, guest registration, guest check out, bell service, room cleaning (e.g., Henn-na Hotel, Tokyo) (Buhalis & Leung, 2018; Lin et al., 2020)
- Navigate the way around the hotel, use the elevator, deliver customer's request to hotel rooms (e.g., Aloft Hotels) (Ivanov et al., 2017; Lu & Tabari, 2019)
- Provide database of information and virtual reality experience of hotel's products and services (e.g., SARA in Singapore hotels) (Naumov, 2019)
- Robots with AI that can communicate and respond to hotel guests, provide information on hotel facilities and services, and suggest tourist destination (e.g., Hilton Hotels and Henn-na Hotel) (Ivanov et al., 2017; Lin et al., 2020; Prentice et al., 2020).

Accordingly, the hotel sector applied robot technology to perform various service delivery and allowing for unique and personalized experiences for satisfying guests efficiently (Naumov, 2019). Despite this, consumer's acceptance towards robot application is still at an immature stage (Yu, 2020). Therefore, hotel managers must invest more time and effort in designing and implementing these technologies, to updating such application in order to encourage more customers accepting and using such service.

The Impact of Technology in the Hotel Sector

Recent times in the post pandemic era has seen accelerated digital applications of technology in the hotel sector to enable a work-anywhere economy and mitigate the potential risk in a hotel's daily operation (Lau, 2020). Hotel businesses continuously reinventing their business model and service strategy which changes the conventional hotel business. Although traditionally, hotels emphasize personal contacts at every service delivery points in the daily operation, the period of uncertainty offers opportunity new technologies and still provide hotel guests with efficient and personalized experience.

Melián-Alzola et al. (2020) stated that the application of technology has helped to improve customer's satisfaction, increase hotel's global market share, enhanced staffs' productivity and performance, standardized the process in daily operations, and significantly helped reduced operating costs. Further, the application of technology is also a key for the development of technological capability that will improve the hotel's capability to respond to changing environment (Melián-Alzola et al., 2020). In addition, technology resources have also led to efficiency in both back-office and front office hotel operation and contributed towards the benefit of various stakeholders in the hotel business (Bilgihan et al., 2011). Moreover, as the travel and tourism industry grow, technology application has invaded the setting and boosted the performance, quality of service delivery, and creating a competitive advantage in the dynamic hotel sector (Samala et al, 2020).

From the perspective of technology application in the hospitality and tourism industry, the Artificial Intelligence technology for instance, has enabled hoteliers to automate service delivery processes and streamline hotel's daily operation and activities. Furthermore, the quality of communication between guests and employees were strengthen, with the technology applied improving the level of personalization to each of the hotel guest and providing efficient responses despite the absence of staff members (Revfine.com, 2021). Various studies have also highlighted the importance and advantageous findings of technology application in the hotel sector that suggest the tendency of hotel customers towards internet and self-service technologies. This is evident in Ivanov and Webster (2017) and Ivanov et al. (2017) findings that revealed most of the customers prefer using self-service technologies, over traditional services. In addition, technology offer a wide range of information than can surpass and outperform human performance in hotel's daily operations and activities.

Conclusion

Technology application is becoming more prevalent in the hotel industry. It is projected that this advancement flourish immensely in the future because of the widespread application of innovative technology to help with service delivery, management of operation, and other processes in the hotel sector. The application of technologies such as AI, service robots, and mobile payment system for example, will bring about significant changes in the hospitality industry. The technological factors can mould the hotel service landscape and the processes that are conducted in hotel businesses. In addition, the application of technology also led to the creation of many new jobs within the industry. It is also forecasted that the hotel sector will see more retraining programs so that the hotel staffs can adapt to the evolving technological advancement.

Furthermore, the technology advancement applied in hotel sector is also an indicator that the industry is making great effort to improve their efficiency in service delivery as well as productivity and performance. With the main objective of technology application to create a personalized experience and satisfaction, the hotel business is surely having better control in its processes and activities. Moreover, with technology application, the automated business process delivery is moving at a greater extent and more streamlined in nature. The hotel businesses must realize that through innovative technology application, they can sustain their competitive advantage in the market, improve communication with hotel guests, improve the performance and service delivery, smooth and efficient transaction for the guests, increase their productivity and efficiency, increase profit, and reduce costs and finally, improve the overall hotel business.

References

Ahmad, R., & Scott, N. (2019). Technology innovations towards reducing hospitality human resource costs in Langkawi Malaysia. *Tourism Review, 74*(3), 547–562.

Ayoobkhan, M., & Kaldeen, M. (2020). An empirical study on cloud computing technology on hotel industry in Sri Lanka. In A. Hassan & A. Shama (Eds.), *The emerald handbook of ICT in tourism and hospitality* (pp. 425–440). Bingley.

Bilgihan, A., Okumus, F., Nusair, K., & Kwun, K. J. W. (2011). Information technology applications and competitive advantage in hotel companies. *Journal of Hospitality and Tourism Technology, 2*(2), 139–153.

Buhalis, D., & Leung, R. (2018). Smart hospitality—Interconnectivity and interoperability towards an ecosystem. *International Journal of Hospitality Management, 71*, 41–50.

Chatterjee, S. (2020). *Robotics/artificial intelligence in hospitality industry: is it a bequest or blight to human race?* https://www.ssrn.com/abstract=3622292. Accessed 20 Mar 2022.

Chin, C. (2020). Hotel manager in Penang sells RM3 food by roadside to survive MCO. *The Star.* https://www.thestar.com.my/lifestyle/travel/2021/02/03/hotel-manager-in-penang-sells-rm3-food-by-roadside-to-survive-mco. Accessed 20 June 2022.

Choo, P. W., & Tan, C. L. (2019). The effect of Hotel Absorptive Capacity on Service Innovation: Knowledge-based Technology as Catalyst. In *The National and International Graduate Research Conference 2017.* Bangkok: University of Bangkok, 1(10), 13–19.

Cobanoglu, C., Yang, W., Shatskikh, A., & Agarwal, A. (2015). Are consumers ready for mobile payment? An examination of consumer acceptance of mobile payment technology in restaurant industry. *Hospitality Review, 31*(4), 6.

Dzulkifly, D. (2020). Muhyiddin: Tourism industry hit hardest by Covid-19, faces RM3.37b loss. *Malay Mail.* https://www.malaymail.com/news/malaysia/2020/03/13/muhyiddin-tourism-industry-hithard-by-covid19to-lose-rm3.37b-while-gdp-s/1846323. Accessed 2 Mar 2022.

Ezzaouia, I., & Bulchand-Gidumal, J. (2020). Factors influencing the adoption of information technology in the hotel industry. An analysis in a developing country. *Tourism Management Perspectives, 34*, 100675.

Gale, J. (2020). Coronavirus may stay for weeks on banknotes and touchscreens. *Bloomberg*. https://www.bloomberg.com/news/articles/2020-10-11/coronavirus-can-persist-for-four-weeks-on-banknotes-study-finds. Accessed 24 Mar 2022.

George, G., Lakhani, K., & Puranam, P. (2020). What has changed? The impact of Covid pandemic on the technology and innovation management research agenda. *Journal of Management Studies, 57*(8), 1754–1758.

Hasanat, M. W., Hoque, A., Shikha, F. A., Anwar, M., Hamid, A. B. A., & Tat, H. H. (2020). The impact of coronavirus (COVID-19) on e-business in Malaysia. *Asian Journal of Multidisciplinary Studies, 3*(1), 85–90.

Ho, T. H., Tojib, D., & Tsarenko, Y. (2020). Human staff vs. service robot vs. fellow customer: Does it matter who helps your customer following a service failure incident? *International Journal of Hospitality Management, 87*, 102501.

Infante-Moro, A., Infante-Moro, J. C., & Gallardo-Pérez, J. (2021). Key factors in the implementation of the internet of things in the hotel sector. *Applied Sciences, 11*(7), 2924.

Ivanov, S., & Webster, C. (2019). Conceptual framework of the use of robots, artificial intelligence and service automation in travel, tourism, and hospitality companies. In S. Ivanov & C. Webster (Eds.), *Robots, artificial intelligence, and service automation in travel, tourism and hospitality* (pp. 1–7). Bingley.

Ivanov, S. (2017). Robonomics-principles, benefits, challenges, solutions. *Yearbook of Varna University of Management, 10*, 283–293.

Ivanov, S. (2019). Ultimate transformation: How will automation technologies disrupt the travel, tourism and hospitality industries? *Zeitschrift Für Tourismuswissenschaft, 11*(1), 25–43.

Ivanov, S. H., & Webster, C. (2017). Adoption of robots, artificial intelligence and service automation by travel, tourism and hospitality companies–a cost-benefit analysis. In *Prepared for the International Scientific Conference "Contemporary Tourism—Traditions and Innovations"*. Sofia: Sofia University, the 19th-21st, October.

Ivanov, S. H., Webster, C., & Berezina, K. (2017). Adoption of robots and service automation by tourism and hospitality companies. *Revista Turismo & Desenvolvimento, 27*(28), 1501–1517.

Karimi-Zarchi, M., Neamatzadeh, H., Dastgheib, S. A., Abbasi, H., Mirjalili, S. R., Behforouz, A., & Bahrami, R. (2020). Vertical transmission of coronavirus disease 19 (COVID-19) from infected pregnant mothers to neonates: A review. *Fetal and Pediatric Pathology, 39*(3), 246–250.

Karjaluoto, H., Shaikh, A. A., Leppäniemi, M., & Luomala, R. (2019). Examining consumers' usage intention of contactless payment systems. *International Journal of Bank Marketing, 38*(2), 332–351.

Khanra, S., Dhir, A., Kaur, P., & Joseph, R. P. (2021). Factors influencing the adoption postponement of mobile payment services in the hospitality sector during a pandemic. *Journal of Hospitality and Tourism Management, 46*, 26–39.

Kim, J. J., Kim, I., & Hwang, J. (2021). A change of perceived innovativeness for contactless food delivery services using drones after the outbreak of COVID-19. *International Journal of Hospitality Management, 93*, 102758.

Kimes, S. E., & Collier, J. (2014). Customer-facing payment technology in the US restaurant industry. *Cornell Hospitality Report, 14*(2), 6–17.

Lau, A. (2020). New technologies used in COVID-19 for business survival: Insights from the Hotel Sector in China. *Information Technology & Tourism, 22*(4), 497–504.

Lee, S. A. (2018). M-servicescape: Effects of the hotel mobile app servicescape preferences on customer response. *Journal of Hospitality and Tourism Technology, 9*(2), 172–187.

Lew, S., Tan, G. W. H., Loh, X. M., Hew, J. J., & Ooi, K. B. (2020). The disruptive mobile wallet in the hospitality industry: An extended mobile technology acceptance model. *Technology in Society, 63*, 101430.

Lin, H., Chi, O. H., & Gursoy, D. (2020). Antecedents of customers' acceptance of artificially intelligent robotic device use in hospitality services. *Journal of Hospitality Marketing & Management, 29*(5), 530–549.

Liu, C., & Yang, J. (2021). How hotels adjust technology-based strategy to respond to COVID-19 and gain competitive productivity (CP): Strategic management process and dynamic capabilities. *International Journal of Contemporary Hospitality Management, 33*(9), 2907–2931.

Liu, Y., & Zhang, N. (2021). Study of hotel AI application and development trends in 5G era. In *2021 4th International Conference on Advanced Electronic Materials, Computers and Software Engineering (AEMCSE)*. IEEE, pp. 1051–1054.

Lu, L., & Tabari, S. (2019). Impact of Airbnb on customers' behavior in the UK hotel industry. *Tourism Analysis, 24*(1), 13–26.

Lukanova, G., & Ilieva, G. (2019). Robots, artificial intelligence, and service automation in hotels. In S. Ivanov & C. Webster (Eds.), *Robots, artificial intelligence, and service automation in travel, tourism and hospitality* (pp. 157–184). Bingley.

Makki, A. M., Ozturk, A. B., & Singh, D. (2016). Role of risk, self-efficacy, and innovativeness on behavioral intentions for mobile payment systems in the restaurant industry. *Journal of Foodservice Business Research, 19*(5), 454–473.

Matemba, E. D., & Li, G. (2018). Consumers' willingness to adopt and use WeChat wallet: An empirical study in South Africa. *Technology in Society, 53*, 55–68.

Melián-Alzola, L., Fernández-Monroy, M., & Hidalgo-Peñate, M. (2020). Information technology capability and organisational agility: A study in the Canary Islands hotel industry. *Tourism Management Perspectives, 33*, 100606.

Meuter, M. L., Ostrom, A. L., Roundtree, R. I., & Bitner, M. J. (2000). Self-service technologies: Understanding customer satisfaction with technology-based service encounters. *Journal of Marketing, 64*(3), 50–64.

Napierała, T., Bahar, M., Leśniewska-Napierała, K., & Topsakal, Y. (2020). Technology towards hotel competitiveness: Case of Antalya, Turkey. *European Journal of Tourism, Hospitality and Recreation, 10*(3), 262–273.

Naumov, N. (2019). The impact of robots, artificial intelligence, and service automation on service quality and service experience in hospitality. In S. Ivanov & C. Webster (Eds.), *Robots, artificial intelligence, and service automation in travel, tourism and hospitality* (pp. 123–134). Bingley.

Prentice, C., Dominique Lopes, S., & Wang, X. (2020). The impact of artificial intelligence and employee service quality on customer satisfaction and loyalty. *Journal of Hospitality Marketing & Management, 29*(7), 739–756.

Revfine.com. (2021). *8 Examples of robots being used in the hospitality industry*. https://www.revfine.com/robots-hospitality-industry. Accessed 20 Mar 2022.

Samala, N., Katkam, B. S., Bellamkonda, R. S., & Rodriguez, R. V. (2020). Impact of AI and robotics in the tourism sector: A critical insight. *Journal of Tourism Futures, 8*(1), 73–87.

Shin, H., & Perdue, R. R. (2022). Hospitality and tourism service innovation: A bibliometric review and future research agenda. *International Journal of Hospitality Management, 102*, 103176.

Smart Card Alliance. (2007). *Proximity mobile payments: Leveraging NFC and the contactless financial payments infrastructure*. https://www.d3nrwezfchbhhm.cloudfront.net/lib/Proximity_Mobile_Payments_200709.pdf. Accessed 20 June 2022.

Sun, S., Law, R., & Schuckert, M. (2020). Mediating effects of attitude, subjective norms and perceived behavioural control for mobile payment-based hotel reservations. *International Journal of Hospitality Management, 84*, 102331.

Teck, T. S., & Karuppiah, N. (2020). Operation strategy as a competitive advantage in hotel industry. *International Business Research, 13*(2), 1–35.

Tuzovic, S., & Kabadayi, S. (2018). The influence of social distancing on employee well-being: A conceptual framework and research agenda. *Journal of Service Management, 32*(2), 145–160.

Wirtz, J., Patterson, P. G., Kunz, W. H., Gruber, T., Lu, V. N., Paluch, S., & Martins, A. (2018). Brave new world: Service robots in the frontline. *Journal of Service Management, 29*(5), 907–931.

Yu, C. E. (2020). Humanlike robots as employees in the hotel industry: Thematic content analysis of online reviews. *Journal of Hospitality Marketing & Management, 29*(1), 22–38.

Dr. Eshaby Mustafa is a Senior Lecturer in the School of Tourism, Hospitality and Environmental Management, Universiti Utara Malaysia. She obtained her first degree in Bachelor of Hotel Management with Honors from UiTM, Shah Alam (Malaysia). Later, she received M.Sc. in Food Management from University of Surrey (UK). She furthered her study in a doctoral program at the same university and was awarded Ph.D. (Consumer Behavior in Food Management). She is interested in the areas of food management in general, with specialization in food choice, food heritage, food service, food culture and food tourism. Other areas of interest include technology in the hotel industry, hospitality management, customer behavior, human resource management, quality management, service operations management, front office management, services marketing, and hospitality education and training. She has published in internationally, peer-reviewed journals while also presented in numerous international conferences. She also supervises postgraduate and undergraduate students in various research topics.

Chapter 7
Digital Advancements in Airline Catering Sector

Fathien Azuien Yusriza

Abstract The COVID-19 pandemic has hastened the digitalization of pre-flight and in-flight services. Digital advancement has proven to improve the effectiveness and efficiency of the supply chain process in airline catering. Digitalization in airline catering is an area that is rarely addressed and discussed in the research, especially in developing countries. Acknowledging this gap, the purpose of this chapter is to emphasize digital advancement from the standpoint of the airline catering sector. The purpose of this chapter is threefold, first is to provide a discussion on the role of digital advancement in the airline catering sector and explain how it helps increase the efficiency and effectiveness of the process. Second, this chapter discusses the current and upcoming digital transformation in airline catering operations; thirdly this chapter provide case analysis of several airline caterers with regards to the implementation of digitalization advancement. This chapter conclude by discussing current studies and opportunity for future studies investigation.

Keywords Digital transformation · Airline catering · In-flight meals · Big data

Introduction

For more than two years, global supply chain challenges have been front-page news. The pandemic exposed numerous underlying concerns and emphasized the need for increased resilience and agility, from major disruptions to soaring customer expectations. Despite the supply chain being shaken by growing geopolitical volatility, inflation, and long-term staff shortages, industry leaders are proactively mitigating risk, minimizing interruptions, and outperforming their competition.

F. A. Yusriza (✉)
Malaysian Institute of Aviation Technology (UniKL MIAT), Universiti Kuala Lumpur, Selangor, Malaysia
e-mail: fathien.yusriza02@s.unikl.edu.my

Politecnico Di Torino (POLITO), Torino, Italy

© The Author(s), under exclusive license to Springer Nature Singapore Pte Ltd. 2023
A. Hassan and N. A. A. Rahman (eds.), *Technology Application in Aviation, Tourism and Hospitality*, https://doi.org/10.1007/978-981-19-6619-4_7

The onboard eating experience is critical to the enjoyment of airline passengers. Airlines are working hard to improve the quality of their in-flight meals and beverages (Rajaratnam & Sunmola, 2021). Airline catering organization is one of the major players in the aviation industry that consist of multi-players such as the airlines, manufacturing, airport, cargo and also MROs organization (maintenance, repair and overhaul). Airline catering plays significant role in the air transport industry as it provides in-flight meals to the passengers or travelers on board (Rahman et al., 2018). Food supply chain in airline catering has started gained popularity in the early 2000s and the use of information technology (IT) system is crucial to monitor the raw materials, the orders, quality control and many other operational processes. In fact, activities involved in in-flight catering business are also involved high volume of meals production every day with serving a number of airlines (Schierholz Foerdertechnik, 2022). It is important for every organization that involved with logistic, distribution and manufacturing to advance their technology application in order to achieve improved operational performance, business performance, improved product quality, improved communication and information sharing (Rahman et al., 2019). The "digital revolution" refers to the transition from mechanical and electronic analogue equipment to modern digital technology. The time period started in the 1980s and is still in effect today. The Information Era officially begins with the digital revolution (Technopedia, 2017).

The pandemic situation has started to steadily improve after two years of catastrophic COVID disturbances to the world as we knew it. According to the Airline News (2022), in 2024, the total number of passengers will exceed 4.0 billion (including multi-sector connecting trips as one passenger), surpassing pre-COVID-19 levels (103% of the 2019 total). Due to the increasing in passenger numbers in future, a digital advancement technology must be added to the operation. Increasing in numbers of passenger will lead to the high expectations and demand. Whether airline caterers can provide fast service or fast-food chains, they must be able to satisfy customers with increasingly high expectations.

Digital advancement is so much in line with the growth of supply chain. Investing in digitalization are important in order to win the market. This is because the technology delivering the promise in improving the business production. For example, in the manufacturing company, when there are large number of data, somehow it will be unmanageable. But, with the digital transformation such as system, has categorized data to several file or folder which then will ease the process of data tracing. Therefore, to improve material requirements planning, production, and product development, airline caterers must take use of the opportunities presented by digital transformation.

A wide range of food sector innovations are providing obstacles for system catering, from vegan diets to dinner delivery. Customers want to be able to eat food that suits their diet no matter where they are, whether they are on an airline or in a fast-food restaurant. They make a big deal out of their meals, which are now more than just about eating. Catering businesses must find new ways to optimize the entire value-added process, from detailed material requirements planning to digital, cloud-based operations.

According to Hitec (1994), the range of items required often proved costly when it came to automating production operations, which is why airline catering has seen minimal mechanization to date. However, with airlines facing severe downward pressure on fares and, as a result, cutting back on their own spending (including catering), and the airline food services business has been seeking for new ways to reduce its own production costs. Therefore, digitalization in airline catering is important as the introduction of a computerized management system not only increases the quality of service provided to clients, but it also considerably improves the efficiency of the operation by automating existing paperwork activities.

Customers of the airline catering sector receive in-flight meals and catering handling services. In a complicated operational environment, they must manage a significant volume of airline meals for all passenger classes, as well as staff meals from the kitchen to the aircraft, and the reverse flow of equipment and unused products (Rajaratnam & Sunmola, 2020). Implementing digital transformation to the operation of catering process will increase the effectiveness and efficiency of the production.

Moreover, flight catering has been undergoing constant change as a result of customer preferences, which has resulted in full-scale patterns with evolving recipes and food service quality. The increasing demands of airline passengers for excellent service and a nutritious diet with a choice-based menu on flight have made food and beverage quality a highlight for domestic and international airline carriers in competing with one another and maintaining their prestige and prominence in their passengers' memories (Moyeenudin et al., 2020).

Role of Digital Transformation in Airline Catering

Catering flights are a critical component of an airline's operations. Meal service has a big influence on customer service quality and costs a lot of money (Megodawickrama, 2018). It is very critical process in airline catering sector. The airline catering industry benefits from sales generated through generally long-term contracts with airline firms for the supply of meals for all flights departing an airport. However, the supply of meals to airlines faces significant challenges due to the fact that the general demand fluctuates frequently to accommodate last-minute bookings and the fact that fresh meals must be supplied to flights in time for departure, whether on time or late (Hitec, 1994).

Flight operations digitalization must be able to bridge disciplines and follow best practises if it is to live up to its promises of reduced time, expense, enhanced efficiency, and improved effectiveness. As aviation has progressed, there have been numerous changes in airline catering, both in the front and back of the aircraft. The changes evolved from manually record the meals data to a system that store customer meals order.

As per, Simple flying (2022) and Airport Technology (2021), airline meals have been around almost as long as commercial flights, with the first instance being on a voyage between London and Paris in 1919. Meal service has altered as the scale and volume of flying has grown. It has made a huge difference to be able to make food onboard. Of course, today's experience is highly dependent on the airline and cabin, with wide disparities in quality. Airline catering possibilities expanded in tandem with the growth of aviation. As flights hour got longer, airlines had to consider onboard meals on regular scheduled international flights.

The airline sector has long struggled to establish a positive reputation in terms of sustainability, and many passengers are increasingly searching for this when choosing a carrier. This, of course, includes on-board meals. Operators' environmental decisions, from food offers to how meals are delivered, produced, and managed after a trip, are becoming increasingly important to passengers, as many airlines have already demonstrated. For example, Emirates Flight Catering, which serves meals to over 100 airlines at Dubai Airport, promises that artificial intelligence technology will help it cut food wastage by 35% (CNN Travel, 2017; Lorraine Elliot notquitenigella, 2010). Intelligent cameras, smart scales, and meters are utilized in the program to analyze components used during food preparation and identify meals that are wasted more frequently.

The digital transformation in airline catering has help smoother the process of meals preparation and help in reducing the food waste. With the correct data captured by the system, caterer can forecast and predict exact number of meals to be prepared before flight departure. Furthermore, over the last few years, the aviation industry has seen significant transformations. The COVID-19 pandemic has wreaked havoc on the tourism industry in general and the aviation industry in particular.

Many inefficiencies afflict today's inflight caterers; systems and managing rapid development and competitiveness have produced a demand for better inflight food services. Airlines must keep track of several caterers, fleet information, galley planning, load planning, menu planning, inventory management, and a variety of other responsibilities. The examples below demonstrate how system caterers, as well as caterers in general, may take advantage of emerging technology to become faster, smarter, and more efficient.

Using Data Analysis to Plan Material Requirements More Efficiently

From meat to vegetables to dairy goods, every system caterer strives to keep precisely enough inventory on hand, since precise material requirements planning is critical for long-term production and on-time delivery. On the one hand, it assures that the things are in stock, while on the other, it reduces the cost of acquiring resources. Customer preferences are becoming more diversified, which means caterers must supply an ever-increasing array of items. System caterers, such as airline caterers and franchise organizations, are finding it increasingly difficult to stock their supply optimally. One solution is predictive analytics. Data analysis can be utilized to identify patterns and contexts for various material requirements, as well as create accurate forecasts about future requirements. This enables airline caterers to reduce not only wastage, but also expensive replacement stock prices.

Transportation, storage, and handling costs, as well as capital investments, are all reduced with a seamless material flow. It also reduces waste, energy use, and the demand for floor space. As a result, resources and working time are better utilized. Finally, airline caterer will be able to reduce their production time. A more efficient material flow leads to a higher bottom line. However, in the future, optimized material flow can help caterer meet more severe sustainability and transparency requirements, lower the carbon footprint, and make better use of scarce raw materials; in other words, airline caterer can run production more sustainably.

Real-Time Transmission of Recipe Modifications to Production

Over the last few decades, significant scientific advances in digital technologies have resulted in the development of new autonomous and self-regulating systems. These advancements have expanded industry output capacity, but the growing diversity of products and rising customer demand for individual or custom-made products at reduced prices necessitate the design and operation of systems capable of handling this growing variety (Coito et al., 2022).

Despite having to deal with an ever-increasing number of unique requests, airline catering recipes and stock lists are nevertheless routinely altered centrally and manually. This implies that staff aren't informed of the changes until later, slowing down output. Furthermore, such adjustments are frequently printed on paper. However, paper-based production is prone to mistakes.

Caterers can reduce the human work required to change production data by digitizing operations, hence speeding up production. This specifically refers to data being collected and altered in a central system. Following that, this clearly presented information regarding food standards—whether organic, halal, or vegan—is sent in real time to tablets situated in manufacturing facilities. This ensures that all staff have access to the most up-to-date information, which is critical for maintaining quality.

Customer Input is Used to Develop New Products Using Big Data

Analyzing enormous volumes of data to find information like hidden patterns, correlations, market trends, and consumer preferences that may help businesses make wise business decisions is known as big data analytics. This process is frequently challenging. Organizations can examine large data sets and discover new insights thanks to data analytics technologies and techniques. Basic inquiries about business operations and performance are addressed by BI queries (Techtarget, 2020).

Customers' satisfaction is influenced by a variety of elements, including aesthetics, portion size, and flavor. So, customer feedback is critical to enhancing products and increasing customer satisfaction. However, it is often difficult to draw generalizations from individual customer opinions—for example, when airline passengers submit comments on menus or catering concepts to flight attendants from several airlines. Filtering out information relevant to product development from comments sent in free-text formats is extremely tough for airline caterers.

Airlines caterers can collect and analyse customer feedback from many airlines utilizing big data analytics approaches. These evaluations can also include responses offered on social media channels. Exploratory data analysis identifies connections between data in a systematic manner. The software can also be taught to evaluate subjective remarks accurately. For product development, the end result is a statistical review and extensive analysis of each meal, which companies may use to build new items successfully.

By implementing big data analysis, now that the operation is under control, automated monitoring operates in the background. As a result, operational employees and supervisors can relax and focus on their tasks. Operators and supervisors will be provided with the tools they need to do their jobs more efficiently by using visualization. This includes easy situational views of the end-to-end process flow that display only the data that is important to each position.

Digital Transformation of Airline Catering: Case Study and Example

AeroChef Web-Based Tool

According to AeroChef Global (2022), AeroChef has proven to be an indispensable software solution for centralised operations management, with business intelligence, analytical dashboards, and management reporting features built-in, allowing for fast decision-making. Order management, menu management, food costing, production planning and forecasting, inventory, dispatch, invoicing, and a variety of other aspects are all covered by the software system. Pre-order meals, sales aboard meals, ordinary drinks, complete tray set dinners, and 5-star cuisines are all available through airlines' catering services. New low-cost and hybrid airlines, new destinations, airports, and a new generation of passengers are all part of the new era of change. In addition, the move has increased demand for in-flight catering and entertainment. Many inefficiencies afflict today's inflight caterers; systems and managing rapid development and competitiveness have produced a demand for better inflight catering services. Airlines must keep track of several caterers, fleet information, galley planning, load

7 Digital Advancements in Airline Catering Sector   95

Features

- Available as 'Hosted SaaS' or 'On Premise' model
- Designed for multiple location management
- Integrations ready with third party systems
- Customizable framework, which is modular and scalable
- Actionable data insights
- Highly Secure
- Real-time data analytics
- Easy to Set Up, Use and Administer

Fig. 7.1 AeroChef web-based tool features. *Source* AeroChef Global (2022)

planning, menu planning, inventory management, and a variety of other activities (Fig. 7.1).

Therefore, airlines with their own in-flight catering production facility can benefit from an integrated system that allows them to effortlessly communicate and simplify information with the caterer. AeroChef ACMS is a web-based tool that assists airlines in managing, monitoring, and controlling operational operations linked to in-flight catering management. Some of the features offer in the software are order management, inventory management, caterer portal, purchase management, MIS report, caterer management, contract management, etc. AeroChef is a cloud-based software which monitor a day-to-day operation of the airline catering and efficiently result to the business improvement.

Following the success of the AeroChef software system for airline catering, the company has expanded its offerings to include more cloud-based catering solutions. AeroChef for Food Catering was created in 2020, based on the experience of assisting in-flight caterers in diversifying into cloud kitchens in order to maintain income and operations during the COVID-19 pandemic. AeroChef was able to take use of the basic technology platform and apply their catering expertise to create simple software for the food service industry. The AeroChef Food Catering system is beneficial to any food catering firm that operates as a central kitchen, cloud kitchen, or has multiple locations.

Monorail Robot for Movement of Meals Production

The application of robotics has rapidly expanded beyond industrial manufacturing to service industries, thanks to the development of artificial intelligence (AI). However, there are a few key issues to consider when adding service robots into the service business. In the airline sector, new products and services have always been an important part of competitive strategy (Jones, 1995). With significant advancements in programming and engineering, robotic systems are increasingly capable of doing nonstandard activities previously designated for humans (Lai & Tsai, 2018) (Fig. 7.2).

How does Emirates manage to serve people per year on nearly 200,000 flights? It's incredible that an airline could make such a large number of productions in a single day. Everything must be unloaded from the incoming flight before the culinary

Fig. 7.2 Industrial size of ware washing machine. *Source* Lorraine Elliot notquitenigella (2010)

activity can begin. Plates, trays, trolleys, spoons, and a variety of other cutlery are all thrown onto the ground to be cleaned. Dishes are sorted into categories and processed by industrial-sized ware washing machines. The dish was washed manually with a considerable manpower in the previous year, which was a decade ago. Emirates caterer currently handles roughly 3 million pieces of tableware every day (CNN Travel, 2017).

Other than cutlery, the trolley that bring passenger meals on board also cleaned here. After cleaned, it will be loaded up onto the buildings by mile-and-half-long monorail to be taken upstairs. The electric monorail system has pick up and drop off point at multiple locations on every floor. This massive inventory technology has saved most of the manpower energy and time. All processes are visualized, controlled, and monitored by a master computer. The master computer can analyse all process data for the development of new transportation methods. More work may be done in less time as a result of digital advancements in airline catering. Work efficiency of a higher standard capable of producing more rationally, efficiently, fast, safely, and cleanly.

DELMIA Quintiq's Supply Chain Planning and Optimization Software (SCP&O)

According to Dassault Systems (2022), planning on a single sheet is impossible. Departments, teams, and even individuals use spreadsheets to stay focused and keep their information feed manageable. Because it is shared, emailed, downloaded, and updated, the masterplan has several versions. As a result, there's a good chance that someone somewhere is making decisions based on obsolete information. To make matters even more complicated, lack of synchronization is sometimes intentional—something that is easy to do when departments plan in divisions.

Let's pretend Sales has presented its prediction. In theory, everyone bases their strategy on such figures. In actuality, there are two types of sales forecasts: official and unofficial. Production believes Sales is being overly optimistic, so it has created its own projection. This means that when it comes to the sales prediction in meetings, everyone has a different number in mind. A key flaw in Excel planning is not doing enough to encourage collaboration. Bottlenecks and excess inventory are common red signals that can be traced back to isolated planning. Supply Chain Planning software from DELMIA Quintiq plans and optimizes supply chain from beginning to finish, giving the power and knowledge, to turn supply chain planning from a cost center to a revenue generator (DELMIA Quintiq, n.d.). Define clear KPIs for the entire organization and link each business function to them. Optimize every step of supply chain, from long-term strategic planning to key details at the point of execution, to achieve consistent and long-term high service, quality, and efficiency levels. The benefit and key features include:

- *Sales and operation planning*

  To bridge the gap between sales and operations, gain end-to-end visibility into elements affecting sales, marketing, finance, and operations. Improve the accuracy of your demand forecasting and supply planning.
- *Production planning*

  High inventory levels, poor delivery performance, low yield, and excessive waste are all barriers to profitability which then can be managed by using DELMIA Quintiq's supply chain planning and optimization software.
- *Logistic scheduling*

  Improve operational efficiency, resource use, and cost reduction.
- *Production scheduling*

  Manage the execution schedule's batching and sequencing to guarantee that the plan is always optimal for meeting service levels at the lowest possible cost.
- *Workforce planning*

  Improve employee satisfaction and productivity while adhering to corporate rules, regulations, and limits.

Malaysia Airlines used to rely primarily on paper-based data. A software to alter a requirement to improve efficiencies through people and truck scheduling is critically needed. Quintic system adaptation allows a corporation to customize the system to meet their own needs. It also allows users the flexibility to customize the system and use it as a platform for changing day-to-day activities. Airline catering is usually dealing with a high volume of ad hoc adjustments, and the Quintic system is one of the systems that allows users to alter drastic data by simply pressing a few keys, and the system then automatically reallocates resources to the relevant aircraft details. By installing the Quintic system, it was able to save labor for airline caterers, achieve a return on investment of less than a year, and reduce truck usage. It also aids airline caterers in planning ahead when a new consumer arrives.

Conclusion, Limitation and Future Research Recommendations

The goal of this paper was to look at the landscape of the digital advancement and speculate on how it would influence how airlines comprehend and market to their customers. New digital advancement ability to collect customer data, along with a continually connected user base, offers enormous promise. The advantages of supply chain optimization simply come down to one critical capability: end-to-end visibility of the complete supply chain rather than isolated silos of data. It is the key to significant cost savings, increased operational efficiency, greater quality, and increased production. It improves airline catering industry's capacity to get closer to customers and understand their values, while machine-learning technologies become more sophisticated, allowing us to better predict their future performance (Amadeus IT Group, 2017). Moreover, in order to maintain consumer loyalty among new digital customers, airlines caterer must meet them "where they are". A proactive, adaptable, and real-time approach to designing offers will spark the interest of new customers and foster brand loyalty. This study can be expanded to look at several case studies in various sizes of airline catering organizations in various areas in order to analyze the global airline catering supply chain. Despite the valuable input this chapter offer, this study also contents a limitation which the source of literature is rarely explored, especially in the context of airline catering. Therefore, future study is called to extend more on how the digital transformation may affect the performance analysis of airline catering supply chain.

References

AeroChef Global. (2022). *Integrated software solution for airlines with catering management*. Retrieved April 28, 2022, from https://www.aerochefglobal.com/airlines.aspx.
Airport Technology. (2021). *In-flight catering: Exploring meal trends for 2021*. Retrieved April 27, 2022, from https://www.airport-technology.com/features/airline-meal-trends-2021/.
Airline News. (2022). *Strong demand recovery in January but impacted by Omicron*. Retrieved April 30, 2022, from https://www.aviationnews-online.com/airline/iata-strong-demand-recovery-in-january-but-impacted-by-omicron/.
Amadeus IT Group. (2017). *Embracing airline digital transformation: A spotlight on what travellers value*. Retrieved April 20, 2022, from https://amadeus.com/documents/en/airlines/research-report/embracing-airline-digital-transformation.pdf?crt=DownloadRequest.
Coito, T., Faria, P., Martins, M. S. E., Firme, B., Vieira, S. M., Figueiredo, J., & Sousa, J. M. C. (2022). Digital twin of a flexible manufacturing system for solutions preparation. *Automation, 3*(1), 153–175.

CNN Travel. (2017). *Airline food: How Emirates airline can dish out 180,000 meals a day*. Retrieved July 22, 2022, from https://edition.cnn.com/travel/article/emirates-flight-catering/index.html.

Dassault Systems. (2022). *Delmia Quintiq supply chain planning: Supply chain planning for business transformation*. Retrieved May 19, 2022, from https://www.3ds.com/products-services/delmia/products/delmia-quintiq/supply-chain-planning/.

DELMIA Quintiq. (n.d.). *The risk-free move from excel to mature supply chain planning: How DELMIA Quintiq enables your team to hit the ground running. When you've reached your system's upper limits*. Retrieved April 5, 2022, from https://easyfairsassets.com/sites/79/2022/03/The-risk-free-move-from-Excel-to-mature-supply-chain-planning.pdf.

Hitec, R. (1994). Management of a catering facility. *Assembly Automation, 14*(1), 28–29.

Jones, P. (1995). Developing new products and services in flight catering. *International Journal of Contemporary Hospitality Management, 7*(2–3), 24–28.

Lai, C. J., & Tsai, C. P. (2018). Design of introducing service robot into catering services. In *ICSRT '18: Proceedings of the 2018 International Conference on Service Robotics Technologies*, March 2018 (pp. 62–66).

Lorraine Elliot notquitenigella. (2010). *All about airline food: Behind the scenes at Emirates airline*. Retrieved July 22, 2022, from https://www.notquitenigella.com/2010/02/03/all-about-airline-food-behind-the-scenes-at-emirates-airlines/.

Megodawickrama, P. (2018). Significance of meal forecasting in airline catering on food waste minimization. In *15th International Conference on Business Management (ICBM)* (pp. 1131–1146). Nugegoda: University of Sri Jayewardenepura Gangodawila.

Moyeenudin, H. M., Parvez, S. J., Anandan, R., & Bindu, G. (2020). Data analytics on gratification of airline passenger with their experience. *International Journal of Recent Technology and Engineering, 8*(5), 1999–2004.

Rajaratnam, D., & Sunmola, F. (2020). Managing business processes in an ERP system context for airline catering logistics. In *10th International Conference on Operations and Supply Chain Management (OSCM)*, 14–16 December (p.10).

Rajaratnam, D., & Sunmola, F. (2021). Supply chain management in airline catering service: Characteristics, challenges and trends. In *Proceedings of the 4th European International Conference on Industrial Engineering and Operations Management*, Rome, 2–5 August (pp. 1831–1842).

Rahman, N. A. A., Mohamed, M. F., Muda, J., Fauzi, M. A., Rahim, S. A., & Majid, Z. A. (2018). Linking halal requirements and branding: An examination of halal flight kitchen provider in Malaysia. *International Journal of Supply Chain Management, 7*(3), 208–215.

Rahman, N. A., Muda, J., Mohammad, M. F., Ahmad, M. F., Rahim, S., & Fernando, M. V. (2019). Digitalization and leap frogging strategy among the supply chain member: Facing GIG economy and why should logistics players care. *International Journal of Supply Chain Management, 8*(2), 1042–1048.

Schierholz Foerdertechnik. (2022). *Airline catering fast, precise and in time*. Retrieved April 28, 2022, from https://www.schierholz.de/en/airlinecatering.html.

Simple flying. (2022). *How has inflight catering evolved over the years?* Retrieved April 27, 2022, from https://simpleflying.com/inflight-catering-evolution/.

Technopedia. (2017). *What does digital revolution mean?* Retrieved July 22, 2022, from https://www.techopedia.com/definition/23371/digital-revolution.

Techtarget. (2020). *Definition of big data analytics*. Retrieved July 22, 2022, from https://www.techtarget.com/searchbusinessanalytics/definition/big-data-analytics.

Fathien Azuien Yusriza graduated from Universiti Kuala Lumpur, Malaysian Institute of Aviation Technology (UniKL MIAT), Subang, Malaysia with a Bachelor's Degree in Aviation Management. She has experience working with global logistics companies and currently pursuing her Master's degree at Universiti Kuala Lumpur—Malaysian Institute of Aviation Technology (UniKL MIAT), Selangor, Malaysia. She is working on her research related to the effectiveness of aviation's supply chain management operation. Her interest to pursue research relating to aviation's supply chain began from the day she completed her undergraduate thesis on the effectiveness of inventory management in airline operation. In the year 2022, she was given the opportunity to participate in an exchange mobility programme in one of the prestige universities in Italy called Politecnico Di Torino (POLITO) for engineering management courses.

Chapter 8
Technology Framework for Rural Tourism Development in Spain

Fernando Mayor-Vitoria

Abstract The growth of the tourism sector in Spain has been constant from the 1960s to the present day at a much higher rate than any other European country and it has only been slightly affected by some specific moments related to the financial crisis of 2008 or the pandemic derived from COVID-19. Tourism has meant many advances in macroeconomic terms for Spain and also some problems related to the environmental impact or the flow of people that have left some rural areas depopulated. In this article, we intend to extol the situation and the importance of rural tourism for Spain and also to talk about how the technological advances of the last decades are totally applicable to this type of tourism and they can help the country to increase and diversify its tourist offer in the short term. In addition, the correct application of technology can help to generate employment at all levels of the supply chain and it should be seen as a generator of sustainable opportunities which can allow Spain to remain a leader in terms of the number of visitors but from the point of view of the conservation and the care of the natural environment.

Keywords Rural tourism · Tourist facility · Standard · Design · Development · Spain

Introduction

Spain is the second country in number of tourism inflows and revenues, the first European destination in terms of tourist inflows, the first destination worldwide in terms of holiday tourism and the fourth destination worldwide in terms of number of international meetings, according to data for 2019 from the International Congress and Convention Association (ICCA) (n.d.). Tourism is a key activity for the national economy, since it represents a very significant figure as a percentage of GDP (Gross Domestic Product) and it contributes in a very high percentage to the employment, and it allows mitigating the structural imbalance of the trade balance.

F. Mayor-Vitoria (✉)
Universidad Internacional de Valencia - VIU, Valencia, Spain
e-mail: fmayor@universidadviu.es

© The Author(s), under exclusive license to Springer Nature Singapore Pte Ltd. 2023
A. Hassan and N. A. A. Rahman (eds.), *Technology Application in Aviation, Tourism and Hospitality*, https://doi.org/10.1007/978-981-19-6619-4_8

At a time when the strategic sectors of the economy must act as levers to contribute to the change of scenario that will consolidate Spain on the path of growth and job creation, tourism must be a priority due to its world leadership, its transversal and driving force in the economy and its orientation towards dynamic and future markets. If the COVID-19 pandemic has revealed anything, it is the enormous dependence of the Spanish economy on tourism, as well as its outstanding capacity as a driver of goods and services for other branches of activity (de la Dehesa Romero, 2003).

Santillán-Núñez et al. (2015) claim that technology has fundamentally altered every aspect of the tourist sector. The power the traveler has attained is one of the major changes. In other words, technology enables the traveler to get far more information, become the main organizer of his or her journey, and reduce reliance on third parties. Tourists are also considerably more demanding given that they have a wider range of alternatives to pick from, which has improved their negotiating position. Tourists are becoming more than just passive observers; they are also content creators who share their work with other travelers. For instance, they can post reviews and comments on digital sites. Travelers may share their experiences through travel blogs, and they can broadcast both positive and negative parts of their journeys on social media. Travelers' increased involvement and expectations for the experiences they wish to have driven businesses to provide better services and more alternatives, which encourages them to invest in innovation in order to keep up with the times.

Despite the aforementioned, travel firms have been able to widen their distribution networks thanks to the Internet. Prior to this, the travel agency's only possible clients were those who passed by the building. However, today any Internet user browsing the Web may utilize a travel agency's services. In this way, travel agencies may work more efficiently thanks to internal technology deployment. Because they can easily access a greater variety of items and information, they may, for instance, provide quotes virtually instantly. In summary, the use of technology has enabled the automation and simplification of several procedures. Additionally, and in line with (Mariani & Baggio, 2021), the digitalization of files has made it easier to gather and analyze data using Big Data initiatives, enabling them to get to know their customers better, complete deals faster, and forge strategic relationships with them.

Another effect of the use of technology in the tourist industry has been the failure and, in many cases, the closure of businesses that were unable to adapt. In other words, not investing in digitization has been a significant disadvantage in this fiercely competitive economy. Traveling alone is one of the largest developments of the past ten years, made possible by technology (Paiva et al., 2021). Dynamic packages, which enable specific services to be booked and adjusted in accordance with the traveler's interests, have supplanted organized package trips. Additionally, having access to more information enables one to experience a place firsthand and learn to know it like a native, rather than just as an outsider who observes it. Eschewing the conventional tourist activities in favor of those more in line with local customs.

Digital company owners' eager to modernize and digitize the tourist industry have taken advantage of the new business prospects made possible by technology advancements. However, in the beginning, they discovered that there were big businesses that controlled a sizable portion of the market and did not need to prioritize the adoption of technology. Particularly, conventional businesses with a long history and intricate hierarchical systems that needed time to develop and remake themselves. As a result, new supply chain enterprises were not developing at the expected rate since existing supply chain participants lacked the required technologies. For instance, due to a lack of sufficiently sophisticated technology, internet travel companies were unable to interface with specific tour operators for years. The absence of digital skills is a further barrier. Traditional businesses are lacking in specialist technology profiles who are aware of the potential that the Internet and the company's digitalization bring. As a result, it was also difficult to put these new techniques into practice.

Furthermore, it should be remembered that the economic crisis that started in 2008 partially coincided with the years in which technology underwent its greatest growth, these advancements (Jóhannesson & Huijbens, 2010). Tourism businesses were in fact severely impacted by the crisis, and their goal at the moment was to keep their doors open rather than close them. Many businesses lacked the funding necessary to invest financially in technology. Therefore, it may be claimed that the financial burden of technology adoption has also been a significant hindrance.

These challenges are now being gradually overcome. To meet the new difficulties, people are receiving training on how to integrate the very best of technology and tourism. In other words, technology application in the travel and tourist industry keeps getting better and more advanced. Large corporations are banking on innovation with all the work that this requires because they understand that they will quickly become outdated without technology. It follows that a thorough implementation strategy is required, from the adoption of new technology and marketing profiles to the employment of software development firms. Without overlooking the equipment required to take full use of the opportunities presented by technology.

In the specific case of rural tourism, technological advances have been key to prevent rural depopulation and boost tourism. It is a very logical equation for most experts that now takes more strength due to the real problem of rural depopulation. According to a study by Spanish Federation of Municipalities and Provinces (FEMP) (n.d.), there are more than 4,000 Spanish municipalities that subsist with less than 1,000 inhabitants and are at risk of extinction in the medium and long term.

In this sense, the recommendation for companies in the sector is to make use of Information and Communications Technology (ICT). According to Instituto Nacional de Estadistica (INE) (2020), during 2019 only 9% of overnight stays in tourist accommodations were in rural tourism accommodations. A figure that can be increased with the use of ICTs, considered a very powerful channel for conveying messages to global audiences. Therefore, they should be used as management, planning and promotion tools, adapting products and services to the new profile of the digital traveler and allowing access to global audiences from rural areas.

Regarding strategies to promote rural tourism, an offer and content must be designed for cell phones. The smartphone is the traveler's best ally, as it is the most widely used device in Spain to access the Internet. 94.6% of Spaniards use their smartphones to go online, do Google searches, watch videos, surf the Internet, check social networks and more, and moreover, in Spain, 35% of purchases made from cell phones are related to travel; for this reason, rural tourism services should pay special attention to offering their services on mobile-friendly websites and even integrate into applications and other tools created specifically for these devices (Ruiz-Palmero et al., 2019).

Facilitating payment is another key to improving the travelers' experience. In a society where paying is as easy as bringing your cell phone close to the terminal or entering your card numbers in an online payment portal, all businesses must adapt, including rural hospitality establishments. The following points will cover some key aspects of the situation of rural tourism in Spain and will also discuss some of the technologies that have the potential to be adapted to the rural environment in the coming years.

Situation of Rural Tourism in Spain

In general, the tourism sector is a key activity for the Spanish economy, both for its contribution to GDP (Gross Domestic Product) and for its capacity to sustain and generate employment; these are some of the indicators which reflect the country's potential is its high supply. According to Gabrielli et al. (2022), Spain is the third largest European country in terms of the number of regulated accommodation places, with more than 3.4 million places in hotels, campsites, tourist apartments and rural tourism lodgings, more than 50% of which are of the highest category, 4 and 5 stars, and more than 17,000 establishments.

Likewise, the tourism sector has traditionally demonstrated an enormous tractor effect on other sectors of the Spanish economy that have benefited from it, such as commerce or real estate, among many others. This relevancy has become evident during the year 2020 because of the effects of the COVID-19 pandemic in Spain. The direct and induced effect of tourism on economic activity has been felt throughout Spain, although with unequal intensity depending on the different characteristics of the various regions and destinations, a fact that is clearly highlighted when the different levels of productive specialization of the territories are analyzed. A productive specialization, in Spain and in a number of its regions (Duro et al., 2021), which also means a high level of dependence on an activity that has not stopped growing in recent years but that is not immune either to the economic situation, or to competition from other destinations, or to the accelerated changes that the travel industry has been experiencing in recent years as a result of sociodemographic changes, digitization and aspects related to greater environmental awareness.

In fact, COVID-19 has highlighted the fragility of the tourism sector in the face of global-scale phenomena (Fragkou, 2021), that are totally alien to it, the result of contexts of growing uncertainty that there is no better way to deal with than by relying on the levers of knowledge and innovation. For example, there are regions that point to tourism as a driving force for other sectors and as an element of dynamization of rural areas (as in the case of Catalonia) or as the main vector of smart growth (as in the case of the Illes Balears).

In the specific case of rural and nature tourism, this is directly linked to the tourist's awareness of environmental aspects, which considers leisure activities in natural areas of specific regions and in which the tourist himself is an active or passive agent of the activity itself. Currently this type of tourism is in a growing phase in Spain and more and more people are practicing rural tourism. According to Instituto Nacional de Estadistica (INE) (2020), the main motivations for a rural getaway are to be in contact with nature (40%), to disconnect from routine (24%) and to socialize with friends or family (14%). Secondary motivations include gastronomy, culture and adventure. The abundance of outdoor options (70%) is the motivation that grows the most compared to 2020. It is followed by the possibility of visiting a cultural environment (49%) and gastronomic richness (45%). These are the three most valued aspects when traveling to a rural destination. In fourth, fifth and sixth place are the friendliness of the people (29%), the existence of a wide range of accommodation (20%) and the fact of knowing that you can practice sustainable tourism (20%), respectively.

According to Instituto Nacional de Estadistica (INE) (2020), the percentage of people who have engaged in rural tourism, has grown by almost 5% from 36% in 2020 to 40.9% in 2021. We have not yet reached the pre-pandemic figures where we saw a penetration of 44% of the Spanish population that had practiced rural tourism in 2019. The average expenditure in rural accommodation stands at €30 (person/night), while last year it was €28. The frequency of consumption has grown significantly over the last year. Those tourists who have made between 3 or more rural getaways a year, grows up to 40% while in 2019 it is observed that those who decide to escape 3 or more times a year was only 33%. Therefore, between these 2 years, where 2019 was a pre pandemic year it is evident that there has been a growth of 7% among those who practice more times a year rural tourism. There has also been a 3% decrease in travelers who only bet on a short-term rural getaway. This growth of the rural tourism is observed especially in summer. In Spain, 72% of rural travelers tend to practice rural tourism between June and September 2021. With respect to 2020, this figure has grown from 56% to the current 72%. This increase of travelers in summer confirms that rural tourism has already been consolidated today as one of the key options to enjoy the main vacations of the year as the summer ones. By regions of Spain, the favorite rural destinations to visit during the year 2022 are in first place: Asturias (19%), Andalusia (16%) and Aragon (11%) and Castilla Leon (8%). When compared with data from 2020, the increase in the region of Andalusia stands out. Also noteworthy is the rise of Aragon, which climbs 4 positions to third place in the top 3 ranking. Cantabria, a favorite until then in third position, drops to fifth place, while Castile rises one position to fourth.

Following Instituto Nacional de Estadistica (INE) (2022), however, rural tourism is also helping Spain to fight against the seasonality of the sector. A fact that indicates the relevance of the rural tourism is that it is not only practiced in summer in a punctual way, but for more than half of the users (57%) they represent their main vacations of the year, therefore, with greater investment of time and budget to this type of tourism. Among those who have not practiced rural tourism in summer 2021, the reasons are different from those exposed in 2020, when more than half of users (51%)

had to cancel it because of COVID-19. This year, on the other hand, the pandemic has not been the main reason, but travelers who have not opted for rural tourism have been mainly because they had not planned it (42%). It is also helping to change the user profile. The typical rural tourist is between 40 and 64 years old. Among men, the percentage of tourists in the 50–64 age bracket is 6 points higher than women (46% vs. 40%), while it drops 9 percentage points (27%) in the case of travelers between 40 and 49 years old. Profiles under 30 years of age are less common among both men and women. Among seniors, men who practice rural tourism stand out with 14%. In this sense, it can be concluded that the typical rural tourist profile is a woman between 40 and 64 years of age. This is of great importance because new followers are being generated. Currently, in the year 2021, the number of new users has increased. Among the new tourists, more than half (52%) recognize that they have changed from sun and beach tourism to rural tourism. It is followed by 23% of travelers who until now chose national urban destinations; 15% who opted for international trips and 10% who for various reasons did not go on vacation, but this year have done so and have chosen rural tourism.

The COVID-19 pandemic also brought with it a new option for telecommuting that is here to stay: teleworking. It landed in March 2020 in many companies under the obligation of the health situation, but its flexibility and ease of reconciling work and family have meant that it has become a priority option for many workers. This meant that at the end of 2020 the owners of rural lodgings already began to consider the option of extending the stays in their houses at the request of those workers who asked for a rural environment for teleworking. According to the latest data on rural tourism in Spain, teleworking is beginning, in an incipient way, to be a trend within the rural tourism sector.

Innovation and Technology for Rural Tourism Development

Nowadays, nobody doubts that technology and tourism are a perfect combo. This combination also has a huge influence on the way we travel, from what destination we choose for our vacations, to what we do when we are there and even in the post-adventure stage. Millennials have also had a lot to do with this paradigm shift. They are passionate about travel and are true fans of new technologies. This combination has given rise to this new context in which social networks, apps or blogs play an important role when it comes to planning a trip. Likewise, the industry, aware of this trend, has adapted its business model and offers to attract this audience.

Mobile Technology

The cell phone is nowadays the main protagonist of the new ways of traveling (Andrade, 2021). The cell phone has become the usual tourist guide, travel agency, locator of the best restaurants and map. It accompanies travelers and tourists during all stages of the purchasing process. For these reasons, there is a need to adapt the company's communication and services to these devices. Many rural hotels have already done so by creating an information service for travelers through instant messaging applications. This system, after confirming the reservation, sends the user the reservation information through this channel as well as additional information about the weather, the arrival route or the state of the roads. The user has access to all the information through the programs they often use in this way.

Augmented Reality and Virtual Reality

The tourist industry in general, and rural tourism in particular, has also been exposed to augmented reality and virtual reality. Due to the fact that there are many potential applications, an increasing number of businesses are thinking about using this technology. Companies in the tourist industry may use it to demonstrate any product to potential clients, such as the inside of a cruise ship cabin or to briefly transfer them to the magnificent Chinese wall. The options are essentially limitless. For instance, it is now feasible to visit some of the world's most isolated locations without ever leaving your house. This is the case, for instance, with Everest, due to the Everest VR program, which enables you to visit the top of the globe without having to do the difficult ascent (Everest Virtual Reality, n.d.). Virtually, it is also feasible to kayak over the Grand Canyon while taking in the views and sounds of the area. In Spain, the rural region of Los Pedroches (Córdoba) is embarking on augmented reality, with the help of various technology companies, to promote rural tourism in its territory, with experiences that will allow visitors to travel back in time and visit the present in a different way. For example, visitors to the Civil War air raid shelter in Villanueva de Córdoba will not only be able to see the two galleries and the central room, which sheltered the town when bombing raids were announced in the area.

Internet of Things

The tourist industry will benefit from a number of advancements thanks to the Internet of Things (IoT) (Car et al., 2019). Examples include adding Internet-connected sensors to physical items like vehicles, baggage, or buildings and using the data they collect to create value. In fact, the Hotel Technological Institute (ITH) predicts that in the near future, the Internet of Things will play a significant role in creating individualized client experiences. Rural motels now give their customers an application that allows them to interact with the thermostat or manage the television in their rooms. Depending on how you use the app, it might choose the TV stations or the temperature of the room before visitors come. There is also luggage that have a gadget that allows the owner to monitor each one's whereabouts from a mobile device, improving traceability at airports.

Voice Assistance

There are well-known voice assistants available today that cater to customer demands, such as Apple and Amazon's Siri and Alexa. There are common queries like "turn on the radio", "open the email", and "what will the weather be like today in my city". However, the tourist industry is likewise utilizing this technology more and more. The introduction of voice assistants that are tailored for this context has made it possible for rural enterprises to start receiving this assistance as well. For instance, IBM just released Watson Assistant (de Silva Oliveira et al., 2019), an AI-powered assistant that offers users a customized and engaging experience. Companies may use and customize it to meet their needs because it is an open technology. For instance, unlike other comparable technologies, Watson will not be the name of the assistant; rather, it will be anything the hotel decides.

Big Data

There is more and more talk about the possibilities that Big Data can offer the rural world (Zhou, 2021), but not yet all the possibilities it offers in the tourism sector have been exposed. However, many companies are already taking advantage of it. For example, large hotel chains use customer information to determine the most appropriate target for a campaign. To determine the most suitable profile and increase success rates, they examine their unstructured database to look at spending patterns, consumption patterns, assessments made, the reason for the trip, nationality, and other factors. They then compare this information to publicly available data from the countries of origin. They may segment their efforts more effectively and maximize the investment spent in doing so.

Blockchain

According to experts, it will be feasible to revolutionize the existing world using blockchain. Although it is directly tied to money, it also appears that it may have an effect on the travel and tourist industry. Although there hasn't been much experience with this technology in the tourism industry, it is thought that it may be helpful for a variety of purposes, including quick and secure payment methods, identification of visitors at the airport, and guaranteeing transparency in visitor opinions (Tirso Pérez & Plasencia López, 2021).

5G Technology

Technology in the rural tourism sector is making inroads with 5G networks. These promise much faster upload and download speeds, wider coverage and much more stable connections. Beyond being able to download content at 20 times faster speeds, 5G will allow the development and implementation of technologies that were limited by 4G. In other words, the connection between smart devices will be much more efficient and we will be able to really start enjoying, for example, the IoTs. Immersive tourism, in which the traveler becomes the protagonist of the experience through technologies, will be possible (Liang et al., 2021). Thus, virtual reality, augmented reality or 360° video will become much more common and accessible. In Spain, rural areas such as Segovia premiered a project that uses 5G and augmented reality so that tourists can move, at least virtually, around San Martin's Church (Segovia) and its surroundings (Segovia et al., 2015).

Conclusion and Recommendations

Rural tourism in Spain is young if we compare it with the European evolution, where it is already in the phase of diversification and maturity. This situation places Spain in an advantageous position. The rural tourism is still an authentic product and linked to an existing agriculture, the houses are giving a good reception and the relation quality-price is, in general, correct. Nevertheless, in the future, rural tourism in Spain must be marketed with unified and homogeneously organized quality labels for the Autonomous Communities. In this sense, technology can help to market a unique product. The rural tourism has to continue betting for the diversification and the territorial complementarity of the products. The regional particularities, the thematizations of the territories, and of the products, a gastronomy and products with denomination of origin, are a good guarantee for the creation of a rural tourism consolidated and recognized in Spain.

The rural tourism is not a competition to the tourism of sun and beach, that continues being protagonist in Spain, but yes it is a good complement and diversifier of the local economies of the interior territories. These new tourism activities have helped to slow down depopulation and revitalize abandoned or isolated areas. However, without the firm commitment of the administration, the local community and the inhabitants of rural areas, rural tourism cannot continue to advance. The new dynamics of rural tourism in Spain are oriented towards social and environmental sustainability, local and regional cohesion in the development of tourism, local involvement in decision-making, product quality and a thematization that allows to fight against seasonalization and diversification of offers and users. Spanish tourism should look in these mirrors, as it can learn from the mistakes and successes of its European neighbors.

Finally, technology is a tool, and it is important that there is a role for a regulator to guide it in a positive direction. The speed of technology has been much faster than that of the Administration, but the regulator must be able to standardize in favor of the sustainability of tourist destinations. Nor can the companies' own responsibility in this regard be overlooked, as well as that of the traveler himself, who must increasingly demand sustainability and act accordingly. Regulation, long-term business vision and social values are essential to guide the proper use of tourism innovation as a positive transforming force.

What is clear is that the future in tourism goes hand in hand with technology. From a business point of view, we see that traditional companies adapted to new trends will coexist in the market, and digital companies that have been born with a technological DNA. From the point of view of the tourist, we see that they are looking for good value for money, comfort and speed. Therefore, companies must meet these needs, and they will do it through technology. Technology makes it possible to be in constant contact with the customer, to know their tastes and preferences better and to offer them personalized solutions quickly.

References

Andrade, P. (2021). Mobile culture for tourism communication. In M. Khosrow-Pour (Ed.), *Encyclopedia of organizational knowledge, administration, and technology* (pp. 1638–1650). IGI Global.

Car, T., Stifanich, L. P., & Šimunić, M. (2019). Internet of things (IoT) in tourism and hospitality: Opportunities and challenges. *Paper presented at the 5th International Scientific Conference ToSEE - Tourism in Southern and Eastern Europe 2019 "Creating Innovative Tourism Experiences: The Way to Extend the Tourist Season"*, Opatija (pp. 163–175).

da Silva Oliveira, J., Espíndola, D. B., Barwaldt, R., Ribeiro, L. M., & Pias, M. (2019). IBM Watson Application as FAQ Assistant about Moodle. In *2019 IEEE Frontiers in Education Conference (FIE)* (pp. 1–8). Covington, KY: IEEE.

de la Dehesa Romero, G. (2003). *Balance de la economía española en los últimos veinticinco años*. Retrieved April 3, 2022, from https://www.eco.uc3m.es/~ricmora/ee/lecturas/Dehesa2003.pdf.

Duro, J. A., Perez-Laborda, A., Turrion-Prats, J., & Fernández-Fernández, M. (2021). Covid-19 and tourism vulnerability. *Tourism Management Perspectives, 38*, 100819.

Everest Virtual Reality. (n.d.). *Home*. Retrieved April 3, 2022, from https://www.everestvirtualreality.com/.

Fragkou, D. (2021). The weakness of mass tourism in the Covid-19 period and the contribution of architecture. In A. Kavoura, S. J. Havlovic, & N. Totskaya (Eds.), *Strategic innovative marketing and tourism in the COVID-19 era* (pp. 131–139). Springer.

Gabrielli, L., Garcés-Mascareñas, B., & Ribera-Almandoz, O. (2022). Between discipline and neglect: The regulation of asylum accommodation in Spain. *Journal of Refugee Studies, 35*(1), 262–281.

Instituto Nacional de Estadistica (INE). (2020). *Estadística de Movimientos Turísticos en Fronteras (FRONTUR)*. Retrieved April 3, 2022, from https://www.ine.es/daco/daco42/frontur/frontur1219.pdf.

Instituto Nacional de Estadistica (INE). (2022). *Última Nota de prensa. Movimientos turísticos en fronteras. Frontur. Junio 2022. España recibe 7,5 millones de turistas internacionales en junio, frente a los 2,2 del mismo mes de 2021*. Retrieved April

3, 2022, from www.ine.es/dyngs/INEbase/es/operacion.htm?c=Estadistica_C&cid=125473617 6996&menu=ultiDatos&idp=1254735576863.

International Congress and Convention Association (ICCA). (n.d.). *Home*. Retrieved April 3, 2022, from https://www.iccaworld.org/.

Jóhannesson, G. T., & Huijbens, E. H. (2010). Tourism in times of crisis: Exploring the discourse of tourism development in Iceland. *Current Issues in Tourism, 13*(5), 419–434.

Liang, F., Mu, L., Wang, D., & Kim, B. S. (2021). A new model path for the development of smart leisure sports tourism industry based on 5G technology. *IET Communications, 16*(5), 485–496.

Mariani, M., & Baggio, R. (2021). Big data and analytics in hospitality and tourism: A systematic literature review. *International Journal of Contemporary Hospitality Management, 34*(1), 231–278.

Paiva, S., Ahad, M. A., Tripathi, G., Feroz, N., & Casalino, G. (2021). Enabling technologies for urban smart mobility: Recent trends, opportunities and challenges. *Sensors, 21*(6), 2143.

Ruiz-Palmero, J., Sánchez-Rivas, E., Gómez-García, M., & Sánchez Vega, E. (2019). Future teachers' smartphone uses and dependence. *Education Sciences, 9*(3), 194.

Santillán-Núñez, M. A., Velarde-Valdez, M., & Obombo-Magio, K. (2015). Tecnologías de Información y Comunicación al servicio del turismo en Mazatlán, Sinaloa, México. *Ciencias Holguín, 21*(1), 1–10.

Segovia, D., Mendoza, M., Mendoza, E., & González, E. (2015). Augmented reality as a tool for production and quality monitoring. *Procedia Computer Science, 75*, 291–300.

Spanish Federation of Municipalities and Provinces (FEMP). (n.d.). *Home*. Retrieved April 3, 2022, from http://www.femp.es/.

Tirso Pérez, M., & Plasencia López, N. (2021). *Blockchain en la industria turística*. Retrieved April 3, 2022, from http://riull.ull.es/xmlui/handle/915/22713.

Zhou, J. (2021). Statistical research on the development of rural tourism economy industry under the background of big data. *Mobile Information Systems, 2021*(3), 1–11.

Dr. Fernando Mayor-Vitoria is an industrial engineer and Ph.D. in economics by the Universitat Politècnica de Valencia and he also holds a MBA and a Master in textile engineering. He has more than twenty years of international business experience in different sectors such as textile, footwear and lighting. Moreover, he is professor at the Universidad Internacional de Valencia (VIU) in the areas of economics and business administration. He has published different papers related to the fields of logistics, big data and decision science as well as books and chapters about operational management and business strategy.

Chapter 9
Iskandar.my: Framework of Mobile Augmented Reality Travel App

Nur Shuhadah Mohd, Maimunah Abdul Aziz, and Hairul Nizam Ismail

Abstract In today's world, Mobile Augmented Reality (AR) technology has been increasingly adopted by tourism industrial players in product development mainly due to the technology's ability in improving tourists' destination interaction through dynamic digital engagement. Mobile Augmented Reality (MAR) travel app, such as 'Iskandar.my', is seen capable to attract users' excitement during travel by augmenting relevant travel-related information media, at the same time still leaving some space for tourist appreciation of the real environment. This research explores the technological framework of 'Iskandar.my' MAR travel apps and elaborates on the service dimension and design dimension of the app. These dimensions of the technological framework would explain the value co-creation experienced by users from the digital engagement and enlighten the possibility of being the antecedent of users' travel satisfaction.

Keywords Mobile augmented reality · Technological framework · Value co-creation · User experience

Introduction

In the current digital age, smartphones have become a must-have device in human daily life (Fannisa et al., 2021). This is due to the rapidly changing innovation and development of technologies worldwide. The various functionalities available within a smartphone are capable of assisting tourist travel movement during travel to better

---

N. S. Mohd (✉)
Kulliyyah of Languages and Management, International Islamic University Malaysia, Muar, Malaysia
e-mail: shuhadah@iium.edu.my

M. Abdul Aziz
UniKL Business School, University Kuala Lumpur, Kuala Lumpur, Malaysia

H. N. Ismail
Faculty of Built Environment and Surveying, Universiti Teknologi Malaysia, Johor Bahru, Malaysia

understand the destination. However, to better engage with the surrounding environment, tourists usually require a more dynamic and interactive experience, as a result from the technological engagement (Kounavis et al., 2012; Edwards-Stewart et al., 2016; Tussyadiah & Zach, 2011) through 3-Dimensional object development (Tülü & Yılmaz, 2013). This is how and when Augmented Reality technology comes into the picture.

Augmented Reality, or denoted as AR is a technology that integrates the virtual objects or medias with real-time environment to enhance the setting of its user experience (Carmigniani & Furht, 2011; Höllerer & Feiner, 2004; Linaza et al., 2012). Through the integration, users are able to obtain real-time information, such as recent updates of social media status and computer-generated data that are overlaid on top of the real-world view of the place visited on users' smartphone screen (Kounavis et al., 2012). This allows users to experience an unconventional form of excitement during destination encountered by integrating tourists-destination interaction in a technological engagement. A good example of MAR app is the windy known Pokemon Go app.

Malaysia is still progressing in its adoption of MAR in mobile applications, especially for tourism-related purposes. A few of the apps available that are still under development include TouristicAR (Obeidy et al., 2018), POCKET MALAYSIA (Sezali et al., 2020), Malaysia Attraction Travel Application (MATA) (Fun et al., 2021), and Iskandar.my (Mohd & Ismail, 2021). Iskandar.my is a destination-specific mobile application developed by Iskandar Malaysia Development Authority (IRDA) in the Southern Region of Malaysia. It is a mobile application developed to facilitate tourists' travel information needs for the execution of leisure activities within the Iskandar Region. The app feature consists of the common Location-Based Services (LBS) and Content-based Services for navigation and information provision purposes, as well as the integration of AR features specifically to augment the historical attractions within the area.

MAR technology is believed to be capable of triggering users' attentiveness towards the physical surroundings of the destination through mobile technological interaction. Using its dynamic layering of digital media on top real-world view, MAR is able to create tourist-destination engagement through exploration activities and games offered by the context-aware feature commonly available in MAR app (Aluri, 2017; Obeidy et al., 2018). With a meaningful destination engagement as such, a memorable experience can be developed, which is significant in establishing emotional attachment and loyalty toward a place (Coghlan & Carter, 2020; Serra-Cantallops et al., 2018). Understanding MAR services and functionalities will facilitate clarifying the technological framework of the MAR app that is highly significant in affecting users' cognitive and emotional experiences. This research, therefore, will explore the technological framework of Iskandar.my MAR app that is related to the user interface from the perspective of service and design dimensions.

Literature Review

Technology and Tourism

Tourism trends nowadays have been altered by the emergence of various technologies to enhance tourists' experience and excitement at a destination (Aluri, 2017). Hence, the better development of apps has changed travel patterns among tourists in which better exposure and enhancing overall experience is essential (Kourouthanassis et al., 2014; Fannisa et al., 2021). The application of technologies such as Virtual Reality (VR) and Augmented Reality (AR) has been applied widely in many countries all over the world. It is seen to be more effective than the metaphor descriptions available on websites (Kourouthanassis et al., 2014), such as Facebook, Twitter, Blogger and Trip Advisor.

Mobile Augmented Reality (MAR)

The vast capabilities of Augmented Reality have made this technology to be increasingly significant in the various fields, including tourism. Augmented Reality itself is referred as a technique of visualization that enables the overlaying of various types of computer-generated data, either in the form of text, audio, video, GPS data or other media formats on top of the physical world view, through the use of specific devices such as smartphones, tablets or similar devices (Kounavis et al., 2012; Shah, 2019). The augmenting of computer-generated data on real-world view is primarily for the purpose of enhancing the user or the domain's understanding on the subject matter in the physical environment. It transforms the subjects into the better view and experience (Shah, 2019). Augmented Reality which falls under the category of mixed-reality is indirectly creating a dynamic and interactive delivery of information through the co-existence of real and virtual environment within a digital information (Bahtar & Muda, 2016; Khalil, 2014). Focusing on mobile augmented reality, the center of attention is on the application of mobile device as the main platform, such as smartphones, in executing the similar capability to ease the use of this visualization technique on the go (Bolter et al., 2013).

AR application had been able to develop rapidly within these years mainly due to the recent advances in mobile related-technology (Linaza et al., 2012; Yovcheva et al., 2012). This can be clearly visible through the increasing numbers of consumer-based mobile AR application that can be easily obtained from online mobile application stores such as Google Play and Apps Store. Looking into the open access of this technology, there seems to be several technological requirements that need to be strictly adhered to ensure the optimization of mobile AR capabilities in enhancing the domain's interaction with its physical environment. In relation to that, enabling technologies play an extremely important role in determining the appropriate functionalities of AR.

MAR and Experience Enhancement

Travelling is highly spatiotemporal in nature, and optimizing the use of tourists' time during the vacation is extremely important in creating meaningful and memorable experience of the destination. Spatial navigation capability alone does not effectively manipulate the spatiotemporal limitation of travelling to fit with the in depth exploitation of tourists surrounding. As experience is highly psychological in character, tourists tend to desire for more interactive social and space encounters through the use of technology. The dynamic interaction with attractions and ability to share travel experience with families and friends through social network are among the important parts in meeting tourist desire and satisfaction in relation to their experience (Kounavis et al., 2012; Linaza et al., 2012).

Although some may question the social acceptability on the increasing density of the mobile technology and the possible issue of users' reservation in operating the new and complex system, the changes is worthwhile with the enhancement that to be made on tourist experience (Brown & Chalmers, 2003). Andersson et al. (2006) justified that the increasing complexity of mobile technology through the adding of new functionalities is sufficient to be overcome by ensuring users continue to value the experience. Pertaining to this demand, several other capabilities had been adapted in mobile technological device, and mobile AR is one of it. Instead of shifting from one functionality to another, tourists actually requiring the simultaneous use of several different functionalities within one application.

As AR generated content able to provide dynamic tourist-destination encounters, the upgrade of its capabilities in meeting tourist diverse interest, improvement of their geographical consciousness and the provision of in depth interpretation of destination, able to assure more insight to tourist experience. In their review on numbers of AR applications had outlined several important functionalities that perceived to be able in adding value to the user experience (see Table 9.1) (Yovcheva et al., 2012). Considering all of the important functionalities, the dynamic tourist-destination encounters and effective tourism interpretation is highly possible to be obtained in mobile AR technology (Yovcheva et al., 2012). As experience formation highly affected by the tourist perception towards their surroundings, computer-mediated interaction that take place in interpreting the destination through the use of mobile AR would psychologically affect impression formation of tourist, which possible in making the destination to be perceived as more attractive than its usual form.

MAR Technological Requirement

In enabling AR to augment and layered on the screen with the real environment background, it requires the device to possess the enabling technologies such as the displays, tracking, registration and calibration systems (Azuma et al., 2001). As MAR

Table 9.1 Important functionalities in AR apps

Past researches	Important functionalities in AR application
Yovcheva et al. (2012)	Search and browse Context-aware push m-commerce Feedback Routing and navigation Tour generation Map services Communication Exploration of visible surroundings Interactive AR Filtering of AR content
Kounavis et al. (2012)	Location-based 3D media Marker-based Images and media Customization
Dickinson et al. (2014)	Information Context awareness Internet of things Tagging Two-way sharing capabilities
Kourouthanassis et al. (2015)	Use the context for providing content: GPS Deliver relevant-to-the-task content: personalization Provide feedback about infrastructure's behavior Support user's procedural and semantic memory: interface usability Inform about content privacy
Ahmad Shukri et al. (2017)	Use the context for providing content Easy learn ability 3D interaction Reduce cognitive overhead
Rashid et al. (2018)	Search and browse Context aware e-commerce Feedback Map and navigation Tour planning Information portal Location aware Interactive AR elements

Source Compiled by the authors (2022)

commonly utilize mobile phone as the most suitable platform, major emphasis to be placed on the tracking system and calibration system used in performing AR capabilities (Rabbi & Ullah, 2013). The identification of users' location and position in generating digital information of the physical environment requires the AR mobile device to be equipped with several tracking systems, such as global positioning system (GPS) and indoor positioning system (especially gyroscope and accelerometers) (Azuma et al., 2001; Kounavis et al., 2012). These technological requirements are crucial in registering the characteristics of physical objects and aligning it with the virtual information that to be augmented (Höllerer & Feiner, 2004; Rabbi & Ullah, 2013).

Extensive calibration capabilities are also required within the device in ensuring the registration of digital information with a certain level of accuracy. As most of the virtual information now-a-days is in real-time basis, the operation of the overall mobile AR systems entails the wireless connection of the Internet (Höllerer & Feiner, 2004; Kounavis et al., 2012). Thus, smartphone and tablet best fit all of the technological capabilities required to operate an MAR application.

The use of mobile application for tourism related purposes are diverse. Either the app consists of context aware service, location-based service, AR technology, or other technological services, the main purpose of the technological adoption is to establish mobile travel guide that can facilitate tourists travel needs and experience (Chuang, 2020; Linton & Kwortnik, 2019). For any mobile travel guide to be considered as useful and effective, the apps often equipped with services that capable in providing relevant information delivery, navigation within destination, m-commerce and sharing capability (Buhalis et al., 2011; Kounavis et al., 2012; Kourouthanassis et al., 2015). Other researchers added a few other recent technologies such as context-aware, tour planning, and interactive AR into the existing list (Dickinson et al., 2014; Rashid et al., 2018; Yovcheva et al., 2012). Table below shows the important functionalities within mobile travel guide as listed by past researches.

Based on the above functionalities, the services provided within general mobile app can be categorized based on the value offering of the different functionalities. Heinonen and Pura (2008) classified the mobile services based on several different factor of users' engagement, which includes the types of consumption, context, social setting, and relationship.

i. Types of consumption: based on the intrinsic and extrinsic motivation of mobile services utilization, such as information and entertainment;
ii. Temporal and spatial context: based on the space–time context when the service is used, such as navigation and ticketing system;
iii. Social setting: based on the kind of interactivity offered by the service, such as game and communication;
iv. Relationship between customer and service provider: based on the different interconnected actions offered by the service, such as context aware and mobile transection (Heinonen & Pura, 2008).

Kennedy-Eden and Gretzel (2012) on the other hand, provide a classification of tourism-related mobile services based on the functionalities. The classification

Table 9.2 Classification of tourism-related mobile service application

Taxonomy of mobile applications (Kennedy-Eden & Gretzel, 2012)	Example of functionalities
1. Navigation: includes GPS and wayfinding	• Routing • Map services • Location-based service
2. Social: includes social network and communication	• Communication • Feedback • Tagging • Two-way sharing capabilities
3. Mobile marketing: includes promotion and alerts	• Context-aware push
4. Security/emergency: includes facilities and other emergency information	• Customization • Personalisation
5. Transactional: includes banking, reservation and shopping	• m-commerce
6. Entertainment: includes games, media, photography and fantasy	• Interactive AR • Exploration of visible surroundings • Images and media
Information: content-based	• Search and browse • Tour generation • Context-aware push • Images and media • Customization

Source Kennedy-Eden and Gretzel (2012)

consists of navigation, social, mobile marketing, security/emergency, transactional, entertainment, and information. Table below shows the classification and some relevant examples of functionalities in past researches (Table 9.2).

Despite the services offered by the mobile application, the way the services and functionalities being design and delivered to the tourists could significantly impact users' perception, experience and satisfaction. In understanding this aspect, Grün et al. (2008) outlined three aspects of design dimension of mobile services delivery that need to be observed in assuring the optimum user experience is achieved by users. The aspects are as listed below:

i. Service delivery: the different processes required to satisfy users service requirement;
ii. Service customization: the extent to which the users' required information can be customized to meet with their specific demand; and
iii. Service initiation: the pull, which is 'user-triggered search process', and push, automatic delivery of information to users, of the system service delivery (Grün et al., 2008).

Methodology

This study is directed to identify the services and design aspects of MAR travel-related application in relation to the rising preference towards AR technology and value creation of tourists' experience. This study is particularly focused on the functionalities offered within the Iskandar.my mobile app and the technological aspects of the AR features that link to the user's interactive destination-engagement upon utilization of the app and possible changes in the users' experience.

The study has been carried out using qualitative research approach. Content analysis approach was adopted to describe the services offered and the design feature of Iskandar.my mobile application. Iskandar.my, a mobile application developed by Iskandar Region Development Authority (IRDA) was chosen due to the limited destination-based travel-related MAR application available for public use in Malaysia. The AR feature as well as the other mobile functionalities offered within Iskandar.my was to analyze using content analysis method.

The content analysis was done to identify two important technological dimensions of the mobile app, service dimension and design dimension. Service dimension looked into the different services provided within the app, while design dimension identified the delivery of the services. Both of these dimensions were adopted from Grün et al. (2008) and Wang and Xiang (2012).

Based on the above strategy, the execution of content analysis was done following a four-step process as listed below:

i. identifying the different services and functionalities available in the mobile app;
ii. classifying the functionalities according to mobile service classification;
iii. identifying the design feature of services available within the summarizing the design features of the functionalities available within the app.

The summary of the technological dimensions identified in Iskandar.my app was mapped out to provide a clear picture of the mobile app service structure.

Findings and Analysis

Service Dimension of 'Iskandar.my' MAR App

The functionality of Iskandar.my app is categorized into seven different contents, as listed below:

1. 'Points of Interest': Provides information on important tourism attractions within the Iskandar region.
2. 'Makan Places': Provides relevant information on food services available within the Iskandar region and introduces local signature dishes.
3. 'Heritage Trail': Provides augmentation of geographical location selected historical attractions through AR technology and context aware feature, which includes

Tun Sri Lanang Park, Central Police Station, Wong Ah Fook Village, Muzium Tokoh Johor, and Balai Cengkih.
4. 'Itinerary': Provides suggestions of general itinerary for tourist activities within the Iskandar region based on user interest.
5. 'Events': Provides information regarding the recent and upcoming events available for the public to join.
6. 'Useful Info': Provides the information on the location of nearest tourist facilities such as accommodations, clinics and automated teller machines (ATM).
7. 'Iskandar News': Provides updates and recent news related to Iskandar Malaysia from various perspectives (Fig. 9.1).

The service dimension of Iskandar.my consist of two main service features, which are content-based service and location-based, in performing the basic function of a travel mobile app. The service deliveries in all of the seven contents in the app are grounded by content-based service as its main feature. Except for 'Iskandar New', the other Iskandar.my app contents are supported with navigation that being integrated with Google Map navigation service, to provide users with the specific spatial location of the related attractions. The overall delivery of the content-based service is integrated with the directory to optional added information including:

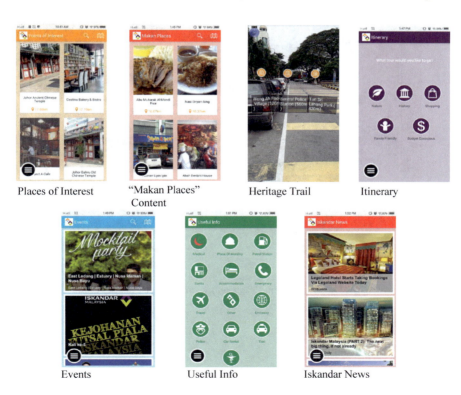

Fig. 9.1 Content of 'Iskandar.my' MAR app. *Source* Findings of the study (2022)

i. 'Did you know?': Detail information of the tourism attraction or activities;
ii. 'Tips and Tricks': Additional tips to ease and enhance tourist travel journey;
iii. 'Travel Info': Information on tourist movement to PoIs and local public transportation;
iv. 'View in Map': Viewing location of attractions and PoIs in map view, distance to attraction and navigate movement through LBS, which integrated with Google Map;
v. 'View Media': Providing variety media information regarding the attraction to enable better visualization of the destination;
vi. 'Contact Details': Information regarding contact details and other relevant information for any query.

On top of that, Iskandar.my provide the assimilation of AR technology in 'Heritage Trail' content, which make the app to be classified as a mobile AR application. Unlike the other contents, the service provided in 'Heritage Trail' is dominated by AR feature. Utilizing navigation as its base, the AR technology make the visualization of important locations of the attractions to be in 3D view, whereas the other content only provides information through 2D media. Figure 9.2 illustrated the overall structure of service dimension and in the contents of 'Iskandar.my'.

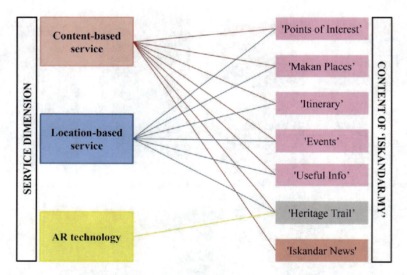

Fig. 9.2 Service dimension for content in 'Iskandar.my' app. *Source* Findings of the study (2022)

9 Iskandar.my: Framework of Mobile Augmented Reality Travel App

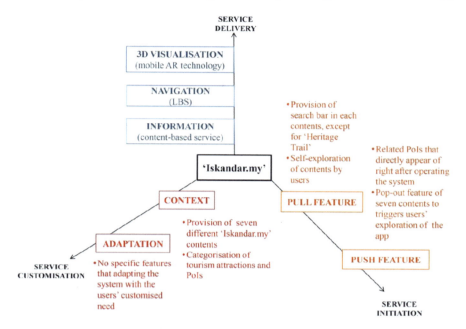

Fig. 9.3 Design dimension of 'Iskandar.my' mobile app services. *Source* Findings of the study (2022)

Design Dimension of 'Iskandar.my' MAR App

The evaluation of Iskandar.my design dimension is done according to the three aspects of design dimension as indicated by Grün et al. (2008). Figure 9.3 illustrated the overall design framework of Iskandar.my app as evaluated by the researcher.

As highlighted, three main mobile services provided in Iskandar.my consist of content-based service, location-based service and AR 3D visualization service. The effective delivery of these services are supported with the service customization and initiation design, which mainly to facilitate tourist utilization of the app. Looking into the aspect of service customization, the app does not offer any feature that enable the adaptation of the mobile service system with the customize need of the users. Customization feature are limited to the proper organization and classification of the internal information through the seven contents provided.

Taking the 'Itinerary' content as the example, all of the tour itinerary offered in the app had been fixed, without feature that enable tailoring of the plans. Customization feature is perceived as important as travel motivation and preferences of differs based on individual tourists, and the capability of a mobile travel guide to provide personalization feature would strongly facilitate tourists planning of travel activities (Chen & Tsai, 2019; Missaoui et al., 2019).

The service initiation of Iskandar.my from the pull and push perspective can be identified through the users' self-exploration of the app. Any service initiation feature such as instructions or step by step guide was unavailable. The pull service that was found available is the provision of 'search bar' on the top view of each content to ease and expedite the information retrieving process. Availability of service initiation elements would provide ease of use and enhance the effectiveness of an app. The provision of push feature capable to impact on the users' behavior towards the mobile service as well as the destination (Susanty et al., 2020). Other than encouraging visitation to the relevant attractions, availability of push feature would increase the reliability of an app, making the information and services provided to be more trusted by the user.

Conclusion

This study identifies the technological dimension of Iskandar.my MAR application. Analysis of the service and design dimension of the app shows that the app offers limited services with restricted customization and service push factor ability. This in directly limit the usability of Iskandar.my by the user. Usability of a product signifies its quality and capability to compete with the other competitor. For mobile application, its usability from several different dimensions, such as service provision, interactivity and functionality, does influence the users' choice of app selection and their reuse intention towards it (Dorcic et al., 2019). Unlike other system, the usability of mobile application is critical to support immediate access to certain specified information and services (Nayebi et al., 2012). Specifically, for travel related purposes, the usability of travel apps is crucial in supporting users' instantaneous demand during travel.

In reference to the service dimension, Iskandar.my focusing on information provision of important attractions and hotspots that are connected with navigation service. The functionalities provided in each content are also identical with some repetitive information indicated lack of interactivity and sensation offered to the user (Fan et al., 2017; Wang et al., 2016). Again, there are six main types of smartphones use during travel to assure meaningful users' experience and satisfaction; and those functionalities are as follows:

1. Communication;
2. Social;
3. Information;
4. Entertainment; and
5. Facilitation (Wang et al., 2016)

Although the services offered in Iskandar.my is quite limited, the app had actually provided two essential functionalities, which are navigation and content-based services. The current services provided are seen sufficient to provide user the basic information and understanding needed about important attractions available in Iskandar region and their whereabouts. This therefore enable users to have an overview of the destination and execute activities planning and decision making (Nilashi et al., 2018; Tan, 2017).

References

Ahmad Shukri, S. A. I., Arshad, H., & Zainal Abidin, R. (2017). The design guidelines of mobile augmented reality for tourism in Malaysia. *AIP Conference Proceedings*. Retrieved March 12, 2022, from https://doi.org/10.1063/1.5005359.

Aluri, A. (2017). Mobile augmented reality (MAR) game as a travel guide: Insights from Pokémon GO. *Journal of Hospitality and Tourism Technology, 8*(1), 55–72.

Andersson, C., Freeman, D., James, I., Johnston, A., & Ljung, S. (2006). *Mobile media and applications, from concept to cash: Successful service creation and launch*. Wiley.

Azuma, R., Baillot, Y., Behringer, R., Feiner, S., Julier, S., & MacIntyre, B. (2001). Recent advances in augmented reality. *IEEE Computer Graphics and Applications, 21*(6), 34–47.

Bahtar, A. Z., & Muda, M. (2016). The impact of user-generated content (UGC) on product reviews towards online purchasing—A conceptual framework. *Procedia Economics and Finance, 37*(16), 337–342.

Bolter, J. D., Engberg, M., & MacIntyre, B. (2013). Media studies, mobile augmented reality, and interaction design. *Interactions, 20*(1), 36–45.

Brown, B., & Chalmers, M. (2003). Tourism and mobile technology. In K. Kuutti, E. H. Karsten, G. Fitzpatrick, P. Dourish, & K. Schmidt (Eds.), *Eighth European Conference on Computer-Supported Cooperative Work* (pp. 335–354). Springer.

Buhalis, D., Leung, D., & Law, R. (2011). eTourism: Critical information and communication technologies for tourism destinations. In Y. Wang & A. Pizam (Eds.), *Destination marketing and management: Theories and applications* (pp. 205–224). CAB International.

Carmigniani, J., & Furht, B. (2011). Augmented reality: An overview. In B. Furht (Ed.), *Handbook of augmented reality* (pp. 3–46). Springer.

Chen, C.-C., & Tsai, J.-L. (2019). Determinants of behavioral intention to use the personalized location-based mobile tourism application: An empirical study by integrating TAM with ISSM. *Future Generation Computer Systems, 96*, 628–638.

Chuang, C.-M. (2020). A current travel model: Smart tour on mobile guide application services. *Current Issues in Tourism, 23*(18), 2333–2352.

Coghlan, A., & Carter, L. (2020). New product design: Creating a digital VR game to promote the conservation of nature-based tourism attractions. In A. Hassan & A. Sharma (Eds.), *The Emerald handbook of ICT in tourism and hospitality* (pp. 167–179). Bingley.

Dickinson, J. E., Ghali, K., Cherrett, T., Speed, C., Davies, N., & Norgate, S. (2014). Tourism and the smartphone app: Capabilities, emerging practice and scope in the travel domain. *Current Issues in Tourism, 17*(1), 84–101.

Dorcic, J., Komsic, J., & Markovic, S. (2019). Mobile technologies and applications towards smart tourism—State of the art. *Tourism Review, 74*(1), 82–103.

Edwards-Stewart, A., Hoyt, T., & Reger, G. (2016). Classifying different types of augmented reality technology. *Annual Review of Cyber Therapy and Telemedicine, 14*, 199–202.

Fan, L., Liu, X., Wang, B., & Wang, L. (2017). Interactivity, engagement, and technology dependence: Understanding users' technology utilisation behaviour. *Behaviour & Information Technology, 36*(2), 113–124.

Fannisa, F., Irawan, H., & Ghina, A. (2021). The development concept of mobile augmented reality (MAR) as an innovation to improve tourism experience (study case in Denpasar City, Bali). In *ICoSMI 2020*, West Java, 14–16 September.

Fun, C. S., Zaaba, Z. F., & Ali, A. S. (2021). Usable tourism application: Malaysia attraction travel application (MATA). In *2021 International Conference on Information Technology, ICIT 2021 - Proceedings*, Amman, 14–15 July.

Grün, C., Werthner, H., Pröll, B., Retschitzegger, W., & Schwinger, W. (2008). Assisting tourists on the move—An evaluation of mobile tourist guides. In *Proceedings - 7th International Conference on Mobile Business, ICMB 2008, Creativity and Convergence*, Barcelona, 7–8 July.

Heinonen, K., & Pura, M. (2008). Classifying mobile services. *All Sprouts Content, 160*. Retrieved March 20, 2022, from https://aisel.aisnet.org/sprouts_all/160.

Höllerer, T. H., & Feiner, S. K. (2004). Mobile augmented reality. In H. A. Karimi & A. Hammad (Eds.), *Telegeoinformatics: Location-based computing and services* (pp. 1–39). CRC Press.

Kennedy-Eden, H., & Gretzel, U. (2012). A taxonomy of mobile applications in tourism. *e-Review of Tourism Research, 10*(2), 47–50.

Khalil, N. (2014). Applications of augmented reality in cultural tourism: The case of Bibliotheca Alexandrina. *Journal of Associations of Arab Universities for Tourism and Hospitality, 11*(3), 182–188.

Kounavis, C. D., Kasimati, A. E., & Zamani, E. D. (2012). Enhancing the tourism experience through mobile augmented reality: Challenges and prospects. *International Journal of Engineering Business Management, 4*(1), 10.

Kourouthanassis, P., Boletsis, C., Bardaki, C., & Chasanidou, D. (2014). Tourists responses to mobile augmented reality travel guides: The role of emotions on adoption behavior. *Pervasive and Mobile Computing, 18*, 71–87.

Kourouthanassis, P. E., Boletsis, C., & Lekakos, G. (2015). Demystifying the design of mobile augmented reality applications. *Multimedia Tools and Applications, 74*, 1045–1066.

Linaza, M., Marimón, D., Carrasco, P., Álvarez, R., Montesa, J., Aguilar, S., & Diez, G. (2012). Evaluation of mobile augmented reality applications for tourism destinations. In M. Fuchs, F. Ricci, & L. Cantoni (Eds.), *Information and communication technologies in tourism 2012* (pp. 260–271). Springer.

Linton, H., & Kwortnik, R. J. (2019). Mobile usage in travel: Bridging the supplier-user gap. *International Journal of Contemporary Hospitality Management, 31*(2), 771–789.

Missaoui, S., Kassem, F., Viviani, M., Agostini, A., Faiz, R., & Pasi, G. (2019). LOOKER: A mobile, personalized recommender system in the tourism domain based on social media user-generated content. *Personal and Ubiquitous Computing, 23*(2), 181–197.

Mohd, N. S., & Ismail, H. N. (2021). Tourists responses to the use of mobile augmented reality for travel. In *Proceedings of the Global Tourism Conference 2021*. Terengganu: Universiti Malaysia Terengganu.

Nayebi, F., Desharnais, J. M., & Abran, A. (2012). The state of the art of mobile application usability evaluation. In *2012 25th IEEE Canadian Conference on Electrical and Computer Engineering (CCECE)*, Nova Scotia (pp. 1–4).

Nilashi, M., Ibrahim, O., Yadegaridehkordi, E., Samad, S., Akbari, E., & Alizadeh, A. (2018). Travelers decision making using online review in social network sites: A case on TripAdvisor. *Journal of Computational Science, 28*, 168–179.

Obeidy, W. K., Arshad, H., & Huang, J. Y. (2018). TouristicAR: A smart glass augmented reality application for UNESCO world heritage sites in Malaysia. *Journal of Telecommunication, Electronic and Computer Engineering, 10*(3–2), 101–108.

Rabbi, I., & Ullah, S. (2013). A survey on augmented reality challenges and tracking. *Acta Graphica: Znanstveni Časopis Za Tiskarstvo i Grafičke Komunikacije, 24*(1–2), 29–46.

Rashid, R. A., Mohamed, H., & Hussin, A. R. C. (2018). Mobile augmented reality tourism application framework. *Lecture Notes on Data Engineering and Communications Technologies, 5*, 108–115.

Serra-Cantallops, A., Ramon-Cardona, J., & Salvi, F. (2018). The impact of positive emotional experiences on eWOM generation and loyalty. *Spanish Journal of Marketing - ESIC, 22*(2), 142–162.

Sezali, S. F., Radzuan, A. M., Mohd Shabudin, N. I., & Afendi, R. A. (2020). POCKET MALAYSIA: Learning about states in Malaysia using augmented reality. *International Journal of Multimedia and Recent Innovation, 2*(1), 45–59.

Shah, M. (2019). How augmented reality (AR) is changing the travel & tourism industry. *Towards Data Science.* Retrieved March 20, 2022, from https://towardsdatascience.com/how-augmented-reality-ar-is-changing-the-travel-tourism-industry-239931f3120c.

Susanty, A., Handoko, A., & Puspitasari, N. B. (2020). Push-pull-mooring framework for e-commerce adoption in small and medium enterprises. *Journal of Enterprise Information Management, 33*(2), 381–406.

Tan, W.-K. (2017). The relationship between smartphone usage, tourist experience and trip satisfaction in the context of a nature-based destination. *Telematics and Informatics, 34*(2), 614–627.

Tülü, M., & Yılmaz, M. (2013). Iphone ile Artırılmış Gerçeklik Uygulamalarının Eğitim Alanında Kullanılması. In *Akademik Bilişim Kongresi* (pp. 23–25). Antalya: Akdeniz Üniversitesi.

Tussyadiah, I., & Zach, F. (2011). The influence of technology on geographic cognition and tourism experience. In R. Law, M. Fuchs, & F. Ricci (Eds.), *Information and communication technologies in tourism 2011* (pp. 279–291). Springer.

Wang, D., & Xiang, Z. (2012). The new landscape of travel: A comprehensive analysis of smartphone apps. In M. Fuchs, F. Ricci, & L. Cantoni (Eds.), *Information and communication technologies in tourism 2012* (pp. 308–319). Springer.

Wang, D., Xiang, Z., & Fesenmaier, D. R. (2016). Smartphone use in everyday life and travel. *Journal of Travel Research, 55*(1), 52–63.

Yovcheva, Z., Buhalis, D., & Gatzidis, C. (2012). Smartphone augmented reality applications for tourism. *e-Review of Tourism Research (eRTR), 10*(2), 63–66.

Dr. Nur Shuhadah Mohd is a senior lecturer in the Department of Tourism, International Islamic University Malaysia. She received her doctorate degree in urban and regional planning, with specialization in tourism planning from Universiti Teknologi Malaysia. Her research interests cover the area of IT in tourism, tourist behavior and tourism planning.

Dr. Maimunah Abdul Aziz is a lecturer at the Tourism Section, University Kuala Lumpur Business School. She has graduated from International Islamic University Malaysia (IIUM), Kuala Lumpur in Ph.D. of Built Environment (Major in Tourism Planning and Development). Her core study area is Tourism Planning and Development, Tourism Policies, Destination and Products Development, Sustainable Tourism, Islamic and Halal Tourism and Tourism Research Methods.

Dr. Hairul Nizam Ismail is currently an Associate Professor and the Director of Urban and Regional Planning in the Faculty of Built Environment and Surveying, UTM. He is also a Registered Town Planner under Board of Town Planners Malaysia (LPBM) and Corporate Member of Malaysian Institute of Planners (MIP) since 2012. Ismail's main research interests are in the fields of urban tourism, urban planning and tourism in developing countries.

Part III
Emerging Issues

Chapter 10
Defender or Attacker? An Approach to Dynamic Sustainability in the Dynamic Business Climate of Rural Tourism

Farah Hida Sharin, Mohd Farid Shamsudin, and Ilham Sentosa

Abstract The aim of the study is for investigating the factors affecting Malaysian SME rural tourism consumers' e-marketplace behavior during the COVID-19 pandemic in Malaysia. This is to measure the influence of product factor, price factor, time saving factor on consumers' rural tourism behavior during the COVID-19 pandemic. This pandemic help in starting to reshape tourism world as more consumers have begun loyalty and retention through online mechanism in greater numbers considering the restricted circumstances. Although some SME rural tourism destination and attraction found it hard and difficult to adapt to the e-marketplace ecosystem, product, price and time saving factors as digital sustainability domain has highlighted as a strategic direction which translated on the predictors of rural tourism business in Malaysia. An advanced quantitative analysis using 1st order confirmatory factor analysis (CFA) of structural equation modeling (SEM) has configured detail pathway on the manufacturing process of the digitainability of rural tourism model. This research has come out with an integrated model that promotes local ecosystems through digitainability rural tourism which accelerate the region's recovery agenda. In conclusion, a business continuity model for Malaysian rural tourism entrepreneurs has been developed using structural equation modeling (SEM) approach, and a multiplier effect for rural economic development will be configured using the the Digitainability of SME's rural tourism.

Keywords Digitainability · SME's rural tourism · Product price and time saving factor · Structural equation modeling

F. H. Sharin (✉)
Universiti Kuala Lumpur (UniKL) Business School, Kuala Lumpur, Malaysia
e-mail: farah.sharin@s.unikl.edu.my

M. F. Shamsudin
Department of Marketing and International Business, Universiti Kuala Lumpur (UniKL) Business School, Kuala Lumpur, Malaysia

I. Sentosa
Department of Management and Entrepreneurship, Universiti Kuala Lumpur (UniKL) Business School, Kuala Lumpur, Malaysia

© The Author(s), under exclusive license to Springer Nature Singapore Pte Ltd. 2023
A. Hassan and N. A. A. Rahman (eds.), *Technology Application in Aviation, Tourism and Hospitality*, https://doi.org/10.1007/978-981-19-6619-4_10

Introduction

COVID-19 tsunami brought a significant effect to the movement of digital economy transformation within 2020 and 2022 in the Southeast Asia region. The present study highlighted strategic direction of further post COVID-19 session through digitainability of supply chain rural tourism model in Malaysia. This study is focusing on the development of a resilient model for SMEs engaged in rural tourism in Malaysia through the application of digitainability. Digitainability is a term that refers to the synthesis of digitalization and sustainability, a field of study that has only recently begun to emerge as a significant new area of research. Digitalization is the process of transforming a business model through the use of digital technologies in order to create new revenue and value-creating opportunities (Sharin et al., 2022). This research confirmed an ecstatic and eager to validate on how the combination of structural equation modeling technique with these two megatrends (digitalization + sustainability) would indicate positive interdependencies in the process of transitioning to a digital business within post pandemic recovery.

Furthermore, rural tourism e-marketplace ecosystem is a form of electronic commerce that allows the activity of buying and selling the physical products and services through an online platform. Rural tourism e-marketplace shopping involves the transfer of funds, money, data and information by the information and communication (ICT) technology. Online stores aim to make customer feel easier to shop by using electronic transactions. When the COVID-19 disease was first detected in Malaysia in January 2020, world trade and commerce, education and many other activities are being halted or have been disrupted (Fig. 10.1).

COVID-19 outbreak has made the world in panic. During the first quarter of 2020, when the pandemic comes to Malaysia, this pandemic has cause businesses in Malaysia faced tremendous losses. Many workers have to leave their jobs and some company need to close their businesses. Related to the digital sustainability on the rural tourism business in Malaysia, the present study configured following research questions: What is the effect of product factor in affecting consumers' rural tourism e-marketplace shopping behaviour during the COVID-19 pandemic?; What is the relationship between the price factor in affecting consumers' rural tourism e-marketplace shopping behaviour during the COVID-19 pandemic?, and What is the impact of time saving factor in affecting consumers' of rural tourism e-marketplace shopping behaviour during the COVID-19 pandemic?. Significantly, rural tourism e-marketplace can provide an online platform for consumers to buy and sell the physical products and services. This online shopping is convenience because they can purchase rural tourism products or services anywhere and anytime. Therefore, this study is important to ensure Rural tourism e-marketplace shopping in Malaysia can be improved in various factors that affecting the consumers' Rural tourism e-marketplace shopping behaviour during the pandemic (Sharin et al., 2022).

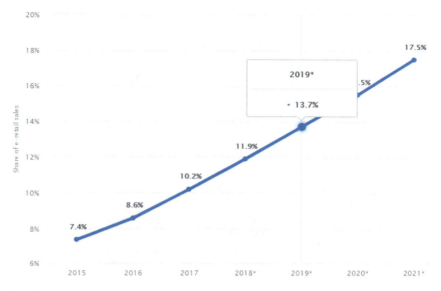

Fig. 10.1 E-commerce share on the total global retail sales 2015 to 2021. *Source* Protocol (2019)

Conceptual Development

The Theory of Reasoned Action (TRA), which later became the Theory of Planned Behavior (TPB), was developed in 1980 to forecast a person's intention to participate in a behaviour at a specific time and location. According to this TRA model, an individual's intention to engage in a behaviour will be influenced by their motivations. The behavioural intention will, however, only be effective if the targeted behaviour is voluntary. The TPB model, on the other hand, created a better description of a behavioural model that depends on both a person's purpose to engage in a certain behaviour and their capacity to exert actual control over the behaviour. Behavioral intents are predicted using the subjective norm, attitude toward behaviour, and perceived behavioural control. This model demonstrated a substantial correlation between these variables in influencing a person's attitude and behaviour regarding their desire to make an online purchase. As a result, we chose to employ TPB as the basis of our research.

A person's overall perspective and appraisal of a product or service while buying on an online marketplace specific to rural tourism might have positive or negative effects. According to earlier research, behaviour is a multidimensional entity that may be understood in a variety of ways (Li & Zhang, 2002). Many academics use many parameters to evaluate consumer behaviour. The first dimension, according to Gozukara et al. (2014), is the consumer's attitude toward a utilitarian incentive (convenience, variety seeking, and the quality of merchandise, cost benefit, and time effectiveness). Happiness, fantasy, escapism, awakening, sensuality, and enjoyment are described as hedonic motivations in the second dimension, while perceived usability and simplicity of use are mentioned in the third dimension by Baber et al. (2014).

Perceived risk is a further factor that affects how consumers behave while purchasing online. In addition, Li and Zhang (2002) noted that there are two distinct categories of perceived risk that affect how consumers behave while purchasing online. The second category of perceived risk associated in e-transactions includes privacy and security, whereas the first category of perceived risk involved in online product and service is defined as money risk, time risk, and product risk (Li & Zhang, 2002). Numerous studies (Samadi & Yaghoob-Nejadi, 2009; Chua et al., 2006; Hassan et al., 2006; Subhalakshami & Ravi, 2015) have claimed that perceived risk, such as financial risk, product risk, non-delivery risk, time risk, privacy risk, information risk, social risk, and personal risk, has a negative and significant impact on consumers' shopping behaviour in rural tourism e-marketplaces.

The research hypothesis entails more than just a hunch when it comes to how two or more variables relate to one another. The hypothesis often starts with a query that is subsequently investigated through background research. Only now do researchers start to formulate a testable hypothesis. The purpose of the research is to ascertain if the hypothesis is correct or incorrect, despite the fact that it predicts what the researchers want to observe. Researchers may investigate a variety of variables during an experiment to identify those that could influence the final result. The following are the three hypotheses created for the study:

Product Factor

If a store offers sufficient details on the items, the majority of customers will consider it trustworthy. Additionally, customers may use internet shopping to compare the attributes of various products or the services provided by the business itself. E-commerce has made transactions simpler than ever before, and consumers benefit from online retailers' increased selection of goods and services (Lim & Dubinsky, 2004; Prasad & Aryasri, 2009). The product may be anything that seeks attention and tries to meet the requirements, wants, or desires of the customer, including goods, services, people, places, ideas, information, and organisations. Customers may find a wide variety of items from across the world that may only be accessible online. Whether they have a physical storefront or not, the majority of businesses have their own websites where they may sell goods or services online. To cut down on retail expenses or to give consumers a wider range of sizes, colours, and features, many traditional merchants sell some items that are only accessible online.

H1. During the COVID-19 pandemic, the product factor has an impact on customers' online purchase behaviour for rural tourism.

Price Factor

Customers who shop online frequently receive better offers, allowing them to purchase the same item at a reduced cost (Rox, 2007). Because internet retailers provide a wide range of goods and services, users have more opportunities to compare costs across websites and discover goods that are more affordable than those offered by local retailers (Lim & Dubinsky, 2004). Using simply their smartphones or other devices, customers may compare any discounts or coupons that the store is offering. Customers may make a good bargain for their product by using the auction or best offer options that some websites, like eBay, provide. Additionally, it turns shopping into a fun and entertaining game of chance and treasure hunt (Prasad & Aryasri, 2009). Consumers' understanding of a product's pricing conveys information about it and gives them a meaningful meaning (Kotler & Keller, 2016). As a result, pricing is a key factor in deciding whether to buy something, especially for frequent transactions. This impacts decisions about the brand, product, and retailer to choose (Faith & Agwu, 2014).

H2. During the COVID-19 pandemic, there is a correlation between the pricing element and customers' online buying behaviour for rural tourism.

Time Saving Factor

These days, customers may use the rural tourism e-marketplace to purchase whenever and wherever they want. Not to worry, e-commerce makes it simpler for consumers to purchase despite their hectic schedules. Customers' lives are made simpler by the convenience of internet shopping since they no longer have to deal with traffic jams, parking lot searches, long checkout lines, or crowded stores (Childers et al., 2001). Compared to traditional brick-and-mortar establishments, purchasing on the rural tourist e-marketplace is more convenient and time-saving for customers. This epidemic has caused a sharp increase in rural tourism and online purchasing. With these new rules, internet buying facilitates easy transaction between customers and enterprises. It could be more challenging for customers to buy in physical stores due to changing consumer lives and hectic schedules.

H3. During the COVID-19 pandemic, customers' e-marketplace purchase habits in rural tourism were impacted by the time-saving factor.

Figure 10.2, configured detail framework and shows a relationship between dependent variable (DV) and independent (IV). Rural tourism e-marketplace shopping behaviour are perceived as dependent variable whereas product factor, price factor and time saving factor are the independent variable that influence the consumers' rural tourism e-marketplace shopping behaviour. This research framework and will serve as a basis for this research and it will help in analyzing and interpretation of the empirical results.

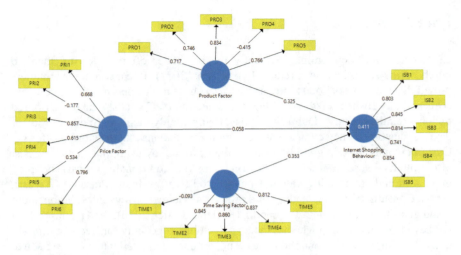

Fig. 10.2 Hypothesised model. *Source* Developed by the authors

Methodology

The primary data comes from two different sources. Primary data are facts discovered by the researcher directly regarding the variables of relevance for the particular goal of the investigation (Uma & Roger, 2013). During the COVID-19 epidemic in Malaysia, the factors influencing consumer purchase behaviour in rural tourism are examined in this study using primary data collecting. A population, circumstance, or phenomena is described in descriptive research, a kind of study. Survey research is the process of gathering data from a sample of people by asking them to fill out questionnaires. This kind of research allows for using several techniques to recruit participant, collect data, and equipment. While causal analysis is a research technique used to establish the cause-and-effect connection between two variables. The primary purpose of this research is to pinpoint the origin of the observed behaviour. Using causal analysis, we determine how changes in one independent variable affect changes in the other. In this study, we used survey research such as quantitative research strategies by using questionnaires with numerically rated items in order to get the data. Researcher used Google forms as our survey platform in making a questionnaire instead of interview survey because of this pandemic. The sample population of our study was consumers ranging from 18 to 47 years old (Table 10.1).

A total of 207 respondents were involved in answering our questionnaire. A questionnaire is employed as a research tool to make data gathering easier when doing fieldwork. Demographic data about the respondents was acquired in the questionnaire's first section. There are six closed-ended questions on the respondents' demographics, such as age, gender, occupation, marital status, the approximate maximum amount spent online, and the most popular online shopping site. The second section of the survey looks at the variables influencing customers' online buying habits when

Table 10.1 Variables and measurements

Measurements	Factor loading
Rural tourism E-marketplace behavior (Neger & Uddin, 2020)	
I like to use online shopping rather than go to physical store during pandemic	0.802
Rural tourism e-marketplace shopping makes the purchasing process easier and more comfortable	0.845
I would recommend my family and friends to use online rural tourism platform to shop during pandemic	0.813
I will use rural tourism e-marketplace shopping platform regularly during pandemic	0.743
Rural tourism e-marketplace shopping during COVID-19 pandemic has given me interesting experiences to shop	0.854
Product factor (Neger & Uddin, 2020)	
Product quality can affect my buying decision	0.702
I focus on the variety of products in choosing the most preferred online rural tourism shopping platform	0.757
I would buy product that has good features	0.857
I would buy product that look aesthetic to me	–
Rural tourism product description is important for me	0.786
Price factor (Neger & Uddin, 2020)	
Discounts and vouchers influence my purchasing behaviour	0.670
I do not mind about the price	–
Online shopping rural tourism platforms offers more affordable price	0.856
I always make price comparison between shops before purchase it	0.617
I likely do online rural tourism shopping during promotions only	0.534
Rural tourism online shopping saves money compared to physical store	0.796
Time saving factor (Neger & Uddin, 2020)	
Delivery time can influence my rural tourism e-marketplace shopping behaviour	–
Fast transaction influences me to purchase rural tourism product online	0.851
I can save time when purchase online shopping rather than traditional shopping	0.857
Online shopping offers the availability to shop anytime	0.835
I like to spend more time on the rural tourism e-marketplace shopping than in physical store	0.819

Source Research findings

travelling in rural areas due to the COVID-19 epidemic. The surveys' 21 questions in all were analysed. According to a Likert-type scale, some of the questions are replied with "Agree" to "Disagree," "Strongly agree" to "Strongly disagree," and "Neutral." The adoption of this approach makes sense since it will aid in the comprehension of a complicated subject through a clear and concise examination of the variables influencing customers' purchase behaviour in rural tourist e-marketplaces during the COVID-19 epidemic. To assess the validity, common comprehension, and response patterns of various respondents, pilot testing is done. Concepts like validity and reliability are applied for assessing a research's calibre. It presents the ways how perfectly a method, methodology, or test can become able to measures something. On the other side, validity is focused on correctness of a measure, when reliability is attached to its consistency.

Findings

In this study, we used 207 respondents for our further analysis. This study assessed the factors affecting consumers' rural tourism e-marketplace shopping behaviour during the COVID-19. All the data from the questionnaire that were collected has been transferred into the SPSS software (Statistical Package for the Social Science) for further analysis. Descriptive statistics (frequencies) were obtained to gather information for demographics (Question 1 to 6) based on age group, gender, occupation, marital status, maximum amount spending on online shopping, and most used shopping platform to shop. The frequency for each demographic characteristic is displayed in the following section. Data from the descriptive statistics shows that the majority of the respondents with the age group 24–29 years old with a percentage of 64.3% (n = 133) followed by 18–23 years old at 20.3% (n = 42), 30–35 years old at 7.2% (n = 15), 36–41 years old at 5.3% (n = 11) and lastly 42–47 years old at 2.9% (n = 6). Data from the descriptive statistics shows that the majority of the respondents are male with a percentage of 65.7% (n = 136) and female at 34.3% (n = 71). Most of the respondents are students with majority percentage of 54.1% (n = 112) followed by employees at 20.3% (n = 42) while unemployed was at 1.4% (n = 3) and freelancers at 0.5% (n = 1) respectively. Most of the respondents are single with majority percentage of 84.5% (n = 175), followed by married people with percentage of 15.5% (n = 32). Majority of the respondents spent between RM100 and RM200 a week at 46.9% (n = 97) followed by people spent less than RM100 a week at 45.9% (n = 95) and lastly people spent more than RM200 a week at 7.2% (n = 15). Most of the respondents used Shopee at 86% (n = 178), followed by respondents that used online website at 5.3% (n = 11), respondents that used Lazada at 3.9% (n = 8), respondent used Zalora at 1.9% (n = 4) and the least was people used Amazon at 0.5% (n = 1). Furthermore, this research had been conducted by using SmartPLS and IBM SPSS as a tool to measure the data collected. SmartPLS was used in order to analyse the significant between the dependent and independent variables. We used 3 variables that contain 21 items as a measurement based on the factor loading (>0.5). The factor loading range from −0.415 to 0.857. Therefore, not all of the items were accepted and valid.

Cronbach's alpha measurement is amount of random when error that exists to use by quantify for a widely-used measure of reliability. Although, the Cronbach's Alpha coefficients of the scale based on the statistical result shows Cronbach's Alpha coefficients product factor, price factor and time saving factor. The Figure shown, the hypothesized factors affecting consumers' rural tourism e-marketplace shopping behaviour during the COVID-19 pandemic. The overall of the model is accepted because $R^2 = 0.411$ means that all of the independent's variables can explain 41.1%

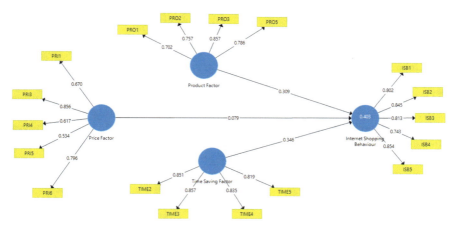

Fig. 10.3 Re-specified model. *Source* Research findings

for consumers' Rural tourism e-marketplace shopping behaviour. Based on the generated model, we confirmed there were four valid and one non-valid product factor which was PRO4. For price factor, there were six items but we decided to take out one item and there were five remaining items. Then, this study confirmed Time1 was found as non-valid item as it did not have the factor loading (>0.5), so for time saving factor, there were four valid items left.

Product factor supported the hypothesis mentioned as it has a significant relationship between product factor in affecting consumers' rural tourism e-marketplace shopping behaviour during the COVID-19 pandemics it as its t-value is 3.4. Product factor such as quality and variety of product played the important role for the respondents to have a satisfaction while shopping online. When a customer recognized

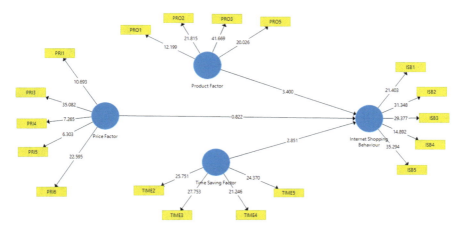

Fig. 10.4 Bootstrapping of structural model. *Source* Research findings

quality, it reflected in customer satisfaction. This survey showed that consumers preferred good product quality while shopping online. Based on the result in this study, price factor did not support the hypothesis mentioned as it had no significant relationship between the price factor in affecting consumers' Rural tourism e-marketplace shopping behaviour during the COVID-19 pandemic because it had t-value at 0.822 which is lower than 1.96. For many consumers, price is not one of the most significant factor that determine where and when to buy. The result in this study supports the third hypothesis, there is a significant relationship between time saving factor in affecting consumers' rural tourism e-marketplace shopping behaviour during the COVID-19 pandemic because its t-value was at 2.851. Time saving factor during online shopping takes consistency, and commitment, to ensure that the platform communicate the desired message to the consumer.

This study had empirically validated the proposed research model. All the hypotheses about the relationship between the variables are developed and tested by reliability test of measurement using Cronbach's Alpha and the partial least squares (PLS) path modeling method (Sharin et al., 2022). The result interpreted that positive factors had an impact that is more significant on the consumers' rural tourism e-marketplace shopping behaviours during COVID-19. Among the three positive factors, time saving factor was the most substantial factor affecting the consumers' rural tourism e-marketplace shopping behaviours during COVID-19. The result indicated that time saving factor was the main interest for the consumers' rural tourism e-marketplace shopping behaviours during COVID-19. On the negative factors, the price factor had the weakest link to affect consumers' rural tourism e-marketplace shopping behaviours during COVID-19. It is indicated that rural tourism e-marketplace shopping consumers are less concerned about the price factor.

Conclusion and Recommendation

The proposed digitainability rural tourism model in this study will be used to study the factors affecting consumers' rural tourism e-marketplace shopping behaviour during the COVID-19 pandemic. The study focused on the positive and negative factors that can influence consumers' rural tourism e-marketplace shopping behaviour during COVID-19. This research confirmed that product factor, price factor and time saving factor significantly impact consumers' rural tourism e-marketplace shopping behaviour during COVID-19. For the recommendation in order to get the exact data, it can be improved by increase the size of the sample, or different type of geographical locations. Since our current situation with the pandemic of COVID-19 has not given the opportunity to do the face-to-face interview. If there is any chance, it will be good to do survey face to face interview so that we can improve the reliability of the data in future studies. As the era technology development as today, every e-commerce platform should compete in focusing more on building links, coordinating with transport unit to be able to deliver goods to consumers as soon as possible to meet their increase needs. Limitations were important to be highlighted as the limited sample size posed the question of generalizability. Since data were collected by Google form and we distributed the link to each people, it is not difficult to ascertain because we got the data from outsider and not only the student university. Furthermore, the use of the convenience sampling technique lacks accurate information. This is because certain subjects do not respond to the most reliable response for themselves, as they may be represented in a less positive way. Another limitation is the demographic background of the participants, since all the respondent from the outside, in this study we had limited the age between 18 and 47 years old, there could be any other people who above that age years old that used online shopping. Last but not least, the reliability of the questionnaire can also be taken into account as a constraint, since it has a restricted response and the questions relevant to a specific variable might not have been detailed enough to provide a satisfactory response.

References

Baber, A., Rasheed, A., & Sajjad, M. (2014). Factors influencing online shopping behavior of consumers. *Journal of Basic and Applied Scientific Research, 4*(4), 314–320.

Childers, T. L., Carr, C. L., Peck, J., & Carson, S. (2001). Hedonic and utilitarian motivations for online retail shopping behavior. *Journal of Retailing, 77*(4), 511–535.

Chua, A., Harn, P., Khatibi, A., & Ismail, H. (2006). E-commerce: A study on online shopping in Malaysia. *Journal of Social Science, 13*, 231–242.

Faith, D. O., & Agwu, M. E. (2014). A review of the effect of pricing strategies on the purchase of consumer goods. *International Journal of Research in Management, Science & Technology, 2*(2), 88–102.

Gozukara, E., Ozyer, Y., & Kocoglu, I. (2014). The moderating effect of perceived use and perceived risk in online shopping. *Journal of Global Strategic Management, 16*, 67–81.

Hassan, A. M., Kunz, M. B., Pearson, A. W., & Mohamed, F. A. (2006). Conceptualization and measurement of perceived risk in online shopping. *The Marketing Management Journal, 16*(1), 138–147.

Kotler, P., & Keller, K. L. (2016). *Marketing management*. Pearson Prentice Hall.

Li, N., & Zhang, P. (2002). Consumer online shopping attitude and behavior: An assessment of research. In *Information System Proceedings of English Americas Conference* (pp. 508–517).

Lim, H., & Dubinsky, A. J. (2004). Consumers' perceptions of e-shopping characteristics: An expectancy-value approach. *The Journal of Services Marketing, 18*(6), 500–513.

Neger, M., & Uddin, B. (2020). Factors affecting consumers' rural tourism e-marketplace shopping behavior during the COVID-19 pandemic: Evidence from Bangladesh. *Chinese Business Review, 19*(3), 91–104.

Prasad, C., & Aryasri, A. (2009). Determinants of shopper behavior in e-tailing: An empirical analysis. *Paradigm, 13*(1), 73–83.

Protocol. (2019). *E-commerce share on the total global retail sales 2015 to 2021*. Retrieved July 28, 2022, from https://www.protocol.gr/blog/e-commerce-share-of-total-global-retail-sales-from-2015-to-2021.

Rox, H. (2007). *Top reasons people shop online may surprise you*. Retrieved March 1, 2022, from http://www.associatedcontent.com/article/459412/top_reasons_people_shop_online_may.html?cat=3.

Samadi, M., & Yaghoob-Nejadi, A. (2009). A survey of the effect of consumers' perceived risk on purchase intention in e shopping. *Business Intelligence Journal, 2*(2), 261–275.

Sharin, F. H., Sentosa, I., & Perumal, R. K. (2022). A chaotic or an orderly of digitalisation. Malaysia's resilient model for sustainable rural tourism. In Hassan, A., Rahman, A. A. A. (Eds.), *Digital transformation in aviation, tourism and hospitality in Southeast Asia*. Routledge. ISBN 9781032324654

Subhalakshami, R., & Ravi, P. (2015). The impact of perceived risk on the online shopping attitude of cosmetic products in Tirunelveli city. *International Journal of Scientific Research, 4*(1), 231–233.

Uma, S., & Roger, B. (2013). *Research methods for business*. Wiley.

Farah Hida Sharin is a Ph.D. Scholar at Universiti Kuala Lumpur (UniKL) Business School, where she specializes in digital marketing intelligence and technopreneurship for rural tourism. She graduated from Universiti Teknologi MARA with a Master of Business Administration (MBA) and a Bachelor of Business Administration (Hons.) in Marketing. Holding various management positions and being involved in policy development since she was 23 led her to pursue a Doctorate of Philosophy (Management) at UniKL Business School currently. Prior to joining the teaching profession, she worked in both the public and private sectors, including city hall, law firms, real estate and property management, and education. Her interest in the development of graduates directed her to become a basic certified counsellor and a certified HRDF trainer. She also realizes her passion in business through managing the company as co-founder and owner. Due to the knowledge and experience, she always been invited to be adjudicator for local and international academic competition such business plan and marketing plan competition. Her current research interest is dynamic business modeling issues using the techniques of System Dynamics (SD) and Structural Equation Modeling (SEM).

Dr. Mohd Farid Shamsudin is an Associate Professor and lecturers and researches in the areas of Marketing. He has 22 years working experience in banking and telecommunication industry. Prior joining UNIKL he was a Senior Product Manager in the largest Telecommunication Company. He acquired enormous industry experience especially related to consumer behavior, product development, relationship marketing and customer services. Currently he is the head of section for Marketing and responsible to oversee Bachelor in Business Administration (Hons.) in Marketing and Bachelor in Business Administration (Hons.) in International Business. Dr. Shamsudin also has more than 5 years teaching experience as a part time lecturer in various local universities for postgraduate studies. He is currently a supervisor for Ph.D. and Master Students and actively participates in writing and attending conferences. He graduated from Multimedia University for his Bachelor in Business Administration followed by MBA from International Islamic University, Malaysia and finally was awarded Doctor of Business Administration from Universiti Utara Malaysia. His interests' areas of research are those related to consumer behavior, relationship marketing, advertising and branding. Among the subject specializes by Dr. Shamsudin are Principle of Marketing, Marketing Management, Strategic Marketing, Advertising and Promotion, Retail Management, Sales Management and Product Development.

Dr. Ilham Sentosa is an Associate Professor, an eco-system developer, researcher, senior lecturer and business consultant with expertise in smart city management, creative technopreneurship and dynamic business modeling issues using the techniques of System Dynamics (SD) and Structural Equation Modeling (SEM). Dr. Sentosa also recognized as an advanced quantitative analyst with interest in latent variable measurement models (factor analysis, item response), longitudinal data analysis (latent growth curves, growth mixture models), parametric and non-parametric analysis using measurement models approaches. He holds the post of Associate Professor at Universiti Kuala Lumpur (UniKL) Business School, Malaysia, where he teaches a graduate course on advanced structural model analysis techniques.

Chapter 11
Technology Application in Airports Reopening and Operations Recovery Due to COVID-19 Pandemic

Rita Zaharah Wan-Chik, Nur Syaza Syazwina Binti Zamri, and Siti Salwa Binti Hasbullah

Abstract Airport business has been severely impacted by the COVID-19 pandemic with travel ban, closed borders and the "new norm" of some standard operating procedures. The implications of the COVID-19 pandemic on airports have driven the adoption of technology that offers value for optimising operations as an approach to airports reopening within the new norm. The purpose of this study is to explore the feasibility of technology adoption in assisting airport industry on the road to recovery following the COVID-19 crisis. It investigates the adoption of technology by airports and its benefits in assisting airports reopening and operations recovery. For this study, a total of 33 literatures on technology adoption by airports between the year of 2020 to 2021 were reviewed. The findings indicated that airports will benefit from adopting three major areas of technology: Artificial Intelligence, biometrics, and the Internet of Things. These technologies benefit airports in a variety of ways such as cost-effectiveness, crowd control, improved efficiency, enhanced passenger experience, reduced contact, improved safety and security, time savings, and assistance for airport workers. Technological adoption in airport operations, on the road to recovery following the COVID-19 crisis, can contribute to the overall perception and distinctiveness of airports, as well as the acceptance of technology.

Keywords Technology adoption · Aviation management · Airport · Operations · Strategies · COVID-19

R. Z. Wan-Chik (✉)
Technical Foundation/Aviation Management Section, Universiti Kuala Lumpur—Malaysian Institute of Aviation Technology (UniKL MIAT), Selangor, Malaysia
e-mail: ritazaharah@unikl.edu.my

N. S. S. B. Zamri
Aviation Management Programme, Universiti Kuala Lumpur—Malaysian Institute of Aviation Technology (UniKL MIAT), Selangor, Malaysia

S. S. B. Hasbullah
Foundation Centre, Universiti Kuala Lumpur—Malaysian Institute of Information Technology (UniKL MIIT), Kuala Lumpur, Malaysia

© The Author(s), under exclusive license to Springer Nature Singapore Pte Ltd. 2023
A. Hassan and N. A. A. Rahman (eds.), *Technology Application in Aviation, Tourism and Hospitality*, https://doi.org/10.1007/978-981-19-6619-4_11

Introduction

COVID-19, an infectious disease, is a global pandemic that started in early 2020 and has affected many lives and companies around the world. While experts disagree about when the epidemic will end, wearing a mask, physical separation, swab tests, and quarantine procedures have all become necessary requirements to follow in order to stop the virus from spreading. The airport industry was threatened by the crisis with a decrease in commerce as a result of the imposition of travel restrictions by countries across the world (Rahman et al., 2021a, b). Airports relocated nearly 1 billion travellers in 2020 as a result of the COVID-19 crisis, indicating a 64.6% drop in worldwide travel traffic (Airports Council International, 2021). According to a survey by Airports Council International (ACI), airports were experiencing the greatest income drop where revenues have plummeted by around 125 billion dollars in 2020, a 66.3% decrease (Low, 2020).

While domestic and international air travel were allowed to resume safely, as recommended by the International Civil Aviation Organization (ICAO) (2021), a core set of precautions has been implemented to protect passengers and staff against COVID-19 and to allow the global aviation to grow during the recovery phase of the pandemic (International Civil Aviation Organization, 2021). As a result, airports will require more than just safety measures to adapt their commercial and operational procedures in order to survive the pandemic and beyond. Using technology to maintain every aspect of the job operation during the COVID-19 pandemic was critical, and the adoption of engaging technologies and innovations in the airport sector may continue or extend beyond COVID-19. There is an increase in studies on consolidating the adoption of technology to assist airports in recovering from the COVID-19 crisis, which is critical for the industry's future. As a result, this review may contribute to our understanding of the utilisation of technology and innovation in the airports reopening and operations recovery in response to COVID-19 pandemic.

Despite the fact that technology adoption is not a new phenomenon in the aviation industry, including airports and airlines, it is still not among the early adopters of the change as Industry Revolution 4.0 approaches. Despite the fact that the aviation industry has been impacted by the digital revolution, which has affected a wide spectrum of businesses and organisations, it has not been a leader in the digital revolution (Cigniti, 2021). Airports must quickly embrace modern technologies if they are to meet expanding client expectations in the future (Jarrel, 2018). Given the current pandemic crisis, crowd control and contact elimination, as well as cleanliness, are the most pressing concerns that airports must address. As a result, the utility and ease of technology adoption could aid airports in their post-COVID-19 recovery efforts. This study examines recent technological developments and its impact on aviation perspectives in relation to airport reopening and operations recovery from pandemic COVID-19 through the existing literature. The findings of the study are critical in assisting airport operators and authorities in gaining greater knowledge and trust in the use of technology in the industry to improve operations and prepare for future pandemic threat.

Travel Restrictions During the COVID-19 Pandemic

The COVID-19 pandemic is a worldwide phenomenon that has hampered several enterprises in a variety of industries, notably the aviation industry (Rahman et al., 2021a). According to a report from the United Nations World Tourism Organization (UNWTO) (2020), travel restrictions linked to COVID-19 were in place in 100% of countries by April 2020, with 83% of those in place for four weeks or longer, and the remaining 49% imposing border closures or flight suspensions lasting more than a month.

Furthermore, international travel has been impeded by border restrictions, which have become more stringent as a result of new COVID-19 variants. In October 2020, the Delta variant was identified in India, while the Omicron variant was discovered in November 2021 in South Africa (World Health Organization, n.d.). Following the discovery of these variants, many governments reacted swiftly, increasing international travel restrictions in an attempt to contain the variant's spread. Southern African travellers, for example, have been denied entry to a number of nations, and testing and quarantine requirements have been increased. In reaction to the outbreak of the Omicron coronavirus variant, at least 42 nations have issued travel restrictions, as shown in Fig. 11.1. Countries such as Australia and Saudi Arabia have halted flights from southern Africa, while Taiwan has tightened quarantine procedures for six African countries (Philip, 2021). As a result, the air travel restrictions have led to the majority of travellers declining to travel if they risk being quarantined upon arrival at their destination (Lee, 2021).

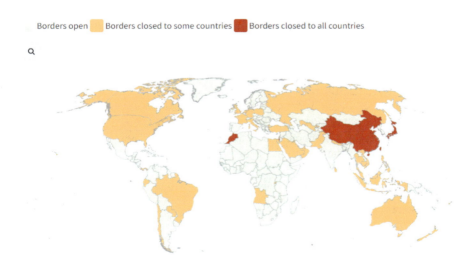

Fig. 11.1 Countries that have imposed travel bans since November 26, 2021 due to the Omicron coronavirus variant. *Source* Duggal and Haddad (2021)

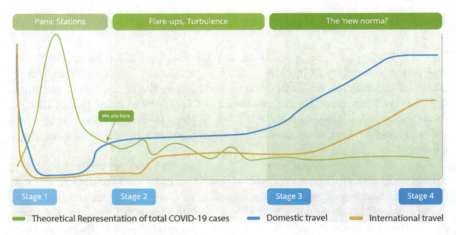

Fig. 11.2 COVID-19 transition stages. *Source* Kriel et al. (2020)

New Normal: Air Travel Reopening

When the borders reopen and air travel resumes, additional health safety procedures and technology will be adopted to reassure travellers about their surroundings' safety. A "new normal" of standard operating procedures was introduced globally which include, among others, the use of personal protection equipment (PPE), maintaining proper hygiene in public with the use of soap or hand sanitizer, and maintaining a specific social distance among people in crowds (Štimac et al., 2020). For air travellers, prior to and after flights, health checks are essential to detect and prevent the virus from spreading without the inconvenience of being quarantined for 14 days (Loo, 2020). In-flight seating designs were revised in accordance with social distancing requirements (IGT Solutions, n.d.), which limit the use of every second seat (Štimac et al., 2020).

Kriel et al. (2020) identified four COVID-19 transition stages in air travelling that make up the transition states from Panic Stations to Flare-ups, Turbulence to the 'new normal'. Figure 11.2 depicts the transition path to the new normal and Table 11.1 explains each of the transition stage.

Considerations for Air Travel Reopening

Players in the aviation industry anticipated the reopening of the skies after the COVID-19 vaccination program were being rolled out globally. As a result, the major goal is to reopen borders, streamline quarantine procedures, and digitise vaccination and testing records (International Air Transport Association, 2021). The Société Internationale de Télécommunications Aéronautiques (SITA) has identified three

Table 11.1 Description of the COVID-19 transition stages

Stage 0	Pre COVID-19
Stage 1	Except for repatriation, the borders are closed. Following government requirements, passengers are subject to managed isolation
Stage 2	Domestic borders reopen, and international travel safe zones connecting countries with trusted routes reopen at some point
Stage 3	International travel is split into two categories: safe and risky. High-level health inspections and social distancing are two trusted methods. Less secure routes require more in-depth testing and passenger separation zones
Stage 4	In the aftermath of COVID-19, a 'new normal' emerges. New measures have been easily implemented at airports (if needed)

Source Kriel et al. (2020)

concerns in their assessment as having a significant impact on aviation as it progresses through the pandemic recovery and beyond: economic pressures, safety and security, and sustainability (SITA, 2021). Travel bubbles will be critical in rebuilding the aviation business and economy as global vaccination rollouts reduce illness rates and encourage countries to make such arrangements (Bloomberg, 2021). Despite the fact that this forecast was based on current COVID-19 pandemic conditions, the Malaysian Aviation Commission (MAVCOM) predicted that the domestic market will remain the principal driver in the industry's recovery, given the likelihood that the interstate travel bubble will persist (Malaysian Aviation Commission, 2021).

Literature Review on Technology Adoption to Assist Airport Reopening and Operations Recovery

For this study, 33 literatures from various types, including academic articles, reports and others, were reviewed to explore on the adoption of technology to assist airports reopening and operations recovery around the globe. The literatures were limited to the year 2020 and 2021 as the COVID-19 pandemic only started in early 2020. Only topics focusing on airports management and operations recovery during the pandemic were chosen for this study. The list of all 33 literatures reviewed for this study is in Table 11.2.

From the analysis of 33 literatures, three technologies have been identified to be the main technologies adopted as part of the airport reopening and operations recovery. The three technologies are Artificial Intelligence (AI), Biometrics, and Internet of Things (IoT) within each having various applications and/or systems as summarized in Fig. 11.3.

Table 11.2 List of the reviewed literature

No.	Researcher	Topic
1	Amankwah-Amoah (2021)	COVID-19 pandemic and innovation activities in the global airline industry: a review
2	Antwi et al. (2021)	Airport self-service technologies, passenger self-concept, and behavior: an attributional view
3	Boranbaev and Assanbek (2020)	The role of information technology in the development of the air transportation market
4	Butcher (2021)	Newark trials biometric self-boarding e-gates
5	Chakraborty et al. (2021)	IoT and AI driven sustainable practices in airlines as enabler of passenger confidence, satisfaction and positive WOM: AI and IoT driven sustainable practice in airline
6	Dresner et al. (2021)	Resilience and efficiency through leadership and cooperation
7	Drljača et al. (2020)	The role and influence of industry 4.0. in airport operations in the context of COVID-19
8	Ebbutt (2020)	Technology's role in rebooting aviation
9	Falconer (2020)	Gearing up for the post COVID-19 era: improving hygiene standards through comprehensive disinfection
10	Gandhi (2021)	SMART preparedness for apparel manufactures for the new (ab) normal
11	Gupta et al. (2021)	Humans and robots: a mutually inclusive relationship in a contagious world
12	Halpern et al. (2021)	Conceptualising airport digital maturity and dimensions of technological and organisational transformation
13	Hornyak (2020)	Meet the robots that may be coming to an airport near you
14	Hoyer et al. (2020)	Transforming the customer experience through new technologies
15	King (2021)	Are health passports the solution to reopening the skies?
16	Kriel et al. (2020)	Departing from COVID-19—a flight path to recovery and reform of the aviation sector
17	Lavorel (2021)	Plotting post-pandemic travel: six technology trends set to transform air travel in 2021
18	Miskolczi et al. (2021)	Technology-enhanced airport services—attractiveness from the travellers' perspective
19	Narongou and Sun (2021)	Intelligent analytics with advanced multi-industry applications

(continued)

11 Technology Application in Airports Reopening and Operations … 149

Table 11.2 (continued)

No.	Researcher	Topic
20	Olaganathan (2021)	Impact of COVID-19 on airline industry and strategic plan for its recovery with special reference to data analytics technology
21	Purcell et al. (2020)	Assessment of risks of SARS-CoV-2 transmission during air travel and non-pharmaceutical interventions to reduce risk
22	Qureshi (2021)	Contactless technology adoption at airports gets accelerated after COVID-19
23	Rahman et al. (2021c)	Biometric technology application in the aviation industry: preliminary findings from passenger perspective
24	Rahman et al. (2021a)	Investigating technology application and new norm in aviation industry: airport perspective
25	Serrano and Kazda (2020)	The future of airports post COVID-19
26	Skotarenko (2021)	Innovative technologies in airports
27	Snow (2020)	Nano needles. Facial recognition. Air travel adapts to make travel safer
28	Souza (2021)	Using biometrics to increase the safety and efficiency of airport processes
29	Štimac et al. (2020)	Analysis of recommended measures in the conditions of the COVID-19 pandemic at Croatian airports
30	Sun et al. (2021)	Technological and educational challenges towards pandemic-resilient aviation
31	Vijayakumar (2021)	Aviation in COVID times: technology trends shaping our industry in 2021
32	Wakim (2020)	How cloud computing can help airports respond to COVID-19
33	Zeng et al. (2020)	From high-touch to high-tech: COVID-19 drives robotics adoption

Source Developed by the authors (2022)

Artificial Intelligence (AI)

Artificial intelligence is defined as the ability to programme computers and other technology-enabled machines to understand and respond in ways that are understandable to humans (Buchanan, 2005). It comprises processes such as data analysis and interpretation, data learning, and task application (Hoyer et al., 2020). Designers of AI systems attempted, to varied degrees, to emulate human traits such as creativity, logical thinking, and information storage (Techslang, 2020). Three key AI concepts are used to gain a full grasp of how artificial intelligence works: machine learning, deep learning, and neural networks. Machine learning is a subset of AI that aims to

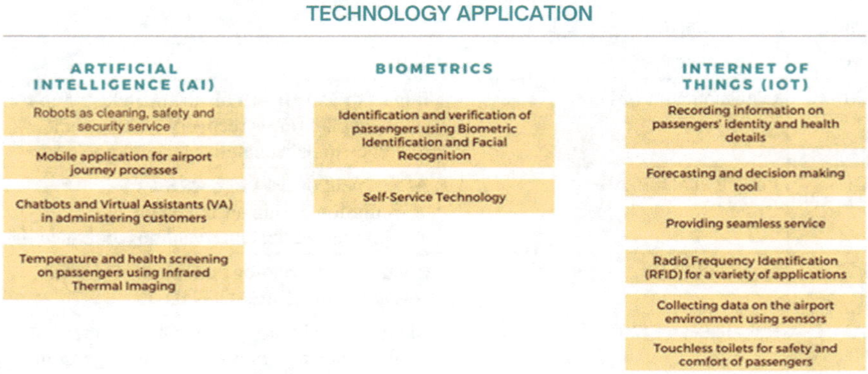

TECHNOLOGY APPLICATION

ARTIFICIAL INTELLIGENCE (AI)
- Robots as cleaning, safety and security service
- Mobile application for airport journey processes
- Chatbots and Virtual Assistants (VA) in administering customers
- Temperature and health screening on passengers using Infrared Thermal Imaging

BIOMETRICS
- Identification and verification of passengers using Biometric Identification and Facial Recognition
- Self-Service Technology

INTERNET OF THINGS (IOT)
- Recording information on passengers' identity and health details
- Forecasting and decision making tool
- Providing seamless service
- Radio Frequency Identification (RFID) for a variety of applications
- Collecting data on the airport environment using sensors
- Touchless toilets for safety and comfort of passengers

Fig. 11.3 Overview of technologies adopted for airport reopening and operations recovery. *Source* Developed by the authors (2022)

enable machines to learn a task without the use of pre-programmed code (Sciglar, 2018); deep learning is a term that refers to a system's ability to collect unstructured data from a variety of sources, analyse it, and then apply it to new problems (Techslang, 2020); and neural networks imitate the functions of the human brain using mathematics and computer science principles, allowing for broad applications (Sciglar, 2018). These three elements have been found to be used in various applications and services for the airport reopening and operations recovery as part of the COVID-19 new normal.

a. *Robots as cleaning, safety and security service*

Passengers' expectations and experiences have changed as a result of the COVID-19 pandemic, demanding an update in airport hygiene, sanitation, and security processes. Airports are deploying robots to assist with cleaning and security services (Skotarenko, 2021). Olaganathan (2021) recommends using automated cleaning robots to disinfect the surface of airports after the cleaning process is completed and this initiative have been used in a number of airports throughout the world (Zeng et al., 2020). Cleaning robots can, in fact, assist airports in maintaining their hygiene standards.

Alternatively, robots can be used to provide airport security services, taking security to a whole new level. Hornyak (2020) suggested security robots that are equipped with artificial intelligence technology that allows them to communicate in multiple languages and recognise faces as well as emergency signals such as shouting instructions. The robots are equipped with a facial recognition system, cameras, fire and smoke sensors, and the ability to communicate with human security workers (Hornyak, 2020; Skotarenko, 2021). If any unusual activity is detected at airport terminals, the robots can promptly alert security authorities.

Additionally, Ultraviolet-C (UVC) surface disinfection can be used to protect the frontline and security checkpoints (Falconer, 2020; Snow, 2020). UVC is a wavelength that destroys the DNA and RNA of viruses, causing them to stop reproducing and eventually die (Snow, 2020). Olaganathan (2021) also suggested that airports use UVC light technology to disinfect handrails on escalators and travellators. UVC technology has proven to be great for fast disinfection, with promises that germs will not be able to develop a natural resistance to it (Falconer, 2020).

According to Gupta et al. (2021), information can be broadcast via flying robots, which can cover a larger area than traditional loudspeakers, and the vision solutions built into the flying robots allow airports to keep a close eye on their passenger count as well as how close they are to one another. To reduce the risk of COVID-19 transmission at airports, ambulances or medical robots that can be operated remotely, have the ability to track high-risk regions, and are equipped with medical equipment can be used (Zeng et al., 2020).

b. *Mobile application for airport journey process assistance*

Although mobile applications are common in the airline industry, the use of mobile technology in the airport sector may be unusual. In response to the pandemic situation, mobile application functions can be enhanced and adjusted to better assist airports and air travellers. One simple approach, for example, is to enhance the application's smartphone alerts, which might assist to alleviate crowding by informing certain customers to board the plane (Snow, 2020). This is far more convenient than sending airport or airline employees to call names one by one. Alternatively, passengers can be vetted and escorted from the airport's point of entry to the boarding gate utilising mobile applications (Sun et al., 2021).

Passengers can also be aided by using a self-check-in kiosk, where they can check-in using the airline's mobile application and obtain their boarding pass and QR code via application notification or email (Chakraborty et al., 2021). Mobile applications should also have a capability for shopping and ordering food at the airport, as shown in Fig. 11.4. When ordering meals through airport delivery services, it is no longer essential to visit a restaurant or fast food stand in the terminal (Purcell et al., 2020). This demonstrates that the improved system of the mobile application will make airport journey processes easier.

c. *Chatbots and virtual assistant (VA) in administering customers*

Artificial intelligence-powered Chatbots are already being used to help with administrative tasks like airline information portals, and the technology is making inroads into airport communications (Miskolczi et al., 2021). Chatbots are a wonderful tool for boosting customer support, due to their capability and capacity to connect with multiple customers at once. Customers should be able to try out AI-based services such as speaking with an AI robot and driving a self-driving car at airports to suit their mobility, communication, and entertainment needs (Miskolczi et al., 2021).

Virtual assistants, on the other hand, play an important role in answering questions regarding services or products and their applications, as well as providing feedback and encouraging further consumption (Hoyer et al., 2020). VA are able to address specific queries from multiple customers and give feedback at the same time. Airports should analyse the feasibility of using VA as well as the type of data that this technological progress would necessitate. However, both technologies, chatbots and VA,

Fig. 11.4 Contactless shopping and food ordering system. *Source* Purcell et al. (2020)

must be integrated and used in a humane manner, to avoid over-automating and thus, losing sight of human connection and terminal involvement (Rahman et al., 2021a).

d. ***Temperature and health screening on passengers using infrared thermal imaging***

Airports can use thermal scanners to detect passengers with high body temperatures as they pass through the terminals. High body temperature is one of the signs that a person is possibly having fever due to COVID-19 infection. Intelligent thermal cameras will make it possible to scan a large number of passengers' body temperatures quickly and discreetly (Štimac et al., 2020). Thermal scanners would generate digital data and will convey this data to the operational control centre and provide passenger's overall health intelligence, as well as notifying airport management when necessary (Olaganathan, 2021).

Biometrics

Biometrics is described as the process of digitally encoding the physical characteristics of a user in order to get access to data or computer systems (Frankenfield, 2020). It involves the automated process of identifying and verifying individuals based on their unique physical characteristics (e.g., face, finger, and iris) and behavioural characteristics (e.g., voice) to distinguish them from one another (Heracleous & Wirtz, 2006). Separating one from a larger group is the act of identifying an individual, whereas verifying an individual's identity entails determining whether or not they are who they claim to be (Corum, 2004). Biometrics is involved with recognising people based on biological and behavioural observations that have been collected in a data gathering system (Corum, 2004; National Research Council, 2010). It is, in essence, the process of identifying a person from a vast number of biometrically recorded individuals.

a. *Identification and verification of passengers using biometric identification and facial recognition*

Biometric identification, which uses physical features such as voice tone, face, and fingerprint, can be used to automatically identify people. Passengers' biometric data will be linked to their boarding pass, allowing them to use only their biometrics to pass through the remaining security checkpoints and into the departure lounge, as well as verifying their identity during check-in (Souza, 2021). While data breaches and security issues will undoubtedly exist, airports can lessen these risks by decentralising data devices.

Facial recognition is the most extensively utilised biometric technology in many airports, and it is well suited for usage in post-pandemic settings (Amankwah-Amoah, 2021). Face recognition technology can be used at the check-in counter and the luggage drop-off area at airports (Serrano & Kazda, 2020). Without the requirement for contact, facial recognition can be utilised to scan passports and conduct health screenings while during the boarding process, a biometric scanner scans the passenger's face to begin the process (Sun et al., 2021).

Biometric technology that depends on a combination of facial and iris recognition for identification, which reduces human participation, can be used to make a contactless transit around the airport more hygienic (Qureshi, 2021). If airports and immigration and customs departments work together to cross-reference images, the images taken prior to boarding can be compared to those already in the database, which has been submitted by all passport holders (Butcher, 2021). Alternatively, airports have the option of deleting any photos taken, and travellers have the option of opting out if they are concerned about showing their travel face.

Facial recognition technology may also be used to detect and verify people based on biological, morphological, and behavioural characteristics (Skotarenko, 2021). Most facial recognition systems have sensors that allow the different aspects of a person's face to be recognised until the person's identity is validated (Snow, 2020).

Passengers may easily utilise their faces as boarding tickets, allowing them to seamlessly transition from taxi to plane (Lavorel, 2021). Passengers stroll past the checkpoint, scan their faces through the facial recognition system, and are cleared by immigration agents without any human interaction or the need for a passport stamp (Qureshi, 2021).

Facial recognition can also be used to identify and authenticate crew members, letting them to use mobile devices to complete check-in processes and mandatory pre-flight safety and security questions (Lavorel, 2021). Facial recognition will be considerably easier to install and run successfully if airports and airlines collaborate to merge their systems to adapt to this technology. Facial recognition has a lot to offer in terms of improving airport operations post-COVID-19, and it's beneficial to both passengers and personnel.

b. *Self-service technology*

Self-service technology has become an integral part of travel experience, from searching for information to purchasing tickets to checking in (Antwi et al., 2021). Passengers can use their face as identity to check in at the self-service kiosk and acquire a luggage tag (Kriel et al., 2020). Passenger data from the passport will be linked with biometrics used as an identification base throughout the entire traffic flow operation at check-in (Drljača et al., 2020). Self-service kiosks can be used to take a passenger's vital signs and provide touch-free health checks and luggage drop-offs, among other things (Qureshi, 2021). Passengers departing, arriving, or transferring at an airport can purchase goods from self-service kiosks located throughout the terminal (Antwi et al., 2021). Airports can also deploy automated boarding pass control systems, as well as automated gate readers and face recognition (Drljača et al., 2020). This allows staff to supervise the entire procedure from a safe distance. As a result, as more self-service technologies are adopted, airport personnel who may be required elsewhere can be used more efficiently.

Internet of Things (IoT)

Patel and Patel (2016) defined the "Internet of Things" as a network in which anything can be connected to the Internet using predetermined protocols and information sensing equipment to exchange data and communicate with one another to enable smart recognition and location, as well as traceability, monitoring, and administrative control. In short, IoT is a system that connects physical items to a network and uses sensors to generate digital data (Halpern et al., 2021). Smart computing systems are built into gadgets and connected to the Internet (Hoyer et al., 2020; Wise & Heidari, 2019).

When sensors are installed in a device or item, they are connected to an IoT platform, which analyses the data and distributes it with apps designed to satisfy specific needs (Clark, 2016). The ultimate goal of the IoT is for devices to self-report in real time, increasing efficiency and providing faster access to crucial data than a system that relies on human input (Kenton, 2021). It aims to enable things to connect with anything and anybody at any time and from any location, ideally through any path/network and using any service.

a. ***Recording information on passengers' identity and health details***

The paper-based passport system is being phased out in favour of a fully digital system. A digital passport is a blockchain-based tool that can speed up airport security checks. Passengers' identities are authenticated in advance using this technology and only those with a real need to know are permitted access to this data, allowing it to be used most effectively in subsequent phases of service delivery (Drljača et al., 2020). Airports, airlines, and governments can collaborate in exchanging baggage content information to pre-clear bags upon arrival and reduce the need for extra bag checks during the journey (Lavorel, 2021). Using a digital passport allows airports to focus on providing a frictionless passenger experience (Sun et al., 2021).

There is also a health passport that airports could take into account. A health passport is based on the idea of creating a digital passport containing up-to-date health information and then sharing it with airports and airlines (King, 2021). If a passenger's phone already has health information on it, he or she could check in and pass through border control e-gates without having to go through additional screening (Kriel et al., 2020). There is also the IATA health passport solution, which consists of two parts: identification management and test results transfer (King, 2021). As a result, with all of the needed health information on the application, travelling will be made easier, demonstrating that the passenger meets all of the requirements for safe travel (Dresner et al., 2021). An airport's endeavour to make air travel easier and safer may include the usage of a health passport. However, no airport or airline can do this on its own as it requires the assistance of the government and health agencies (Kriel et al., 2020).

b. ***Forecasting information using decision-making tool***

Predictive and prescriptive analytics using big data can be used by airports to improve data-driven decision-making and increase efficiency (Olaganathan, 2021). Airports would be able to transform customer feedback and data into meaningful insights, and would then be able to deliver that data to customers in order to keep them informed and aware of their interactions when near airports (Narongou & Sun, 2021). Airports must have a data-driven, personalised e-commerce strategy that finds, groups, and engages customers with customised promotions based on their data (Olaganathan, 2021). As a result, poor decision making is reduced, giving an advantage over the broad use of data to optimise an airport's operational functions (Narongou & Sun, 2021). Using big data analytics during the post-COVID-19 reopening period is a smart step since it allows airports to foresee the aviation industry, which will aid them in making commercial decisions.

c. ***Providing seamless service using cloud technology***

Travelers can exert control over the sharing and use of their personal data by using digital identity technology. The identity holder can only provide the information required for a specific transaction or interaction, which adds another layer of security and flexibility (Wakim, 2020). Furthermore, data from sensors can be collected and stored in the cloud using cloud technologies or a digital platform that is unified across all devices in the system (Halpern et al., 2021). A software modification can also be done once in the data centre and then scaled across many passenger touchpoints using cloud infrastructure (Wakim, 2020). Overall, cloud computing may be used in conjunction with other technologies like biometrics and mobile apps to help airports provide seamless service to passengers throughout this vital period of the recovery. The services provided by cloud computing are depicted in Fig. 11.5.

d. ***Radio frequency identification (RFID) for various applications***

For electronic contactless payments, RFID is the most widely utilised technology. Passengers can shop or buy food using contactless payment methods enabled by credit or debit cards (Purcell et al., 2020). RFID tags can now be affixed to travellers' luggage as digital bag tags (Halpern et al., 2021) or to any purchasing products at duty-free stores (Hoyer et al., 2020). Passengers will utilise an application installed on their mobile devices to access this technology.

Passengers can use a mobile application to track their luggage from start to finish, which includes the ability to report mishandled or misplaced luggage, trigger an alarm in the event of theft, and be told when the baggage is ready to be picked and from which carousel (Halpern et al., 2021). Passengers can also scan RFID tags connected to shopping merchandise with their smartphone cameras or other smart devices to do a fast check to verify the prices, colours, sizes, or availability of the products they are interested in before asking for help from staff (Hoyer et al., 2020). This demonstrates that airports may utilise RFID technology for a variety of applications.

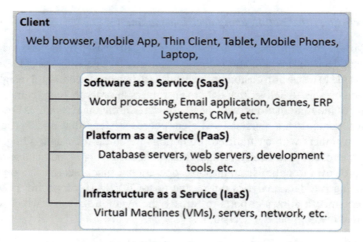

Fig. 11.5 Services provide by cloud computing. *Source* Narongou and Sun (2021)

e. *Collecting data on the airport environment using sensors*

Sensor technology can be used by airports to gather information about their physical surroundings. Purcell et al. (2020) recommended that airports look at adopting autonomous sensors that can detect substantial passenger congestion and quickly adjust air supply to certain areas. Passengers could board without interacting with on-ground crews if proximity sensors are installed across an airport and linked to an airline's phone apps (Kriel et al., 2020). Sensor data can then be shared in real-time with travellers to help them make social distancing decisions (Gandhi, 2021; Halpern et al., 2021). Sensors can also be used for other purposes, such as smart energy monitoring, building maintenance, and waste management (Halpern et al., 2021). As a result, airports are able to derive findings from data analysis quickly and efficiently, and put those conclusions into practise without disrupting airport operations.

f. *Touchless toilets for the safety and comfort of passengers*

Sensors can be linked to a mobile app on the passengers' phones to create touchless bathrooms. Passengers will use an app on their smartphones to find public restrooms, check how crowded they are, join a virtual queue, and be notified when it is their turn to use the restroom (Kriel et al., 2020). This method will maintain a safe physical distance in the restroom while protecting the passengers.

User detection sensors can be put in airport toilets to control automated flushing systems for lavatories and urinals (Purcell et al., 2020). Some of the most basic 'touchless' installations that permit successful handwashing without coming into contact with harmful fomites include automatic faucets, soap dispensers, and flushing (Kriel et al., 2020; Purcell et al., 2020). The touchless restroom will, in theory, help the airport run more efficiently while also improving passenger safety and comfort.

The Benefits of Adopting Technology for Airports Reopening

26 of the 33 studies examined emphasised the advantages of employing technologies to help with airport reopening and operations recovery due to COVID-19 crisis. Cost-effectiveness, better crowd control, improved efficiency, enhanced passenger experience, reduced contact, improved safety and security, time savings, and assistance for airport workers are among the eight primary benefits cited.

Cost-Effectiveness

Airports have suffered a drop in sales and revenue as a result of the coronavirus pandemic. Accordingly, the use of technology may assist airports to cut expenses in their operations (Amankwah-Amoah, 2021). Finger and facial recognition are two examples of technology that can help airports cut expenses by doing operations faster than humans and reducing the quantity of manual processes (Serrano & Kazda, 2020).

Cloud computing may be able to help lower the financial risk of using flawless software (Lavorel, 2021). Airports can choose from a number of cloud computing providers, and they pay for the model that best suits their needs. Airports can also save money on software repair because data and programmes are stored and accessed over the internet.

Because of the high number of people employed at airports, keeping personnel costs under control is crucial. As a result, airports can reduce labour costs by installing technology such as self-service kiosks (Boranbaev & Assanbek, 2020), as this technology does not require personnel assistance. This does not mean that airports must lay off employees, particularly during a pandemic, but it does reduce the risk of overpayment with minimal effort. It would be operationally more effective if airports could station personnel at locations where their skills are most needed.

Better Crowd Control Management

Airports are usually congested, but a pandemic situation is exceptional and necessitates extra vigilance. As a result, airports benefit from crowd management technologies such as smartphone apps, facial recognition, touchless bathrooms, and RFID. Face recognition screening automation, for example, can prevent long lines from forming (Skotarenko, 2021), leading in less crowding at check-in counters (Wakim, 2020). Passengers will feel protected and at ease in less crowded areas.

It is possible to reduce crowds lingering around the gate or in line on the jet bridge, which is a dangerous zone with little air circulation, putting people at risk of the transmission of COVID-19 by developing a mobile application to alert passengers to board the plane (Snow, 2020). Everyone will be able to freely travel between the departure area and other parts of the airport once airports are able to keep crowds under control. Meanwhile, for airport shopping, restaurants, and fast food stalls, RFID facilitates faster payment, reducing crowding and exposure time for virus transmission via airborne (Purcell et al., 2020). A decrease in crowd size could depict that airports are managing crowd effectively, which is a real necessity during a pandemic situation.

Improve Efficiency in Various Aspects

Airport operators can improve operational and process efficiency by overhauling their current operations and processes with the use of AI technologies (Rahman et al., 2021c). For example, by eliminating the need for passports and boarding cards manually, operations can be streamlined by using facial recognition to identify passengers and speed their itineraries (Halpern et al., 2021; Skotarenko, 2021).

To be more specific, increased processing efficiency leads to shorter wait times, increased social distance (Lavorel, 2021), improved hygiene (Falconer, 2020), and a less stressful environment for all passengers. Boosting efficiency means offering a more effective way of monitoring passengers to ensure that they are not only bio-safe, but also secure, have adequate documents, and can cross customs more swiftly. In an ideal world, technology would make airport management responsibilities easier to complete and more efficient (Dresner et al., 2021).

Apart from that, airport efficiency may be improved by utilising flexible big data analytics, which allows airports to get insights into various types of clients from many nations and specific geographic locations in order to make changes and maximise Return on Investment (ROI) (Olaganathan, 2021). It will help the airport operator to improve and enhance passenger predictions using more modern methods by merging it with AI technology (Rahman et al., 2021c). This enables airport managers to make informed decisions based on collected data and forecasts.

Customer behaviour can also be discovered using real-time reactive analytics, according to Olaganathan (2021), which will help to promote impulse purchases and secure reluctant buyers. Souza (2021) noted that consenting to the sharing of personal data allows travellers to enjoy a customised travel experience that is suited to their individual needs. Airports' business models will alter drastically as they obtain a better understanding of their clients and can give tailored products and services based on the data (Drljača et al., 2020). Airports will be able to tailor products and services as a result of their ability to analyse and forecast, resulting in enhanced efficiency.

Furthermore, airports can improve efficiency by employing facial recognition to provide the highest level of hygiene (Amankwah-Amoah, 2021), reduce the number of times customers must present identification (Snow, 2020), and improve customer service quality (Boranbaev & Assanbek, 2020). The availability of health and digital passports enables a frictionless journey, which benefits both passengers and staff. Improved efficiency can be demonstrated by reduced boarding wait times with biometric identification (Souza, 2021) or a lower risk of luggage mishandling upon arrival (Lavorel, 2021). Finally, by aiding customers with problems or proposing alternatives, optimising their consumption and experience will increase efficiency (Hoyer et al., 2020).

Enhance Passengers' Experience

Another benefit that airports will receive from using technology is that they will be able to improve passenger experience (Rahman et al., 2021c; Serrano & Kazda, 2020; Wakim, 2020) by providing customers with the opportunity to suit their demands by embracing technology. In fact, AI-based services that cater to environmentally conscious clients can improve customer views of airport operations (Miskolczi et al., 2021). Many technologies improve the travel experience by delivering specialised and personalised benefits as well as engaging with customers in a way that allows for maximum revenue growth (Souza, 2021). It is expected that providing customers with broad, detailed, and relevant information that can be used for decision-making will improve the entire passenger experience (Hoyer et al., 2020).

Furthermore, using facial recognition, self-service technology, and digital passports, travellers' experiences may be improved by making their movements more fluid (Rahman et al., 2021c). As a result of the shorter wait time, passengers will feel less bored and stressed. Furthermore, as a result of the increased quality of services provided by technology, passengers' trust and contentment (Chakraborty et al., 2021) will increase, as will their emotions and behaviour (Halpern et al., 2021). For example, security robots can communicate with passengers and personnel in a range of languages and recognise emergency indicators, allowing them to assist passengers and employees in a variety of situations.

Increasing passenger confidence in flying during a pandemic will improve customer's experience (Chakraborty et al., 2021). As a result, deploying technologies to rebuild customer confidence and restructure air travel while also boosting airport capabilities in the long run is crucial (Olaganathan, 2021). Customers will be able to plan their travel into and through airport facilities with confidence thanks to mobile applications that perform a variety of functions and provide critical information. In fact, it is the combination of multiple technologies that will have the most impact on improving the passenger experience.

Reduce Contact Between Passengers and Staff

Using technology at all touchpoints at the airport, as opposed to manual operation, will likely reduce physical contact (Štimac et al., 2020) between passengers, airport workers, and shared surfaces (Butcher, 2021), resulting in less face-to-face engagement. For example, instead of having personnel complete the temperature check manually, which would take time, smart thermal cameras may be used to assess the temperature of the enormous number of passengers passing through. With the use of a mobile application that serves as a boarding permit, the airport will be able to eliminate the requirement for passengers and workers to contact any surfaces while minimising the risk of infection (Lavorel, 2021). The fewer human touchpoints at the airport, the lower the chance of virus infection (Chakraborty et al., 2021; Serrano & Kazda, 2020). These technologies can assist airports in their post-COVID-19 reopening efforts and are critical for future passenger and crew health safety.

Safety and Security

Airport safety and security is a critical issue that must be addressed. Using technology at airports will increase safety and security while also streamlining and speeding up the process (Rahman et al., 2021c). This is a big advantage since technology protects people not only from COVID-19 infection but also from other potential threats. Passengers' safety and airport structure functioning will be ensured by technology such as smart scanning cameras and biometric identification, which will also enable high-level automated security inspections (Skotarenko, 2021).

One of the most common security problems is fraud. Using technology like finger recognition, which requires passengers to scan their fingertips and then the system instantly verifies them, fraud may be avoided (Rahman et al., 2021c). There are also a variety of different technologies that can prevent passengers' personal information from falling into the wrong hands (Lavorel, 2021) and lower the risk of cybercrime because data can only be accessed with authorisation (Lavorel, 2021). These technologies will vastly improve airport safety and security while also reducing the possibility of human error.

Time Savings

The length of time spent at the airport will be critical in reducing the risk of infection. It is consequently recommended that airports embrace technologies to help them complete their responsibilities more quickly and efficiently. Because health passports are linked to passenger IDs, King (2021) claims that passengers can swiftly and easily demonstrate that they are virus-free before boarding the airline. Face recognition, which confirms travellers' IDs using their faces, saves time for both passengers and airport personnel (Butcher, 2021).

At airport retail outlets, automated transactions utilising IoT technology should be noted on the price tag. Customers will save time (Hoyer et al., 2020) by automatically charging their mobile payment app accounts for the prices of the things they are purchasing during check out, in addition to making life easier. More technology can be used to reduce wait times and speed up the passenger and baggage screening process (Štimac et al., 2020).

Support Airport Personnel

Technology adoption has made airport staff's jobs easier in many ways, including no longer have to execute their duties manually which would have exposed them to the virus transmission risk. Operators can better plan and execute a full hygiene and maintenance programme using IoT technologies (Ebbutt, 2020). Meanwhile, enormous amounts of historical data are being retrieved to help human operators on the ground make the best decisions possible (Vijayakumar, 2021). A less stressful and safe workplace will be established by developing or automating various processes to assist staff in airport operations, time will be saved on superfluous activities, and employees will be happier with their work performance.

Airport employees profit immensely from the assistance offered by robots, which help them with a variety of tasks in the airport environment. Skotarenko (2021) suggested that airport security officials use robots with facial recognition systems, cameras, and sensors to help them provide enough security. According to Gupta et al. (2021), robots can help officials manage crowds and identify people with elevated body temperatures, which could indicate the presence of the virus. Falconer (2020) underlined that robots ease staff duties by automating repetitive disinfection labour, freeing up more human operators for more vital tasks, and enhancing cleanliness significantly. Rather than completely replacing human operators with robots, it would be preferable if humans and robots collaborated on a fair task distribution. After all, robots help to relieve some of the strain on employees by reducing service delays and slowdowns.

Conclusion

The goal of this study was to look into the technology that airports can employ to help with airport reopening and operations recovery following the COVID-19 disaster. From the 33 literature reviewed, it was found that a number of technologies generated from AI, biometrics, and IoT can assist airports in their efforts to reopen and on the road of recovery. The majority of the studies look at how different types of technology are being implemented in airports.

Cleaning, security procedures, airport route operations, customer administration, and health screening could all benefit from AI. Biometrics, on the other hand, can help identify and authenticate passengers in a variety of ways, as well as provide self-service check-in and baggage drop-off technology. Meanwhile, IoT can be used to create digital or health passports, forecast, collect, and safeguard data, and other passenger safety and comfort applications.

Apart from that, all of these technologies will provide considerable benefits to airports in a variety of ways. Cost-effectiveness, crowd control, improved efficiency, enhanced passenger experience, reduced contact, improved safety and security, time savings, and assistance for airport workers are the eight primary benefits cited.

In conclusion, air travel will become more convenient, smart, and safe for everyone as a result of technological advancements. This will inspire more people to fly again, resulting in increased income for airports. Airport operations will almost certainly be streamlined as a result of technological adoption in the post-COVID-19 age. This may help to improve not just technology's acceptability, but also airports' overall perception and originality on their operations and services.

References

Airports Council International (ACI). (2021). *The impact of COVID-19 on the airport business—And the path to recovery*. Retrieved May 14, 2022, from https://aci.aero/2021/11/01/the-impact-of-covid-19-on-the-airport-business-and-the-path-to-recovery-3/.

Amankwah-Amoah, J. (2021). COVID-19 pandemic and innovation activities in the global airline industry: A review. *Environment International, 156*, 106719.

Antwi, C. O., Ren, J., Owusu-Ansah, W., Mensah, H. K., & Aboagye, M. O. (2021). Airport self-service technologies, passenger self-concept, and behavior: An attributional view. *Sustainability, 13*(6), 1–18.

Bloomberg. (2021). Singapore sees safe reopening of Changi as key to survival. *New Straits Times*. Retrieved May 22, 2022, from https://www.nst.com.my/business/2021/03/671341/singapore-sees-safe-reopening-changi-key-survival.

Boranbaev, S. N., & Assanbek, G. D. (2020). The role of information technology in the development of the air transportation market. *Евразийский Союз Ученых, 4*(73), 25–27.

Buchanan, B. G. (2005). A (very) brief history of artificial intelligence. *AI Magazine, 26*(4), 53.

Butcher, L. (2021). Newark trials biometric self-boarding e-gates. *Passenger Terminal Today*. Retrieved May 18, 2022, from https://www.passengerterminaltoday.com/news/biometrics/newark-trials-biometric-self-boarding-e-gates.html.

Chakraborty, S., Chakravorty, T., & Bhatt, V. (2021). IoT and AI driven sustainable practices in airlines as enabler of passenger confidence, satisfaction and positive WOM: AI and IoT driven sustainable practice in airline. In *Proceedings - International Conference on Artificial Intelligence and Smart Systems (ICAIS) 2021*, Coimbatore, 25–27 March (pp. 1421–1425).

Cigniti. (2021). *The future of air travel in a new age of technology*. Retrieved May 12, 2022, from https://www.cigniti.com/blog/aviation-future-technology/.

Clark, J. (2016). What is the Internet of Things (IoT)? *IBM Business Operations Blog*. Retrieved May 22, 2022, from https://www.ibm.com/blogs/internet-of-things/what-is-the-iot/.

Corum, C. (2004). Biometrics 101: Understanding the basics of this crucial technology. *SecureID-News*. Retrieved May 15, 2022, from https://www.secureidnews.com/news-item/biometrics-101-understanding-the-basics-of-this-crucial-technology/.

Dresner, M., Aliu, O. B., Gittens, A., & Papatheodorou, A. (2021). Resilience and efficiency through leadership and cooperation. *Hermes Air Transpot Oganisation*. Retrieved May 28, 2022, from http://hermes.aero/wp-content/uploads/2021/09/R21-R-1.pdf.

Drljača, M., Štimac, I., Bračić, M., & Petar, S. (2020). The role and influence of industry 4.0. in airport operations in the context of COVID-19. *Sustainability, 12*(24), 1–18.

Duggal, H., & Haddad, M. (2021). Visualising the global air travel industry. *Al-Jazeera*. Retrieved May 23, 2022, from https://www.aljazeera.com/economy/2021/12/9/visualising-the-global-air-travel-industry-interactive.

Ebbutt, L. (2020). Technology's role in rebooting aviation. *Mott Macdonald*. Retrieved May 22, 2022, from https://www.mottmac.com/views/technologys-role-in-rebooting-aviation.

Falconer, R. (2020). Gearing up for the post COVID-19 era: Improving hygiene standards through comprehensive disinfection. *Airport Business by ACI*. Retrieved May 11, 2022, from http://www.airport-business.com/2020/08/gearing-post-covid-19-era-improving-hygiene-standards-comprehensive-disinfection/.

Frankenfield, J. (2020). Biometrics. *Investopedia*. Retrieved May 21, 2022, from https://www.investopedia.com/terms/b/biometrics.asp.

Gandhi, A. (2021). *SMART preparedness for apparel manufactures for the new (ab) normal*. Retrieved May 11, 2022, from https://ssrn.com/abstract=3866503.

Gupta, A., Singh, A., Bharadwaj, D., & Mondal, A. K. (2021). Humans and robots: A mutually inclusive relationship in a contagious world. *International Journal of Automation and Computing, 18*(2), 185–203.

Halpern, N., Budd, T., Suau-Sanchez, P., Bråthen, S., & Mwesiumo, D. (2021). Conceptualising airport digital maturity and dimensions of technological and organisational transformation. *Journal of Airport Management, 15*(2), 182–203.

Heracleous, L., & Wirtz, J. (2006). Biometrics: The next frontier in service excellence, productivity and security in the service sector. *Managing Service Quality, 16*(1), 12–22.

Hornyak, T. (2020). Meet the robots that may be coming to an airport near you. *CNBC*. Retrieved May 17, 2022, from https://www.cnbc.com/2020/01/10/meet-the-robots-that-may-be-coming-to-an-airport-near-you.html.

Hoyer, W. D., Kroschke, M., Schmitt, B., & Kraume, K. (2020). Transforming the customer experience through new technologies. *Journal of Interactive Marketing, 51*, 57–71.

IGT Solutions. (n.d.). *The new normal for travel in a post COVID-19 world*. Retrieved May 12, 2022, from https://www.igtsolutions.com/blog/the-new-normal-for-travel-in-a-post-covid-19-world/.

International Air Transport Association (IATA). (2021). *Optimism for travel restart as borders reopen*. Retrieved May 15, 2022, from https://airlines.iata.org/news/optimism-for-travel-restart-as-borders-reopen.

International Civil Aviation Organization (ICAO). (2021). *Effects of novel coronavirus (COVID-19) on civil aviation: Economic impact analysis*. Retrieved May 27, 2022, from https://www.icao.int/sustainability/Documents/Covid-19/ICAO_coronavirus_Econ_Impact.pdf.

Jarrel, J. (2018). The future of digital technology in the aviation industry. *International Airport Review*. Retrieved May 25, 2022, from https://www.internationalairportreview.com/article/76057/future-digital-technology/.

Kenton, W. (2021). The Internet of Things (IoT). *Investopedia*. Retrieved May 15, 2022, from https://www.investopedia.com/terms/i/internet-things.asp.

King, H. (2021). Are health passports the solution to reopening the skies? *Passenger Terminal Today*. Retrieved May 21, 2022, from https://www.passengerterminaltoday.com/features/are-health-passports-the-solution-to-reopening-the-skies.html.

Kriel, E., Reiss, B., Baker-Holland, S., & Farrell, D. (2020). Departing from COVID-19—A flight path to recovery and reform of the aviation sector. *Aurecon*. Retrieved May 15, 2022, from https://www.aurecongroup.com/thinking/thinking-papers/covid-19-aviation-sector-reform.

Lavorel, D. (2021). Plotting post-pandemic travel: Six technology trends set to transform air travel in 2021. *SITA*. Retrieved May 24, 2022, from https://www.sita.aero/pressroom/blog/plotting-post-pandemic-travel/.

Lee, K. (2021). Future of aviation: Beyond COVID or with COVID? *McKinsey*. Retrieved May 24, 2022, from https://www.mckinsey.com/industries/travel-logistics-and-infrastructure/our-insights/back-to-the-future-airline-sector-poised-for-change-post-covid-19.

Loo, B. (2020). The new normal of air travel: Face masks, blocked seats, mandatory health checks and more. *Klook*. Retrieved May 28, 2022, from https://www.klook.com/en-PH/blog/safety-measures-flying/.

Low, T. K. (2020). COVID-19: Strategizing airport operations for the new norm. *Airports Council International. ACI Insights*. Retrieved May 15, 2022, from https://blog.aci.aero/covid-19-strategizing-airport-operations-for-the-new-norm/.

Malaysian Aviation Commission (MAVCOM). (2021). *2021 air passenger traffic to contract between 22.9 and 29.1 per cent year-on-year*. Retrieved May 15, 2022, from https://www.mavcom.my/en/2021/04/28/2021-air-passenger-traffic-to-contract-between-22-9-and-29-1-per-cent-year-on-year/.

Miskolczi, M., Jászberényi, M., & Tóth, D. (2021). Technology-enhanced airport services—Attractiveness from the travelers' perspective. *Sustainability, 13*(2), 1–18.

National Research Council. (2010). *Biometric recognition: Challenges and opportunities*. The National Academies Press.

Narongou, D., & Sun, Z. (2021). Big data analytics for smart airport management. In *Intelligent analytics with advanced multi-industry applications* (pp. 209–231).

Olaganathan, R. (2021). Impact of COVID-19 on airline industry and strategic plan for its recovery with special reference to data analytics technology. *Global Journal of Engineering and Technology Advances, 7*(1), 033–046.

Patel, K. K., & Patel, S. M. (2016). Internet of Things-IOT: Definition, characteristics, architecture, enabling technologies, application & future challenges. *International Journal of Engineering Science and Computing*, 6122–6131.

Philip, S. V. (2021). Omicron curbs from Japan to Spain wreak havoc on air travel. *Bloomberg*. Retrieved May 15, 2022, from https://www.bloomberg.com/news/articles/2021-11-28/airlines-scramble-to-navigate-fast-degrading-travel-outlook.

Purcell, W. M., Marcus, L., Spengler, J., & McCarthy, J. (2020). *Assessment of risks of SARS-CoV-2 transmission during air travel and non-pharmaceutical interventions to reduce risk*. Retrieved May 1, 2022, from https://npli.sph.harvard.edu/crisis-research/aviation-public-health-initiative-aphi/.

Qureshi, D. (2021). Contactless technology adoption at airports gets accelerated after Covid-19. *Theairportshow*. Retrieved May 1, 2022, from https://www.theairportshow.com/en-gb/event-news/contactless-technology-adoption-at-airports-gets-accelerated-after-covid-19.html.

Rahman, N. A. A., Sa'don, M. A. A. M., Nur, N. M., Rahim, S. A., & Ahmad, M. F. (2021a). Investigating technology application and new norm in aviation industry: Airport perspective. *Turkish Journal of Computer and Mathematics Education, 12*, 2273–2278.

Rahman, N. A. A., Wan-Chik, R. Z., Anuar, N. F., Nur, N. M., & Ahmad, M. F. (2021b). Adapting techniques and challenges by air cargo players in Covid 19 pandemic and the post recovery strategy adopted. *Journal of Tianjin University Science and Technology, 54*(12).

Rahman, N. A. A., Rosshahdan, A. M., Mohammad, M. F., Abdul Majid, Z., & Mokhtar, A. Z. (2021b). Biometric technology application in the aviation industry: Preliminary findings from passenger perspective. *Turkish Journal of Computer and Mathematics Education (TURCOMAT), 12*(11), 2279–2288.

Sciglar, P. (2018). What is artificial intelligence? Understanding 3 basic AI concepts. *Robotics Business Review*. Retrieved May 2, 2022, from https://www.roboticsbusinessreview.com/ai/3-basic-ai-concepts-explain-artificial-intelligence/.

Serrano, F., & Kazda, A. (2020). The future of airports post COVID-19. *Journal of Air Transport Management, 89*, 101900.

Skotarenko, Z. A. (2021). Innovative technologies in airports. *National Aviation University*, 95–97.

Snow, J. (2020). Nano needles. Facial Recognition. Air travel adapts to make travel safer. *National Geographic*. Retrieved May 1, 2022, from https://www.nationalgeographic.com/travel/article/the-future-of-flying-is-going-high-tech-due-to-coronavirus-cvd.

Société Internationale de Télécommunications Aéronautiques (SITA). (2021). *A 'new normal': The changing face post-Covid-19*. Retrieved May 15, 2022, from https://www.sita.aero/resources/White-papers/the-changing-face-of-air-transport-post-covid-19/.

Souza, C. E. G. (2021). Using biometrics to increase the safety and efficiency of airport processes. *International Airport Review*. Retrieved May 11, 2022, from https://www.internationalairportreview.com/article/160306/biometrics-safety-efficiency-airport-processes/.

Štimac, I., Bracic, M., Pivac, J., & Oleksa, I. (2020). Analysis of recommended measures in the conditions of the COVID-19 pandemic at Croatian airports. *Transportation Research Procedia, 51*, 141–151.

Sun, X., Wandelt, S., & Zhang, A. (2021). Technological and educational challenges towards pandemic-resilient aviation. *Transport Policy, 114*, 104–115.

Techslang. (2020). *What are the basic AI concepts?* Retrieved May 15, 2022, from https://www.techslang.com/what-are-the-basic-concepts-in-ai/.

United Nations World Tourism Organization (UNWTO). (2020). *Covid-19 related travel restrictions a global review for tourism*. Retrieved May 15, 2022, from https://www.unwto.org/news/covid-19-travel-restrictions.

Vijayakumar, L. S. (2021). Aviation in COVID times: Technology trends shaping our industry in 2021. *ADB SAFEGATE*. Retrieved May 19, 2022, from https://blog.adbsafegate.com/aviation-in-covid-times-technology-trends-shaping-our-industry-in-2021/.

Wakim, B. (2020). How cloud computing can help airports respond to COVID-19. *Aviation Pros*. Retrieved May 11, 2022, from https://www.aviationpros.com/airports/airport-technology/article/21162612/how-cloud-computing-can-help-airports-respond-to-covid19.

Wise, N., & Heidari, H. (2019). Developing smart tourism destinations with the Internet of Things: Managerial approaches, techniques, and applications. In M. Sigala, R. Rahimi, & M. Thelwall (Eds.), *Big data and innovation in tourism, travel, and hospitality: Managerial approaches, techniques, and applications* (pp. 21–29). Springer.

World Health Organization (WHO). (n.d.). *Tracking SARS-CoV-2 variants*. Retrieved May 15, 2022, from https://www.who.int/en/activities/tracking-SARS-CoV-2-variants/.

Zeng, Z., Chen, P. J., & Lew, A. A. (2020). From high-touch to high-tech: COVID-19 drives robotics adoption. *Tourism Geographies, 22*(3), 724–734.

Dr. Rita Zaharah Wan-Chik is a Senior Lecturer at the Malaysian Institute of Aviation Technology, Universiti Kuala Lumpur. Previously she was teaching at the Malaysian Institute of Information Technology under the same university. She received her Ph.D. in Information Studies from the University of Sheffield, UK, in 2013. She has taught Information Technology-related courses, which includes Internet of Things (IoT) and Data Analytics, Cyber Law, Data Mining and Data warehousing, Management Information Systems, and Operating Systems, among others. She has also experienced working in the industry for a few years before joining the academia world. Her research interest includes Information Technology Adoption in Aviation, Information Behaviour and Semantic Data Analytic.

Nur Syaza Syazwina Binti Zamri is a student researcher at the Malaysian Institute of Aviation Technology, Universiti Kuala Lumpur. She is currently in studies under the Bachelor of Aviation Management (Hons.) programme. She has been assisting in the department's research activities mainly on topics related to aviation management.

Siti Salwa Binti Hasbullah received the Master of Computer Science from National University of Malaysia in 2008. She is currently a lecturer in Malaysian Institute of Information Technology, Universiti Kuala Lumpur. She has been in academia for almost 11 years now, mostly teaching Information Technology and Businesses-related courses such as Computer Organization, Business Intelligence, Business Enterprise Management and Project Management. She has also experienced working in the industry for a few years before joining the academia world. Her current research interests include Artificial Intelligence, Sentiment Analysis, Natural Language Processing, Information Retrieval, and Semantic Data Analytic.

Part IV
Directions for Future Research

Chapter 12
Artificial Intelligence Technology in Travel, Tourism and Hospitality: Current and Future Developments

Zaharuzaman Jamaluddin and Abdul Khabir Rahmat

Abstract Artificial intelligence (AI) is appearing in almost all field of travel and tourism, present in various types of applications for instance the care of critical business processes, ease human experiences and support important governance features. AI has been object of research in travel, tourism and hospitality has gained tremendous impact on making lives easier for travelers around the globe. Tourism companies have applied AI in projecting tourism arrivals, demands, expenses and hotel occupancy, identification of destination points and evaluation of online reviews. This paper presents an overview on current implementation of AI technology in travel, tourism and hospitality based on operation, facility management, supply chain and marketing. In term of company view, they protected data acquisition, the provision of rich service, support customer engagement and improved employee productivity and efficiency. Furthermore, AI technology could increase the perceived service quality through new attractive and interactive manners of service delivery, connecting and engaging with customers. This paper also stresses on potential AI implementations in tourism industry in the future such as self-driving vehicle, crops and forest monitoring, AI in pest control, decision support system, forest protections, virtual reality and AI dimension travel tourism.

Keywords Travel · Tourism · Hospitality · Artificial intelligence technology

Introduction

Artificial intelligence (AI) has created an exciting opportunity for travel, tourism, and hospitality during the pandemic and endemic, clear path for new business models, new customer engagement, and new value formation chances (Koo et al., 2021). These technologies facilitate human experiences, support critical business processes,

---

Z. Jamaluddin (✉)
Faculty of Business and Accountancy, Universiti Selangor, Selangor, Malaysia
e-mail: zaharuzaman@unisel.edu.my

A. K. Rahmat
Malaysia Institute of Transport, Universiti Teknologi MARA, Selangor, Malaysia

and enable important governance aspects. From the customer perspective, AI and robotics can provide structured automated services and enhanced experiences. From a firm perspective, they support customer engagement, the delivery of rich service, secure data acquisition, and increased employee productivity and efficiency (Alt, 2021). The advances AI allows companies from various sectors to have costs reduction, operations streamline, waste elimination, and enhance productivity and efficiency, which leads to vast transformations in the businesses approach (Ivanov, 2019). The introduction of AI improving competitiveness by contribute positively to the financial results of a company. It elaborates on the decisions key personals have to considers when implementing cost-benefits analysis of the use of AI technology by travel, tourism and hospitality companies.

At present, various AI applications have been developed and introduced in many areas of the travel, tourism and hospitality industry, as well as language translation applications, voice recognition, personal travel devices, robots, personalization and recommender systems, business forecasting systems, and natural language processing network. AI is widely available to travel, tourism and hospitality for numerous reasons. Many of the tourists need to make variety decisions about future tours, for example, selection a destination point, types of transportation, choice of accommodation and other recreation activities (Sun et al., 2019). Therefore, these decisions will have an impact on satisfaction result that evaluate by the tourist in every single trip. However, the network of destinations, transportation, accommodation and activities currently available provides an almost infinite variety of options that require assistance. Travel organizations and agents facing similar challenges when trying to find the best fit between customers and travel packages that suit their needs. In addition, organization has near infinite supply of potential customers with AI technology. Therefore, matching demand with a product is a very complex process that seems well fit with the capabilities of AI.

This chapter attempts to show that AI technologies be able to improve business operations and services. The first section of this chapter gives overview of the recent AI application and the benefits in travel, tourism and hospitality. The remaining part of this chapter will be highlight on future development of AI technologies in travel, tourism and hospitality.

Defining Artificial Intelligence

AI is usually defined as a set of technologies that can imitate human intelligence in the process of problem solving (Lai & Hung, 2018). In another study, Huang and Rust (2018) defined AI is the ability of a computer or a robot controlled by a computer to do jobs that are generally done by humans because they require human intelligence and wisdom. According to a definition provided by Kaplan and Haenlein (2019), AI as a computer system ability to correctly interpret data, learn from data characteristics and to use those learnings pattern to achieved desired goals and tasks through flexible adjustment. The concept of AI has evolved over time, from initial conceptualizations in which AI was defined as having some form of intelligence, to more recent definitions and conceptualizations in which AI is defined as being able to act autonomously on large amounts of data (Buhalis et al., 2019).

AI systems require four basic elements to work: data, programs, hardware, and interconnectivity between the different systems. Its applications usually require large hardware capacities such as processing and storage to run adequately. Big data form one of the key foundations of AI since big data provide the necessary input for AI systems to improve by learning, to find and understand patterns of behavior, and to generate insights. Big data in travel, tourism and hospitality usually comes from two sources: the environment and the tourist. The environment is the source of meteorological data, events occurring at the destination, and information obtained in real time from sensors, Internet of Things, and transactions. Tourists provide data before, during, and after their trip in five ways: online activities, offline activities, biometric and emotional data, wearables, and user-generated content (Li et al., 2018).

Artificial Intelligence in Travel, Tourism and Hospitality

AI research in travel, tourism and hospitality has gained momentum. Researchers have applied AI (neural networks, machine learning) in forecasting tourism arrivals/demand/expenditure and hotel occupancy, identification of destination attributes, analysis of online reviews (Kirilenko et al., 2018; Santos Silva et al., 2016). This view is supported by Ivanov et al. (2017), who writes that the practical application of robots and service automation by travel, tourism and hospitality companies, and outlined the potential areas of their adoption. Another important practical application of AI in travel, tourism and hospitality has been quite extensive are self-service technologies such as check-in or information kiosks at hotels or airport, ticket machines at train stations, self-ordering kiosks and conveyor belts in restaurant probably due to the early adoption of this technology in the industry (Ahn & Seo, 2018; Bogicevic et al., 2017; Kelly et al., 2017). They are much less expensive and sophisticated than robots, hence they are widely used worldwide and travellers are accustomed to them although they may prefer to be served by human employees rather than use kiosks.

The most important and visible impact on operations of a travel, tourism or hospitality company from the adoption of AI technologies is the change of the service provider—service is delivered by a robot, a computer programme, a kiosk, or other than human beings. The participants in the services are different and human employees have a decreasing role it. This requires the reengineering of service delivery processes—new processes, activities, procedures, controls need to be implemented, new service operations manuals have to be developed and introduced to reflect the new service provider. However, the service delivery system would be more structured and less flexible compared to human-delivered services. The use of AI also means an increased role of the customers in the service delivery as they now perform some of the activities in the service delivery process that were once performed by the company's employees. Moreover, the use of AI leads to increased service capacity of travel, tourism and hospitality companies—more customers can be served simultaneously and for a particular period of time, thus improving productivity as well. As AI can work 24/7, do not get ill, complain, shirk from work, the scheduling and planning of operations becomes much easier and predictable. Furthermore, AI technologies mean improved environmental sustainability of operations due to reduced use of resources, less waste, elimination of unnecessary activities, and less energy consumption due to better energy demand forecasts (Casteleiro-Roca et al., 2018). Ivanov et al. (2019) identify the possibilities for restaurants and hotels dominate the existing hospitality literature on adoptions of service robots, although impacts will occur across the industry.

In facilities management, the premises of hotels, restaurants and airports, among others, would be used by a wide variety of mobile robots such as robot rail guides, security robots, wheeled robot waiters, companion robots, pet robots, room service deliver robots, robotic vacuum cleaners, underwater robot pool cleaners and entertainment robots. Regardless whether these mobile robots belong to the customers or to the hospitality companies, the latter would need to ensure the robot-friendliness of their premises, i.e. accessible for mobile robots (Ivanov & Webster, 2017). However, Tan et al. (2016) point out that robot operates as how much the environment layout takes into account depends on where the robot needs to operate such as on cleanliness and tidiness need predetermined routes for robot movement and sensors to help robot navigation. According to Decker et al. (2017) mentioned that service robot has already mostly replaced humans in a range of jobs that exceed the physical capabilities of humans.

The adoption of AI technologies allows the integration of the information systems of suppliers and travel, tourism and hospitality companies. This has already started in the beginning of the century, when tourism websites introduced back-to-back connections. These connections allow, for example, the inventory of hotels, rooms and their availability from one website to be visualised in another website. When a customer makes a booking in the second website, the booking goes directly to the first website without the need for human intervention. The integration, however, was mostly on the website level. AI technologies allow much further integration—for example a booking made by a customer through a travel chat bot of one company could be automatically registered into the booking system of that company's supplier (e.g. hotel chain).

AI technologies transform the marketing of travel, tourism and hospitality companies in various ways (Gentsch, 2019). In regards to product and service quality, the adoption of robots would change customers' expectations about what constitutes a travel/tourism/hospitality product which may require a redefinition of its scope. Some hotel guests might consider that robot repair or robot rental services should be part of a hotel's offer, similar to swimming pools, spa centres, souvenir shops, and be available against additional payment. Additionally, AI could improve the perceived service quality through new attractive characteristics and interactive methods of service delivery, communicating and engaging with customers' chat bot, and service kiosks, for instance, could communicate in different languages and do this 24/7 (Ivanov et al., 2018a). A diversity of robotic utilisation for digitilisation have been adopted by hospitality operators, theme parks and museums to deliver unique experiences, enhance service quality, and improve business processes (Tung & Au, 2018). Some travel agent has already use elements of AI, which help to analyze large volumes of data and learn from their own and other people's experience of fulfilling customer orders. AI can create value for the customers by making the service delivery process funny and entertaining. However, we should acknowledge that not all companies will succeed in the implementation of AI technologies (Ivanov et al., 2018b). In addition, when examining the technologies application by travel agent, we have to analyse the particulars activities, deriving their function and implemented in the everyday work (Buhalis & Leung, 2018).

Future Developments

There are various potential AI implementations in tourism industry in the future. We have identified our future expectation based on current technologies used in other sectors and industry such as medical, agricultural, enforcement and town planning. We divide the findings based on technologies in transportation for tourism, tourism attraction location, tour operator management system, AI as tour attraction.

Transportation of Tourism and Hospitality

Firstly, self-driving vehicle or autonomous vehicle is expected to be largely utilised in future transportation (Iyer, 2021). China for example, have built a new township in Zhuzhou Hunan which use virtual track to guide the vehicle (Debeunne & Vivet, 2020). Car developers are also in the race to make self-driving vehicle, it is one of the most anticipated AI and machine learning to be applied in tourism and hospitality. It can be the attraction by itself where luxurious and premium transportation such as train and limousine were equipped with AI driverless vehicle (Martínez-Díaz & Soriguera, 2018; Newman et al., 2019).

Secondly, with AI, it can overcome the issue of manpower shortages or human made errors. Thus, making imbalance or the concern of ensuring staff to be available all the time is eliminated or at least reduced. Imagine if this system is at full-fledged up and running, drivers who are fatigue is no longer a concern, as driverless vehicle took over.

Third, application of AI in transportation which is also important in the context of tourism is smart city traffic management and planning. Countries like Malaysia, Singapore, London, Paris, Berlin, Seoul, Barcelona are among countries which have installed sensors, cameras and software to monitor and manage traffic flow. Especially within city areas which are also the place for tourist attraction.

Fourth, there are also the technology of AI face detection. It will be used to identify a tired driver, which suggest alarm to wake up or alert the tour company to take further action. Similarly, facial detection technology can be used in transport terminals. With continuous advancement of AI technology, tourist and operators will enjoy safer journey as crowded area such as airports are enabled with this fast responding to the potential threats. Camera installed with advanced software will immediately identify a suspects and provide the detail of a person, such system is definitely the next in thing. With heightening concerns on terror acts within mass public area. Such technology will be crucial elements not just in daily work life, but also in tourism industry (Hasan & Sallow, 2021).

Tourism, Attraction and Location

Tourists spots with agriculture focus and attraction such Cameron Highlands may also enjoy AI advancement, where their crops will be monitored for freshness and better management of irrigations, harvests, fertilisation and pest controls. With that other crops such as paddy field or any kind of green tourism will not be frustrated seeing dying trees or yellowish leaves and this technology apply to forest monitoring, where health and growth of flora and fauna can be monitored and protected by using AI (Talaviya et al., 2020).

On top of enjoying fertile and premium grade harvests at optimized costs, AI technology helps local authority and community to analyse the condition of hillside type attractions and the condition of soil. With deploying drones, buckled with GPS system for prevention of possible landslides and early warning of potential floods avoid tourist or help to reduce the risk of potential hazards at the tourist area.

Tour Operator Management System

Next, AI technologies also helps tour operators and suppliers to manage a better tourist experience with Decision Support Systems. With AI decision support system, AI processes big data information feed via social media or marketing force made in the market. With detailed algorithm analysis the system may predict with high accuracy on tourist behaviour, what will they buy during the tour activities, how much will they spend, their preferences, language, weather condition. Such comprehensive system enables operators and each members in the value chain have a better ideas of making decision which maximises their profits, happiness and cleaner environment (Rahmat et al., 2019).

AI as Tour Attraction

AI combined with Virtual reality offers tourism experience by itself. Where VR and AI may offer tourist to travel to imaginative dimension. Few years back, with AI embedment in characters created to replace a family member who have already passed away. Similarly, with the same technology, people with disability were given the experience similar to movie AVATAR which allows them to be in other person characters. Thus, beyond this invented therapy, open up a larger possibility of dimension of its application in tourism industry (Iyer, 2021; Samala et al., 2020).

Conclusion

There can be unimaginable innovations and potentials of AI in tourism and hospitality industry. We might see it in different industry (i.e., logistics, medical, agriculture) and if it is applied in tourism industry may perform or enjoyed better. This indicated that with AI and machine learning, it helps operators to operate in a situation where they have limitation in manpower and sources. The AI offers stability, efficiency and quality compared to human. For customers, our review reveals that AI offer various new excitement, prior to that, with AI both customers and operators, even government would enjoy a safer, greener, healthier and cost efficient tour experience. But with so many benefit that AI brings, we must also acknowledge that in future, with extensive unique skills training, human touch or human skills may be considered as premium and more exclusive in the tourism industry. Chatbot for instance, may not answer to you directly on what you want, and as a user, answering simple questions by a robot may be an insult to some. In achieving moment of truth for customer satisfaction in tourist activities, we suggest more work to be done and look at this void.

References

Ahn, J. A., & Seo, S. (2018). Consumer responses to interactive restaurant self-service technology (IRSST): The role of gadget-loving propensity. *International Journal of Hospitality Management, 74*, 109–121.

Alt, R. (2021). Digital transformation in the restaurant industry: Current developments and implications. *Journal of Smart Tourism, 1*(1), 69–74.

Bogicevic, V., Bujisic, M., Bilgihan, A., Yang, W., & Cobanoglu, C. (2017). The impact of traveler-focused airport technology on traveler satisfaction. *Technological Forecasting and Social Change, 123*, 351–361.

Buhalis, D., & Leung, R. (2018). Smart hospitality—Interconnectivity and interoperability towards an ecosystem. *International Journal of Hospitality Management, 74*, 41–50.

Buhalis, D., Harwood, T., Bogicevic, V., Viglia, G., Beldona, S., & Hofacker, C. (2019). Technological disruptions in services: Lessons from tourism and hospitality. *Journal of Service Management, 30*, 484–506.

Casteleiro-Roca, J. L., Gómez-González, J. F., Calvo-Rolle, J. L., Jove, E., Quintián, H., Martín, J. F. A., Perez, S. G., Diaz, B. G., Calero-Garcia, F., & Méndez-Perez, J. A. (2018). Prediction of the energy demand of a hotel using an artificial intelligence-based model. In *Lecture notes in computer science* (p. 10870). Springer

Debeunne, C., & Vivet, D. (2020). A review of visual-LiDAR fusion based simultaneous localization and mapping. *Sensors, 20*(7), 2068.

Decker, M., Fischer, M., & Ingrid, O. (2017). Service robotics and human labor: A first technology assessment of substitution and cooperation. *Robotics and Autonomous Systems, 87*, 348–354.

Gentsch, P. (2019). *AI in marketing, sales and service. How marketers without a data science degree can use AI, big data and bots.* Palgrave Macmillan.

Hasan, R. T. H., & Sallow, A. B. (2021). Face detection and recognition using Open CV. *Journal of Soft Computing and Data Mining, 2*(2), 86–97.

Huang, M. H., & Rust, R. T. (2018). Artificial intelligence in service. *Journal of Service Research, 21*(2), 155–172.

Ivanov, S., & Webster, C. (2017). Designing robot-friendly hospitality facilities. In *Proceedings of the Scientific Conference "Tourism. Innovations. Strategies"*, Bourgas, 13–14 October.

Ivanov, S. (2019). Ultimate transformation: How will automation technologies disrupt the travel, tourism and hospitality industries? *Zeitschrift Für Tourismuswissenschaft, 11*(1), 1–16.

Ivanov, S., Gretzel, U., Berezina, K., Sigala, M., & Webster, C. (2019). Progress on robotics in hospitality and tourism: A review of the literature. *Journal of Hospitality and Tourism Technology, 10*(4), 489–521.

Ivanov, S., Webster, C., & Berezina, K. (2017). Adoption of robots and service automation by tourism and hospitality companies. *Revista Turismo & Desenvolvimento, 27*(28), 1501–1517.

Ivanov, S., Webster, C., & Garenko, A. (2018a). Young Russian adults' attitudes towards the potential use of robots in hotels. *Technology in Society, 55*, 24–32.

Ivanov, S., Webster, C., & Seyyedi, P. (2018b). Consumers' attitudes towards the introduction of robots in accommodation establishments. *Tourism, 63*(3), 302–317.

Iyer, L. S. (2021). AI enabled applications towards intelligent transportation. *Transportation Engineering, 5*, 100083.

Kaplan, A., & Haenlein, M. (2019). Siri, Siri, in my hand: Who's the fairest in the land? On the interpretations, illustrations and implications of artificial intelligence. *Business Horizons, 62*(1), 15–25.

Kelly, P., Lawlor, J., & Mulvey, M. (2017). Customer roles in self-service technology encounters in a tourism context. *Journal of Travel & Tourism Marketing, 34*(2), 222–238.

Kirilenko, A. P., Stepchenkova, S. O., Kim, H., & Li, X. (2018). Automated sentiment analysis in tourism: Comparison of approaches. *Journal of Travel Research, 57*(8), 1012–1025.

Koo, C., Xiang, Z., & Gretzel, U. (2021). Artificial intelligence (AI) and robotics in travel, hospitality and leisure. *Electron Markets, 31*, 473–476.

Lai, W. C., & Hung, W. H. (2018). A framework of cloud and AI based intelligent hotel. In *Proceedings of the 18th International Conference on Electronic Business* (pp. 36–43). Guilin: ICEB.

Li, J., Xu, L., Tang, L., Wang, S., & Li, L. (2018). Big data in tourism research: A literature review. *Tourism Management, 68*, 301–323.

Martínez-Díaz, M., & Soriguera, F. (2018). Autonomous vehicles: Theoretical and practical challenges. *Transportation Research Procedia, 33*, 275–282.

Newman, P., Hargroves, K., Davies-Slate, S., Conley, D., Verschuer, M., Mouritz, M., & Yangka, D. (2019). The trackless tram: Is it the transit and city shaping catalyst we have been waiting for? *Journal of Transportation Technologies, 9*, 31–55.

Rahmat, A. K., Faisol, N., Yajid, A. A., & Badrillah, M. I. M. (2019). Manufacturers satisfaction on third party logistics providers' service quality. *International Journal of Control and Automation, 12*(5), 131–141.

Samala, N., Katkam, B. S., Bellamkonda, R. S., & Rodriguez, R. V. (2020). Impact of AI and robotics in the tourism sector: A critical insight. *Journal of Tourism Futures, 8*(1), 73–87.

Santos Silva, M., Albayrak, T., Caber, M., & Moutinho, L. (2016). Key destination attributes of behavioural intention: An application of neural networks. *European Journal of Tourism Research, 14*, 16–28.

Sun, S., Wei, Y., Tsui, K. L., & Wang, S. (2019). Forecasting tourist arrivals with machine learning and internet search index. *Tourism Management, 70*, 1–10.

Talaviya, T., Shah, D., Patel, N., Yagnik, H., & Shah, M. (2020). Implementation of artificial intelligence in agriculture for optimisation of irrigation and application of pesticides and herbicides. *Artificial Intelligence in Agriculture, 4*, 58–73.

Tan, N., Mohan, R. E., & Watanabe, A. (2016). Toward a framework for robot-inclusive environments. *Automation in Construction, 69*, 68–78.

Tung, V. W. S., & Au, N. (2018). Exploring customer experiences with robotics in hospitality. *International Journal of Contemporary Hospitality Management, 30*(7), 2680–2697.

Dr. Zaharuzaman Jamaluddin is a Deputy Dean of Academic and Lecturer at the Faculty of Business and Accountancy, Universiti Selangor, Shah Alam Campus, Selangor, Malaysia. Dr. Zaharuzaman obtained his Bachelor degree in Industrial Technology from Universiti Sains Malaysia, a Master degree in Business Administration from Universiti Teknologi Mara and Ph.D. in Quality Management from Universiti Kebangsaan Malaysia. He has 20 years in industrial experiences and 7 years of academic/research experiences. At present he is teaching courses on current issue in business and quality management. On research activities, he publishes more than 15 journals in topic of quality management and business management. At present he having one ongoing research grant as project leader. Regarding post graduate supervision, he has 2 students completed study, 1 wait for Viva Voce and 12 students ongoing research.

Dr. Abdul Khabir Rahmat is a Coordinator/Researcher and Lecturer at the Malaysia Institute of Transport, Universiti Teknologi MARA, Shah Alam, Malaysia. Dr. Rahmat is a professional Technologist certified by Malaysia Board of Technologist. He is also Head of CILT Malaysia Selangor Section NexGen and active members of Council of Supply Management Professionals. His research interest is in the field of Logistics Service Quality, Logistics Performance, Service Marketing, Logistics of Humanitarian Mission, Transport and Tourism to name a few.

Chapter 13
Contactless Hospitality Technology in Post-COVID-19 Era: Future Research Clusters

Nor Aida Abdul Rahman, Azizul Hassan, Md Fauzi Ahmad, and Reshminder Kaur Satvindar Singh

Abstract The global travel, tourism and hospitality sector is facing the effect of pandemic COVID-19 outbreak. Health and the safe of travelers' issue has become the critical focus and crucial in hospitality recovery plan. The sudden COVID-19 outbreak has led to accelerated adoption of technology for both travelers and hospitality service providers. This chapter aims to explore type of contactless technology used in hospitality industry and proposed a research cluster for future research agenda. Among the technology discuss in this chapter are Virtual Reality, Chatbots, Robotic, contactless payment, voice search, mobile check-in, recognition technology and many more.

Keywords Contactless technology · Hospitality · COVID-19 · Research cluster · Tourism and travel

Introduction

The emergence of COVID-19 in late 2019 have imposed negative consequences to many business sector worldwide including travel, tourism, aviation, as well as hospitality sector. It was reported by World Tourism Organization (UNWTO) (2020) that the movement of the international travelers has been dropped tremendously due to COVID-19 outbreak in the first 10 months of year 2020. The number of

N. A. A. Rahman (✉)
Technical Foundation/Aviation Management Section, Universiti Kuala Lumpur—Malaysian Institute of Aviation Technology (UniKL MIAT), Selangor, Malaysia
e-mail: noraida@unikl.edu.my

A. Hassan
Tourism Consultant Network, The Tourism Society, London, UK

Md F. Ahmad
Faculty of Technology Management, Universiti Tun Hussein Onn Malaysia, Johor, Malaysia

R. K. S. Singh
Universiti Kuala Lumpur—Malaysian Institute of Aviation Technology (UniKL MIAT), Selangor, Malaysia

© The Author(s), under exclusive license to Springer Nature Singapore Pte Ltd. 2023
A. Hassan and N. A. A. Rahman (eds.), *Technology Application in Aviation, Tourism and Hospitality*, https://doi.org/10.1007/978-981-19-6619-4_13

travelers worldwide has been decreased to 900 million which equal to USD 935 billion in export revenue worldwide. Many significant impact has been reported due to COVID-19 including health issue, economy recession, lockdown, downsizing practices, border closure and many more (Dogra, 2022). This critical impact reflects the important of activities in managing business and operation. Hospitality sector is a service industry sector that provides broad categories of services. It is closely connected with travel and tourism activities among the service categorized under hospitality sector are event planning, hotel and lodging, restaurants or food and drink services, bars, casinos, theme parks and other entertainment activities.

Technology advancement in hospitality specific rarely discussed in previous literature especially focusing in current pandemic era of COVID-19. Contactless technology is part of industry 4.0 revolution. According to Frank et al. (2019), Industry 4.0 technology was introduced by Germany federal government in early 2011 and has become a global reference for technology revolution for all countries in the world (Pfeiffer, 2017). Bloom et al. (2014) and Xu et al. (2014) highlight that this newly emerged technology such as automation, smart manufacturing and internet of things has successfully transform many business organizations to smart business and improved their organizational performance. The service industry including hospitality and air travel are critical in current era due to the need of going contactless or touchless activity in travel due to pandemic COVID-19. As highlighted by Chen et al. (2021), the influence of COVID-19 disease has changed the hospitality activities from physical face-to-face to online activities and contactless. It is vital for hospitality to fully go for contactless hospitality services to accommodate current needs of travelers to ensure their safety and health.

Davahli et al. (2020) stress that among the key control effort in controlling COVID-19 to spread are travel restriction, new normal standard operating procedure (SOP), social distancing practices and touchless activities. Recent article by Baum et al. (2020) also highlight similar conclusion whereby the need of hospitality players to regain customer confident in hotel operations with touchless activity and appropriate technology. Having noticed the importance of contactless technology in the hospitality sector, this study aims to highlights the type of contactless technology needed in hospitality sector in current COVID-19 era.

Technology Revolution and Advancement in Hospitality Sector

One of the major component for hospitality industry development is technology and industry 4.0 revolution. Technology landscape generally could be viewed from two main perspective namely large scale application and small scale usage which relate with data analysis for decision making process (Deloitte, 2019). Sivarajah et al. (2020) and Kumar (2021) emphasize on the technology usage in service industry is important that can help business organization to actively transform and facilitate their business activity remotely. As mentioned earlier, technology advancement in travel, tourism and hospitality sector has been discussed in previous literature substantially. Advanced technology such as Artificial Intelligence (AI), block chain technology, biometric application, cyber security, robotics is among popular frontiers technology discuss in the travel and tourism sector literature. However, in the context of hospitality industry, it is still under developed. Lee (2022) argues that there is a strong need for a future studies to discuss on the technology themes discussed in current and previous tourism and hospitality literature such as smart technology, AI and industry 4.0 (Buhalis, 2019). These frontier technologies are widely discussed in many sector such as health and medical sector, transportation, construction, tourism and many more. Given the significance of the technology application to improve business organization performance and operation, Kim et al. (2019) recommend scholars to urgently evaluate the role of frontiers technology in overcoming business issues which is rarely explored by previous scholars in hospitality context.

Even though there are quite a number of paper that discuss technology in the field of travel, tourism and hospitality, however, it has not been widely discussed in the field of hospitality especially contactless technology related to COVID-19 crisis (Rahman et al., 2020, 2021). Technology usage in hospitality in COVID-19 era is vital to facilitate the travelers travel activity and improved safety and uncertainty. The role of technology in present era is undeniable as the organization need to improve its efficiency and build their reputation via technology application and advancement.

COVID-19 has caused critical business, social and economic issue for every country in a globe. The increased number of people get affected, disruption in operation and supply chain activity in many businesses in every industries is very challenging to adapt. This pandemic outbreak has affected more than 200 countries worldwide with millions of death that lead to business disruption and business closure. No one has a good understanding on what currently had happened and the new norm in social and business activities has created great tense to every party involved. For instance, living and working in new norm due to pandemic COVID-19 outbreak is very challenging and force the business entities especially in hospitality and travel industry to shift their business model holistically. Since pandemic COVID-19 creates new touchless phenomena, the use of technology seems to be very significant for hospitality business organization to adopt appropriate technology to manage their operation and business for future sustainability. Mobile technology, chatbox and biometric recognition are among the popular technology tools in pandemic COVID-19 era.

As far as we concern, this new norm with appropriate digital or technology advancement, it will lead to the effective management and recovery plan for those affected from the pandemic, including hospitality industry players. Therefore, with this background, the hospitality organization in any sub sector (restaurant, hotel and lodging, entertainment etc.) need to have effective strategic plan to manage their business and operation, and changed their operation from physical face-to-face interaction to online or contactless technology. Investigating the technological application framework for hospitality sector in this pandemic era is justifiable as it will allow the hospitality organization to be aware with the main challenges and recover from any negative impact to their organization due to pandemic. Next section will deliberate on past research in the field of hospitality in relation to technology application.

Past Research on Technology in Hospitality Sector

The emergence of smart technology in the field of hospitality starts as early 1990s. Early work from Gamble (1991) highlights the importance of technology application as a key strategy to have a proper planning and consistency in business operation. It is acknowledged that technology has become the essential to manage business operation, information sharing, communication and daily business monitoring worldwide. Technology allow the business organization in the hospitality to innovate new products, new service, improved process which lead to business sustainability (Chung, 2021; Sivarajah et al., 2020; Müller et al., 2018). Having reviewed the literature, there are 173 documents has been published in Scopus database that study technology in the hospitality context. In this search in Scopus database, the researcher uses two keywords in title namely "technology" and "hospitality". As can be seen in Fig. 13.1, the distribution of previous study that has been published in hospitality sector related to technology from year 1991 until 2022.

Another frontier technology available in hospitality sector are video technology. 3D video technology is also used in many hotels to showcase every angle of their hotel facilities to their guest such as pool, restaurant, bar, room, meeting lounge, lobby and many more. In current pandemic era, hotel tour using 3d video is very useful and allow the guest or travelers to feel safe and no need to think about social distancing precaution during physical tour. Again, guest expectation due to COVID-19 pandemic has been changed and they always want a hotel to provide excellence digital experience throughout their stay.

From the literature review study, we can see that that the top five authors that write about technology in hospitality sector are led by Law, followed by Buhalis, Leung, Ahn and Bilgihan. Figure 13.2 show documents by the authors published in

Filter by year

☐ 2022	(4) >	☐ 2012	(8) >	☐ 2001	(4) >
☐ 2021	(25) >	☐ 2011	(6) >	☐ 2000	(4) >
☐ 2020	(18) >	☐ 2010	(8) >	☐ 1999	(1) >
☐ 2019	(15) >	☐ 2009	(3) >	☐ 1998	(2) >
☐ 2018	(11) >	☐ 2008	(7) >	☐ 1996	(1) >
☐ 2017	(6) >	☐ 2007	(2) >	☐ 1995	(1) >
☐ 2016	(12) >	☐ 2006	(4) >	☐ 1993	(1) >
☐ 2015	(7) >	☐ 2005	(3) >	☐ 1991	(1) >
☐ 2014	(11) >	☐ 2004	(3) >		
☐ 2013	(4) >	☐ 2002	(1) >		

Fig. 13.1 Numbers of article published in the field of hospitality on technology application in Scopus database from 173. *Source* The authors (2022)

Scopus database on technology in hospitality industry. While Fig. 13.3 shows the top 10 country that study on technology topic in the hospitality sector.

In the hospitality sector, technology helps to improve business strategy and help business to run smoothly and provide personalization experience to the guest. The most important reason for hospitality businesses to adopt new technology is to satisfy customer demands and give guests the most pleasant experience possible. In this pandemic and for post pandemic era, technology is very significant to support contactless and touchless experience to the travelers. As recognized, health and cleanliness has become the top priority to the travelers in this era. In the next section, multi type of contactless technology will be discuss and reflects the future research cluster for future research agenda.

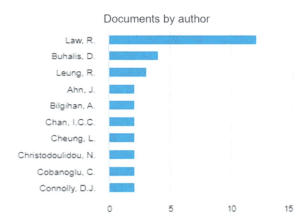

Fig. 13.2 Top 10 authors published on technology topic in hospitality context. *Source* The authors (2022)

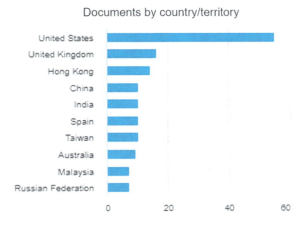

Fig. 13.3 Top 10 countries that published on technology in hospitality sector. *Source* The authors (2022)

Multi Types of Contactless Technology in Hospitality Sector: Future Research Clusters

There are multi type of technology advancement in hospitality sector that is appropriate to be empirically research by future scholars. Hsu and Tseng (2022) recommend that current dynamic environment because of COVID-19 tragedy could not allow conservative or traditional way in running or practicing hospitality business. Frontiers technology are needed to transform industry into smart hospitality industry (Buhalis & Leung, 2018). Hsu and Tseng (2022) suggest 10 technologies to focus in hospitality namely AI technology, Robotics and Chatbots, Internet of things, Clod computing, basic ICT, Big data analytics, Cybersecurity, XR and simulation, integration of IT system and additive manufacturing. All of these technology strategy proposed by Hsu and Tseng (2022) could lead to achieving technology competency from both individual and organizational perspective. As defined by Bartram et al. (2002:7), technology competence refers to "set of behaviors that are instrumental in the delivery of desired results or outcomes". It is important for hospitality form to evaluate the competency of their workers and their firms, to sharpen their weaknesses, improved the performance of incompetent workers and for future organizational planning.

Touchless technology such as QR code for check in and food ordering are also part of the frontiers technology that can be further research in the field of hospitality. This has been performed in hospitality sector in many countries which can be achieved via using specific mobile app. In fact, it is also used as a payment mechanism in hospitality context. With contactless technology, it provides easy experience to the travelers to pay for any service they use with secure and hygienic manner. As emphasized by Hao (2021) and, the demand for contactless payment is more increased due to COVID-19 as the travelers are become motivated to use the technology for health and safety reason. However, as recommended by Hao (2021) and Hao and Chon (2021), the hospitality managers should always monitor the complexities of the system or technology use to ensure the travelers know how to use this technology and have clear understanding to use it. Similarly, Rahimizhian and Irani (2021) state that contactless technology that help in reducing physical contact and optimize business operation have an added value to the hospitality business players. As the tourism, travel, aviation and hospitality sector is expose and sensitive to health disease issue, therefore adopting contactless technology could increase the confidence level of the travelers to travel again during post pandemic year. In line with past studies on technology trend and traveler attitude, Webster and Ivanov (2019) highlight the difference of the travelers' attitude with different technology acceptance level.

Another technology that can be researched is the application of AI technology in hospitality sector and the Chatbot application among the travelers. According to Van Doorn et al. (2017), AI technology is not only help the organization to trigger their operational problem, but also work in improving direct interaction with the customers or travelers. In fact, in the airline sectors also, Chatbots technology were widely used by the airliners for various functions. As highlighted by Ghosh and Chakravarty

(2018), more than 42% airport across the region plans to adopt Chatbot technology. Chatbot technology is a technology that is programmed to emulate dialogues with human beings using language text and voice methods (Xcubelabs, 2017). Align with definition provided by Ramachandran (2019), AI-based Chatbots can also be defined as an abbreviation for chat robot that uses AI technology and an internal computer software to create conversation with people. Chatbots as an integration of intelligent backend systems and interface. Many research directions could be exploring with regards to this contactless technology of Chatbot in hospitality. For instance, to evaluate the efficiency of Chatbot application in hotel sector and air travel, to examine user experience of AI technology Chatbots, and how this technology helps the industry to recover faster after post pandemic era.

The popularity of mobile technology since 2013 is constantly growing with the rise of COVID-19 cases. As to date, there are still a lack of research that study on mobile technology in the field of travel, tourism and hospitality (Dorcic et al., 2019). As highlighted by them, even though many hospitality providers offer mobile application to their guest, many of them have not utilized it. Apart from mobile technology, there are other technology that can be explored by future scholars such as voice search, augmented reality, internet of things, hospitality 4.0 infrastructure and many more.

Conclusion

To conclude, even the technology application in hospitality sector start as early as 1960s, however there are many other areas that needs to be examined (Coussement & Teague, 2013; Lee, 2022). COVID-19 outbreak has led to increased need to go for contactless experience in hospitality industry by the travelers. Contactless technology could provide more personalized, safe and pleasant experience to the travelers. With the accelerating demand of contactless technology by the travelers, there is always an issue and challenges that can be study. More researchers are call to examine issue on contactless technology in hospitality context. As discussed, a part of issue of operational performance and the efficiency of the technology adoption, future researcher also could examine issue of privacy, safety and security of each technology highlighted.

References

Bartram, D., Robertson, I. T., & Callinan, M. (2002). Introduction: A framework for examining organizational effectiveness. In I. T. Robertson, M. Callinan, & D. Bartram (Eds.), *Organizational effectiveness: The role of psychology* (p. 2). Wiley.
Baum, T., Mooney, S. K., Robinson, R. N., & Solnet, D. (2020). COVID-19's impact on the hospitality workforce—New crisis or amplification of the norm? *International Journal of Contemporary Hospitality Management, 32*(9), 2813–2829.

Bloom, N., Garicano, L., Sadun, R., & Van Reenen, J. (2014). The distinct effects of information technology and communication technology on firm organization. *Management Science, 60*(12), 2859–2885.

Buhalis, D. (2019). Technology in tourism-from information communication technologies to eTourism and smart tourism towards ambient intelligence tourism: A perspective article. *Tourism Review, 75*(1), 267–272.

Buhalis, D., & Leung, R. (2018). Smart hospitality—Interconnectivity and interoperability towards an ecosystem. *International Journal of Hospitality Management, 71*, 41–50.

Chen, S.-H., Tzeng, S.-Y., Tham, A., & Chu, P.-X. (2021). Hospitality services in the post COVID-19 era: Are we ready for high-tech and no touch service delivery in smart hotels?. *Journal of Hospitality Marketing and Management, 30*(8), 1–24.

Chung, S.-H. (2021). Applications of smart technologies in logistics and transport: A review. *Transportation Research Part E: Logistics and Transportation Review, 153*, 102455.

Coussement, M. A., & Teague, T. J. (2013). The new customer-facing technology: Mobile and the constantly-connected consumer. *Journal of Hospitality and Tourism Technology, 4*(2), 177–187.

Davahli, M. R., Karwowski, W., Sonmez, S., & Apostolopoulos, Y. (2020). The hospitality industry in the face of the COVID-19 pandemic: Current topics and research methods. *International Journal of Environmental Research and Public Health, 17*(20), 7366.

Deloitte. (2019). 4 Trends that will help executives create a better world. *Forbes Insights*. Retrieved April 9, 2022, from https://www.forbes.com/sites/insights-deloitte/2018/01/31/4-trends-thatwill-help-executives-create-a-better-world/#555bec1e335d%0A.

Dogra, S. (2022). Covid-19: Impact on the hospitality workforce. *Hospitalityinsights*. Retrieved April 3, 2022, from https://hospitalityinsights.ehl.edu/covid-19-impact-hospitality-workforce.

Dorcic, J., Komsic, J., & Markovic, S. (2019). Mobile technologies and applications towards smart tourism—State of the art. *Tourism Review, 4*(1), 82–103.

Frank, A. G., Dalenogare, L. S., & Ayala, N. F. (2019). Industry 4.0 technologies: Implementation patterns in manufacturing companies. *International Journal of Production Economics, 210*, 15–26.

Gamble, P. R. (1991). An information technology strategy for the hospitality industry of the 1990s. *International Journal of Contemporary Hospitality Management, 3*(1). https://doi.org/10.1108/09596119110138349.

Ghosh, J., & Chakravarty, R. (2018). Expedition 3.0: Travel and hospitality gone digital. *KPMG and FICCI*. Retrieved April 23, 2022, from https://home.kpmg/in/en/home/insights/2018/03/ficci-exp edition-travel-hospitality-technology-innovation-india-digital.html.

Hao, F. (2021). Acceptance of contactless technology in the hospitality industry: Extending the unified theory of acceptance and use of technology 2. *Asia Pacific Journal of Tourism Research, 26*(12), 1386–1401.

Hao, F., & Chon, K. K. S. (2021). Contactless service in hospitality: Bridging customer equity, experience, delight, satisfaction, and trust. *International Journal of Contemporary Hospitality Management, 34*(1), 113–134.

Hsu, H., & Tseng, K.-F. (2022). Facing the era of smartness: Constructing a framework of required technology competencies for hospitality practitioners. *Journal of Hospitality and Tourism Technology, 13*(3), 500–526.

Kim, Y., Lee, J., & Ahn, J. (2019). Innovation towards sustainable technologies: A socio-technical perspective on accelerating transition to aviation biofuel. *Technological Forecasting and Social Change, 145*, 317–329.

Kumar, S. (2021). The effect of CORONA-COVID-19 on hospitality sector. *Journal of Statistics and Management Systems, 24*(1), 163–174.

Lee, M. (2022). Evolution of hospitality and tourism technology research from Journal of Hospitality and Tourism Technology: A computer-assisted qualitative data analysis. *Journal of Hospitality and Tourism Technology, 13*(1), 62–84.

Müller, J. M., Kiel, D., & Voigt, K.-I. (2018). What drives the implementation of industry 4.0? The role of opportunities and challenges in the context of sustainability. *Sustainability, 10*(1), 247.

Pfeiffer, S. (2017). The vision of 'industrie 4.0' in the making—A case of future told, tamed, and traded. *NanoEthics, 11*(1), 107–121.

Rahimizhian, S., & Irani, F. (2021). Contactless hospitality in a post-Covid-19 world. *International Hospitality Review, 35*(2), 293–304.

Rahman, N. A. A., Hassan, A., & Rahman, M. S. U. (2021). Tourism and air transport sustainability in Bangladesh: The role of technology. In A. Hassan (Ed.), *Tourism marketing in Bangladesh: An introduction* (pp. 42–50). Routledge.

Rahman, N. A. A., Rahim, S. A., Ahmad, M. F., & Hafizuddin-Syah, B. A. M. (2020). Exploring Covid-19 pandemic: Its impact to global aviation industry and the key strategy. *International Journal of Advanced Science and Technology, 29*(6s), 1829–1836.

Ramachandran, A. (2019). *User adoption of Chatbots.* Retrieved April 28, 2022, from https://ssrn.com/abstract=3406997.

Sivarajah, U., Irani, Z., Gupta, S., & Mahroof, K. (2020). Role of big data and social media analytics for business to business sustainability: A participatory web context. *Industrial Marketing Management, 86*, 163–179.

Van Doorn, J., Mende, M., Noble, S. M., Hulland, J., Ostrom, A. L., Grewal, D., & Petersen, J. A. (2017). Domo arigato Mr Roboto: Emergence of automated social presence in organizational frontlines and customers' service experiences. *Journal of Service Research, 20*(1), 43–58.

Webster, C., & Ivanov, S. H. (2019). What do people think robots should do in hospitality and tourism? Preliminary findings from a global study of market segments. In *Proceedings of the AIRSI2019 Conference "Artificial Intelligence and Robotics in Service Interactions: Trends, Benefits, and Challenges*, Zaragoza (pp. 55–71).

World Tourism Organization (UNWTO). (2020). *Impact assessment of the COVID-19 outbreak on international tourism.* Retrieved April 5, 2022, from www.unwto.org/impact-assessment-of-the-covid-19-outbreak-on-internationaltourism.

Xcubelabs. (2017). *5 ways chatbots are changing the face of travel industry.* Retrieved April 23, 2022, from www.xcubelabs.com/blog/chatbots-travel-industry/.

Xu, L. D., He, W., & Li, S. (2014). Internet of things in industries: A survey. *IEEE Transactions on Industrial Informatics, 10*(4), 2233–2243.

Dr. Nor Aida Abdul Rahman is an Associate Professor, Universiti Kuala Lumpur (UniKL), Kuala Lumpur, Malaysia, and Head of Aviation Management, Universiti Kuala Lumpur—Malaysian Institute of Aviation Technology (UniKL MIAT), Selangor, Malaysia. She has worked as internal and external trainer in management, supply chain, Halal logistics and postgraduate research. Her research work has appeared in several reputable academic journals such as Industrial Marketing Management, Journal of Humanitarian logistics and supply chain, International journal of quality and reliability management, International journal of supply chain management and others. She has also published a number of book chapter and refereed conference proceedings, and part of the editorial team of book project with Routledge. She is a panel of WG in MS2400 Halal Supply Chain standard & TC10 for Halal supply chain standard (SMIIC). She earned Ph.D. degree in Management (supply chain management) from Brunel University, London, UK. She is also serving as Academic Advisor in college, a chartered member for Chartered Institute of Logistics and Transport Malaysia (CILTM), HRDF Certified Trainer, Chairman (Academic Committee) for Malaysian Association of Transportation, Logistics and Supply Chain Schools (MyATLAS), Vice President (Research Journal) for Institute for Research in Management and Engineering UK (INRME), JAKIM Halal Certified Trainer, UniKL Halal Professional Board and a member of Academy of Marketing, UK.

Dr. Azizul Hassan is a member of the Tourism Consultants Network of the UK Tourism Society. Dr. Hassan has been working for the tourism industry as a consultant, academic, and researcher for over two decades. His research interest areas are technology-supported marketing for tourism and hospitality, immersive technology applications in the tourism and hospitality industry, and technology-influenced marketing suggestions for sustainable tourism and hospitality industry in developing countries. Dr. Hassan has authored over 150 articles and book chapters in leading tourism outlets. He is also part of the editorial team of 25 book projects from Routledge, Springer, CAB International, and Emerald Group Publishing Limited. He is a regular reviewer of a number of international journals.

Dr. Md Fauzi Ahmad is an academic staff at Universiti Tun Hussein Onn Malaysia (UTHM). He started his career as a Quality Engineer and has been assigned to various areas, such as product quality assurance (PQA), quality control (qc), product planning and sales departments. He has contributed to establishing company strategy for improving customer satisfaction and other major improvement.

Reshminder Kaur Satvindar Singh graduated with M.App Linguistics from Universiti Putra Malaysia in 2010. She has been lecturing at Universiti Kuala Lumpur-Malaysian Institute of Aviation Technology since 2008. She has experience in Curriculum Design & Development, ESP, Language Testing and Assessment and Interactive Learning. She has been actively involved in language training and testing based on ICAO standards for Air Traffic Controllers at DCA Malaysia. She is currently pursuing her Ph.D. with Universiti Malaya, Malaysia She also provides consultation and short courses for Aviation companies and International students. Over the years, she has also been involved in research work and publication in ESP, PBL and Communication.

Printed in the United States
by Baker & Taylor Publisher Services